if you love me

In Memory of My Feelings

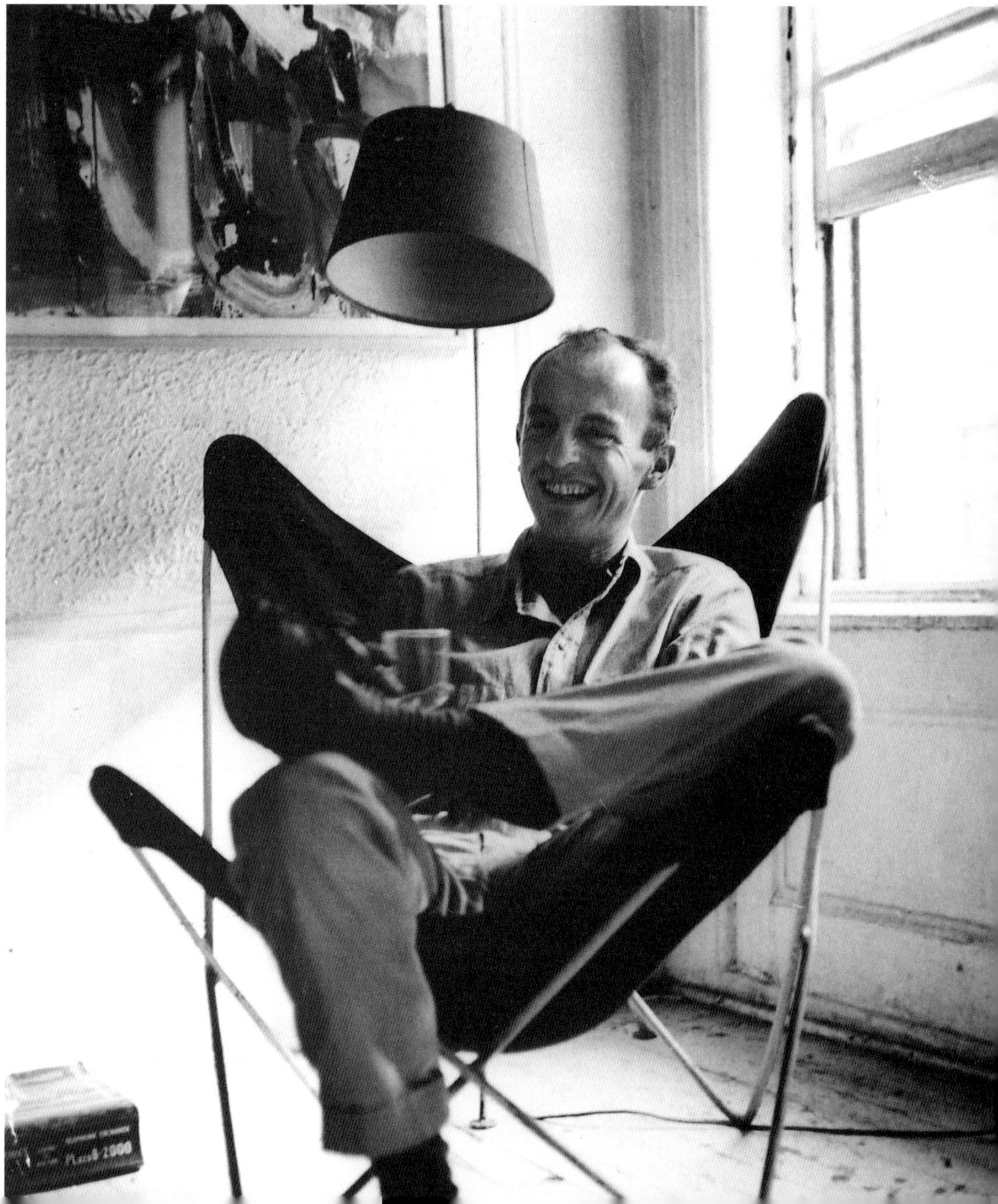

Fred W. McDarrah
Frank O'Hara in his flat,
441 East 9th Street,
September 26, 1959

In Memory of My Feelings: Frank O'Hara and American Art

RUSSELL FERGUSON

The Museum of Contemporary Art, Los Angeles
University of California Press Berkeley Los Angeles London

This publication accompanies the exhibition
"In Memory of My Feelings: Frank O'Hara and American Art,"
organized by Russell Ferguson and presented at The Museum of Contemporary Art, Los Angeles,
July 11–November 14, 1999.

"In Memory of My Feelings: Frank O'Hara and American Art" is made possible in part by generous support from the Dedalus Foundation, Inc.; the National Endowment for the Arts, a federal agency; Beatrice and Philip Gersh; and the Thorton S. Glide, Jr. and Katrina D. Glide Foundation.

Published by
The Museum of Contemporary Art, Los Angeles
in association with
University of California Press
Berkeley and Los Angeles, California
and University of California Press, Ltd.
London, England

Cover:
Alex Katz,
Frank O'Hara,
1959–60

Library of Congress Cataloging-in-Publication Data
Ferguson, Russell.
In Memory of My Feelings: Frank O 'Hara and American art/Russell Ferguson.
p. cm.
Exhibition catalog.
Includes bibliographical references.
ISBN 0-520-22243-1
1. Art. American—New York (State)—New York Exhibitions. 2. Art. Modern—20th century—New York (State)—New York Exhibitions. 3. O'Hara, Frank Exhibitions. 4. Poets, American—20th century Biography Exhibitions.
I. O'Hara, Frank. II. Los Angeles Museum of Contemporary Art. III. Title.
N6535, N5F47 1999 99-23375
709. 73 07479494—dc21 CIP

Printed in Germany
9 8 7 6 5 4 3 2 1

Director's Foreword

"In Memory of My Feelings: Frank O'Hara and American Art" is a splendid addition to a series of historical explorations that have defined the character and mission of The Museum of Contemporary Art. In the spirit of "Reconsidering the Object of Art: 1965-1975," and "Out of Actions: Between Performance and the Object, 1949-1979," "In Memory of My Feelings" makes an invaluable contribution to our understanding of contemporary art, and provides us with the opportunity to revisit and rethink one of the most mythologized periods in American art. In addition, it brings the work of an extraordinary poet and thinker into a new and compelling light.

This exhibition owes its existence to the intelligence, dedication, and perseverance of Associate Curator Russell Ferguson. Russell first conceived of this show several years ago, and his passionate commitment to both the work of Frank O'Hara and to the world in which O'Hara flourished has provided MOCA with an extraordinary exhibition for which we are most grateful. "In Memory of My Feelings" is notable for its juxtaposition of artists who are conventionally regarded as inhabiting entirely separate sectors of recent art history. Here the masters of Abstract Expressionism stand next to the inventors of Pop; the still-under-recognized abstract painters of a slightly younger generation are placed alongside artists who continue to pursue the figurative tradition. Ferguson makes such juxtapositions compelling by allowing them to spiral around the charismatic figure of Frank O'Hara, a man of boundless interests and enthusiasms who serves here as a link between the disparate members of a group who were, after all, close contemporaries.

No exhibition is possible without the generosity of the institutions and individual collectors who graciously loan their works and entrust us with their care, and to them we express the deepest thanks. On behalf of the museum staff and the Board of the Trustees I would like to express our gratitude to those individuals and institutions who generously provided funding for the exhibition: the Dedalus Foundation, both for monetary support and for their important loans to the exhibition; the National Endowment for the Arts, who provided the earliest support to the exhibition; Beatrice and Philip Gersh, whose dedication to the museum is unmatched; and The Thornton S. Glide, Jr. and Katrina D. Glide Foundation.

We are particularly grateful to MOCA's Board of Trustees, led by Chair Audrey M. Irmas, President Gilbert B. Friesen, and Vice Chairs Ruth Bloom, Robert C. Davidson, Jr., and Clifford J. Einstein for their indomitable spirit and unending commitment and support to the museum.

This publication and exhibition were conceived under the directorship of Richard Koshalek, and I would like to personally express my thanks for his enthusiasm and great dedication to the museum. I am grateful for the opportunity to open my tenure with this excellent exhibition and look forward to working with the museum's entire staff in maintaining the institution's stellar reputation and leading it into an even greater future.

—Jeremy Strick

Director

July 1999

Acknowledgments

In the organization of this exhibition and publication I have relied upon the generous support of an enormous number of people. It is a testament, I think, to the great affection that those who knew Frank O'Hara have for his memory, and to the high regard that his poetry continues to command, that so many people were eager to help make this project a reality. It is a pleasure to offer them my thanks here.

The Dedalus Foundation has been a generous supporter of this project from an early stage. My sincere thanks go to Richard Rubin, Joan Banach, Jack Flam, and Dore Ashton for their help, not just with funding but also for their important loans to the exhibition, their insights into the art of the period, and for access to the Robert Motherwell archives. The exhibition received its earliest funding from the National Endowment for the Arts. This backing was crucial not just in fiscal terms, but also as recognition of the project's significance by others in the field. Beatrice and Philip Gersh have always been among The Museum of Contemporary Art's most dedicated supporters, and I am particularly happy that they have chosen to contribute to this project. The Thornton S. Glide, Jr. and Katrina D. Glide Foundation has also been very generous in its support of the exhibition.

From the inception of this project I have enjoyed the help of my colleagues at The Museum of Contemporary Art, from the Board of Trustees to every member of the museum's staff. "In Memory of My Feelings" was begun when Richard Koshalek was director of MOCA, and it is opening shortly after his departure. Richard was an enthusiastic supporter of the exhibition from the beginning, and I am deeply grateful for all his help in moving it forward. Even more important to me than his support for this particular exhibition, however, has been the opportunity I have had to work with him over the last eight years. I have learned an incalculable amount in that period, not least that making exhibitions should be an enjoyable experience. Richard Koshalek is one of the great museum directors.

Jeremy Strick is just beginning as Richard's successor, and this publication is the first to appear under his leadership. He has been highly supportive of the exhibition since the announcement of his appointment, for which I am very grateful. I look forward to working on future projects with him as director.

My thanks go also to Kathleen S. Bartels, assistant director, and Jack Wiant, chief financial officer, for their consistent help with countless organizational issues. Erica Clark, director of development, and her staff, especially Jillian Spaak, grants officer, directed the crucial search for funding.

Paul Schimmel, MOCA's chief curator, has encouraged me in every way since I came to the museum as editor in 1991. His support for this project has been whole-hearted, and is much appreciated. It has certainly been influenced by his own projects focusing on transitional periods in American art, especially "Hand-Painted Pop," which he organized with Donna De Salvo in 1992. My colleagues Ann Goldstein and Connie Butler also helped me a great deal in thinking about the exhibition. Stacia Payne handled coordination of the exhibition tour precisely and efficiently.

No one worked harder on the research for and implementation of this project than Michael Darling. His title of research assistant barely hints at the scope of responsibilities he cheerfully shouldered. He tracked down hard-to-find references as swiftly as he located elusive works of art. He dealt with lenders as effectively as he coordinated all the in-house aspects of the exhibition. In addition, he was unfailingly willing to discuss any aspect of the content of the project with me, from overarching themes to the slightest of nuances, and from each of those conversations I emerged clearer in my thinking about whatever we discussed. I cannot imagine having completed the project without his help on every detail of it.

This publication was brought into existence through the dedication and hard work of Stephanie Emerson, MOCA's editor, assisted by Jane Hyun. Both Stephanie and Jane displayed throughout the process the combination of professionalism and good humor that makes working with them such a pleasure. I also owe a great debt of thanks to John Alan Farmer, who read and commented on my text with his customary sensitivity and sense of structure. Michael Darling, Karin Higa and David Joselit also read drafts of my text and I benefited from their comments. The book was designed by Lorraine Wild, with Amanda Washburn and Bele Ducke. As usual, Lorraine has made a beautiful publication in which the design is completely in tune with the content. Deborah Kirshman at the University of California Press has been a wonderful collaborator as co-publisher. I appreciate her commitment and that of her colleagues at the Press. My thanks also to Brian Forrest, Scott Darling, Zoë Van Baaren, and James Isberner, who took new photographs on our behalf, and to Peter Kirby, who made film stills.

MOCA's chief registrar, Robert Hollister, and the registrar in charge of this exhibition, Rosanna Hemerick, handled the myriad details of bringing works of art from all over the country safely together in one place at the right time. I am constantly amazed at their calm in the face of such organizational complexity. John Bowsher, exhibitions production manager, and Jang Park, chief exhibition technician, oversaw the installation of the exhibition, along with Zazu Faure, exhibition production associate, and Barry Grady, Joe Howard, Shinichi Kitahara, and Valerie West, exhibition technicians. David Bradshaw installed the film and video elements.

My thanks also go to Kim Kanatani, director of education, and Caroline Blackburn, adult programs coordinator, for the extensive program of talks, workshops and readings that they organized around the exhibition. Sylvia Hohri, director of marketing and public relations, and Katherine Lee, media relations coordinator, were tireless in their efforts to publicize it. Beth Gruenberg expertly arranged the opening reception. Anna Boyiazis and Danielle Foushee are responsible for the graphic design related to the exhibition. Annie Reiniger and Stuart Comer were enthusiastic in developing related products for our store. In addition I would like to thank my colleagues Kim Cooper, Colette Dartnall, Julia Langlotz, Julie Lazar, Sheila Low, Ed Patuto, Alma Ruiz, and Brent Zerger.

One of the very great pleasures of organizing this exhibition has been the opportunity to meet and talk with many of the artists whose work is included in it. Norman Bluhm's death in February of this year deprived the American art world of a truly legendary figure, a man whose huge talent as a painter was matched by his zest for life and his generosity of spirit. I am very grateful to have been able to spend some time in his company, as well as that of his wife Cary and daughter Nina. He is greatly missed.

Jane Freilicher, Mike Goldberg, Alex Katz, and Alfred Leslie also were kind enough to spend long periods discussing their work and their memories of Frank O'Hara with me. All more than lived up to my expectations that they would be fascinating and engaging people. It was exciting finally to meet the artists whose work I have admired for so many years.

I also had the opportunity to meet and talk with a number of others who knew O'Hara well. Bill Berkson was helpful far beyond any of my expectations. He provided me with all manner of documents and information. More importantly, the time I spent talking with him yielded a trove of insights into O'Hara's poetry and his personality. Joe LeSueur was also a charming and generous host when I visited him, and shared his memories and reflections. The *Homage to Frank O'Hara* that Bill and Joe edited in 1978 was in many ways the starting point of this exhibition, and it remains a moving and essential volume. Others who took time to talk with me about their memories of O'Hara include James Eliot, Grace Hartigan, Kenneth Koch, Jack Larson, William Lieberman, Lewis MacAdams, Alvin Novak, Ron Padgett, and Tony Towle.

It was also a pleasure to get to know Maureen O'Hara, Frank O'Hara's sister and the executrix of his estate. She has been a most generous supporter of this project from the very beginning, and I am deeply grateful for the enthusiasm which she has brought to many different aspects of the exhibition.

I imposed upon a large number of people and institutions for loans, including many of those named above. I was often asking for works that are literally priceless to their owners. I cannot overstate how grateful I am to those who entrusted their works to us. My deepest thanks, therefore, go to John Bergman; Bill Berkson; the family of Norman Bluhm; Carmen Fernandez of Channel Thirteen; Richard Rubin and Joan Banach at the Dedalus Foundation; Mr. and Mrs. Richard P. Doerer; Michael Goldberg; Lynn Gumpert, director, and Michèle Wong, registrar, at the Grey Art Gallery and Study Center, New York University; Jasper Johns; Elizabeth Hazan; Frank Del Deo and Jennifer Samet at Hirschl and Adler Modern; Kenneth Koch; Jack Larson; Margo Leavin; Alfred Leslie; Joe LeSueur; Tara K. Reddi at Marlborough Gallery; Luke Matthiessen; Fred W. McDarrah; Mr. and Mrs. Earl McGrath;

Anna O'Sullivan, Michele R. Heinrici, and Amy Young at the Robert Miller Gallery; Robert Fitzpatrick, director, and Elizabeth A. T. Smith, chief curator, at the Museum of Contemporary Art, Chicago; Peter Namuth at Hans Namuth, Ltd., Elizabeth Broun, director, Jacquelin Serwer, curator of contemporary art, and Melissa L. Kroning, registrar, at the National Museum of American Art; Alan Fern, director, Liza Karvellas, exhibition coordinator, and Suzanne Jenkins, registrar, at the National Portrait Gallery; Colin Still of Optic Nerve; Ariel Follett O'Hara and J. Philip O'Hara; Maureen O'Hara; Ron and Pat Padgett; Larry Rivers; Charling Chang Fagan, library director, and Patti Owen, archivist, at Sarah Lawrence College; Dr. Robert Bertholf, curator of the Poetry and Rare Books Collection at the State University of New York, Buffalo; Mr. and Mrs. Eugene V. Thaw; Roger M. Berkowitz, director, at the Toledo Museum of Art; James Mundy, director and Joanne Potter, registrar, at the Frances Lehman Loeb Art Center at Vassar College; and Dan Wagoner.

I am very happy that the exhibition will be seen not only at MOCA, but also at the Wexner Center for the Arts, Columbus, Ohio, and at The Parrish Art Museum, Southhampton, New York. At the Wexner my deep thanks go to Sherri Geldin, director, and Donna De Salvo, curator at large, for their commitment to the project. At the Parrish, I am equally grateful to Trudy Kramer, director, and Alicia Longwell, curator, for their participation.

Fred Dewey, the director of Beyond Baroque in Los Angeles, collaborated with Lewis MacAdams and Kenward Elmslie on readings in conjunction with the exhibition, and Mark Salerno dedicated a special issue of his magazine *Arshile* to the work of Frank O'Hara. I am very grateful for their collegial approach to the exhibition.

I discussed O'Hara's life and work with many people, and drew heavily on those conversations for the ideas in this book. Marjorie Perloff is the author of an indispensable critical study of O'Hara's work, *Frank O'Hara: Poet Among Painters,* which shaped my thinking about his work. Marjorie was also incredibly generous in giving me access to her own research materials for that book, and in sharing her more recent thinking on O'Hara. I owe her an enormous debt of gratitude. Terence Diggory has also written brilliantly on O'Hara and his milieu, and he too was more than generous in sharing his thoughts with me. One of the first people I discussed the project with was John Yau, a wonderful poet who carries on a fine tradition by also writing frequently about art. My discussions with him were illuminating. Others from whose comments I benefited include Alison Gingeras, Lynn

Gumpert, Bruce Hainley, Klaus Kertess, David Lehman, Molly Nesbit, Robert Rosenblum, Manny Silverman, and Lynn Zelevansky.

There are many others who deserve my sincere thanks for their contributions to this project. Among them are Dr. Daisy Aldan, Charles Altieri, Paule Anglim, Jenny Augustyn, Jeffry Bailey, Lucinda Barnes, Wendy Brandow, Eric Brown, Rudy Burkhardt, Darlene Butler, May Castleberry, John Cheim, Amada Cruz, Denise Fasanello, Katy Flanagan, Marc Foxx, Vincent Katz, Lynn Kearcher, Gina Koziatek, Karen LaGatta, Gerard Malanga, Peter Namuth, Kay Pallister, Roberto Peccolo, Kathy Ritter, Bridgette Saylor, Linda Hooper, Daisy Kramer, Odyssia Skouros, Allan Stone, Claudia Stone, Kippy Stroud, Sarah Taggart, Sherry Thompson, Garner Tullis, Dianne Vanderlip, Barry Walker, and Aletha Zapf.

Finally, I want to give my thanks to Karin Higa, who probably now knows more about Frank O'Hara than she ever planned to. Without her constant support I could not have undertaken this project.

—Russell Ferguson

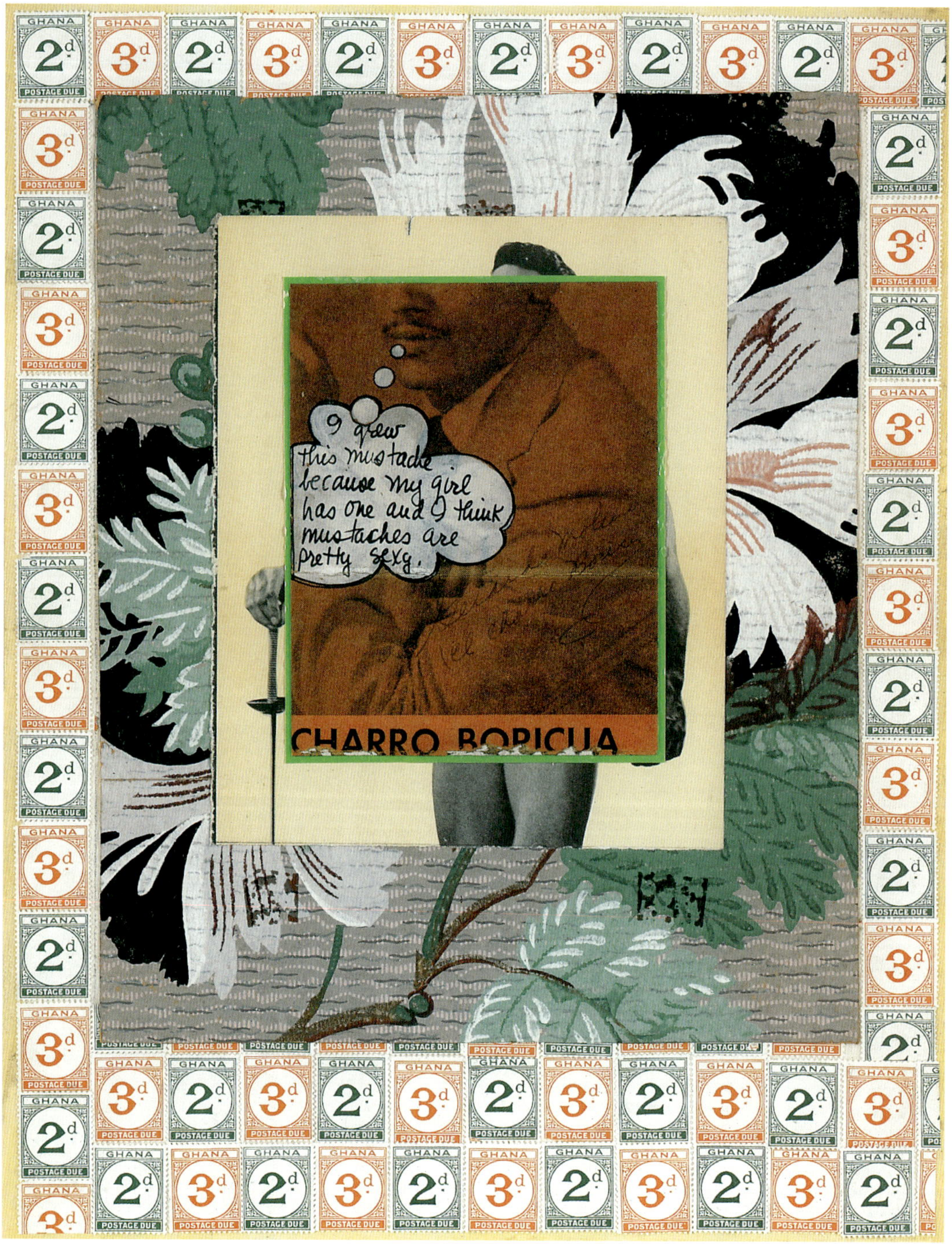

Joe Brainard and Frank O'Hara

"I Grew This Mustache. . .", 1964

In Memory of My Feelings: Frank O'Hara and American Art

Don't be bored

Frank O'Hara was one of the most important poets of his generation. Born in 1926, he had originally trained as a pianist, but as a Harvard undergraduate changed his focus to poetry. He moved to New York in 1951 and became deeply involved with the art world there. He worked at the front desk of The Museum of Modern Art (MoMA) until 1953, when he became an editorial associate at *Art News* for two years. He returned to MoMA in 1955 as an assistant in the International Program, and in 1960 became Assistant (later Associate) Curator in the Department of Painting and Sculpture. In 1966 he was struck by a jeep on the beach at Fire Island, sustaining injuries that led to his death. Throughout his career as a critic and curator, O'Hara wrote the poetry that is the primary basis for his reputation today.

This book is not, however, a study of his poetry. Nor is it a biographical study.[1] Its aim, rather, is to use the charismatic figure of O'Hara as a lens through which to take another look at the most mythologized period in American art. Despite much recent scholarship, the oversimplified narrative remains only too familiar: a heroic generation of Abstract Expressionist pioneers followed by a much weaker "second generation," and then by the explosion of Pop. In that version of history, there is little room for the strong tradition of realist and figurative painting that continued throughout the period. Nor does it easily accommodate idiosyncratic figures who cannot be easily pigeonholed, such as Joe Brainard or Alfred Leslie.

The real lives of artists, and their relationships with those they consider their peers, are much more complex than the processes of art history sometimes render them. In looking at the extraordinarily rich texture of the New York art world from the early fifties until 1966 through the lens provided by Frank O'Hara, I want to suggest one alternative path through the period. Other focal points would yield other narratives, but the milieu that is visible in O'Hara's writing and in the work gathered for this exhibition will, I hope, be compelling enough to communicate with those who look back at it today from a distance of almost forty years. This account is devoted to the artists who made up much of his circle, among whom he was by turn acolyte, friend, model, muse, collaborator, and critic. O'Hara's poetry has of course a much greater scope than that circle. But it is also true that his artist friends are everywhere in the poetry. His friendships and his work are in fact inseparable. For O'Hara poetry had no meaning except in the context of a life fully lived, just as living life fully for him meant always to be engaged with poetry and with art.

To be fully engaged did not mean the pursuit of any doctrinaire position. O'Hara was notorious, in fact, for the rapidity with which he could shift his position. He often preferred the vigorous cut and thrust of argument itself to the conclusions drawn from it. In art he rejected absolutely any rigid identification with one tendency in painting over another. He had no time for critical approaches that would declare certain areas off limits for serious artists. O'Hara was consistently eclectic in a period when an exclusionary reductivism was increasingly becoming the critical norm. His passionate engagement with the work of an enormously diverse group of artists could not have been more different from the prescriptive criticism practiced by Clement Greenberg. Greenberg saw the future in an art that was self-referential and devoted to the special qualities of its medium. There was little room here for strongly expressed personal feelings. "The ambitious contemporary artist," Greenberg wrote, "distrusts more and more of his emotions."[2] It is hard to imagine a position further from that of O'Hara, who trusted *only* his emotional responses. The composer Morton Feldman has said that, "It is interesting that in a circle that demanded partisanship above all, he was so totally accepted. I suppose we recognized that his wisdom came from his own 'system'—the dialectic of the heart."[3] O'Hara, as an artist himself—a poet—perhaps identified with the individuals who struggled to create as much as with their completed works. As the painter John Button put it, "Frank's respect, his admiration, his judgment, and his love seemed inseparable."[4] He was always open to whatever he saw emerging from the studios in which he was a constant visitor, resistant only to work that he felt lacked true passion. As he said about the sculpture of David Smith, "Don't be bored, don't be lazy, don't be trivial and don't be proud. The slightest loss of attention leads to death."[5] This sense of constant attentiveness to the shifting nuances of his physical and emotional worlds was at the heart of both his poetry and his relationships with his countless friends.

With regard to his own work, O'Hara was both self-effacingly modest and supremely confident. His poems, he wrote, might "just shrivel up, turn brown and blow away. But on the other hand, if we can't make leaves, neither can god poems."[6] While he was in no doubt about the quality of his poetry, he made only the most cursory attempts to disseminate it, sometimes simply putting completed poems away in a drawer, and often not even keeping copies of poems he sent to friends. When he did publish, it was predominantly in the most fleeting of little magazines. Feldman recalls that:

> He never talked about his own work; at least, not to me. If ever I complimented him on something he had done he would answer, all smiles, "well,—thank you." That was the end of it. As if he were saying, "Now, you don't have to congratulate me about a thing. Naturally, everything I do is first rate, but it's you who needs looking after."[7]

Such self-effacement was not simply a matter of politeness. On a deeper level O'Hara's very sense of self was constantly refracted through his relationships with other people, their work and their needs. He was always available. "At times Frank seemed to be a priest who got into a different business," Alex Katz wrote. "Even on his sixth martini–second pack of cigarettes and while calling a friend, 'a bag of shit,' and roaring off into the night. Frank's business was being an active intellectual. He was out to improve our world whether we liked it or not.... The frightening amount of energy he invested in our art and our lives often made me feel like a miser."[8]

It is probably impossible to capture in print the essence of a charismatic figure like O'Hara, no matter how many of his friends' voices are invoked. "I remember him coming into a crowded party, and he just seemed to have a spotlight on him," said Lewis MacAdams.[9] "He talked and I listened," James Schuyler remembered. "His conversation

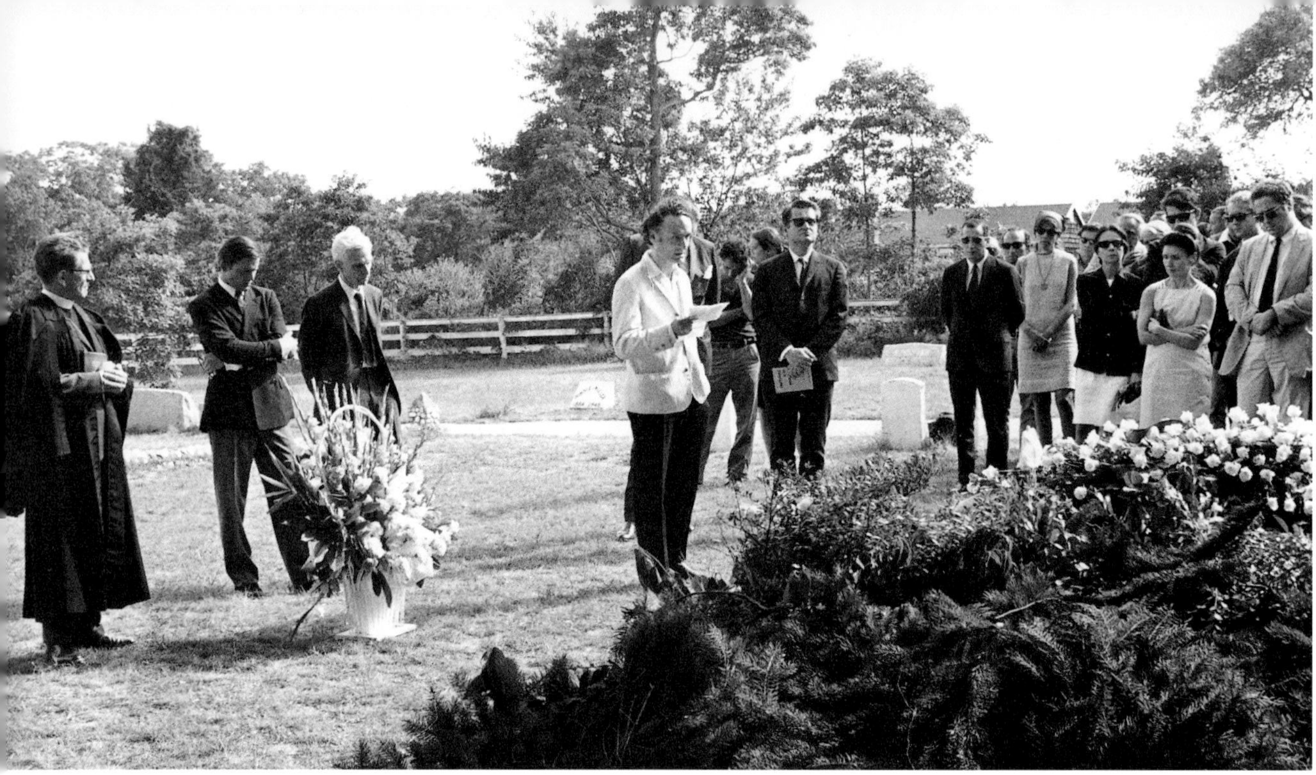

was self-propelling and one idea, or anecdote, or *bon mot* was fuel to his own fire, inspiring him verbally to blaze ahead, that curious voice rising and falling, full of invisible italics, the strong pianist's hands gesturing with the invariable cigarette."[10] Philip Guston recalled how O'Hara's flights of language could make even Guston's own studio, previously "a giant ashtray," into a site of new inspiration. "Frank was in his most non-stop way of talking, saying that the pictures put him in mind of Tiepolo. Certain cupola frescoes. Suddenly I was working in an ancient building, a warehouse facing the Giudecca. The loft over the Firehouse was transformed. It was filled with light reflected from the canal. I was a painter in Venice."[11] Guston's portrait drawing of O'Hara goes to the edge of caricature to catch him in the act of holding forth in this way. Guston's line traces the elegant curve of O'Hara's neck and head, his broken nose, and his lips, parted to deliver the next sparkling line.

At O'Hara's funeral, Larry Rivers said, "Frank O'Hara was my best friend. There are at least sixty people in New York who thought Frank O'Hara was their best friend."[12] That sentiment was echoed repeatedly by those who knew him. Everyone he befriended felt the greatest intimacy with him, even as they recognized that his intimacy was exclusive only for the time that they were with him. As John Gruen wrote, "When Frank talked to you he made you feel everything *you* did was of vital importance and interest—at least for the moment."[13]

Larry Rivers speaking at Frank O'Hara's funeral,
Springs Cemetery, Long Island, New York
July 27, 1966

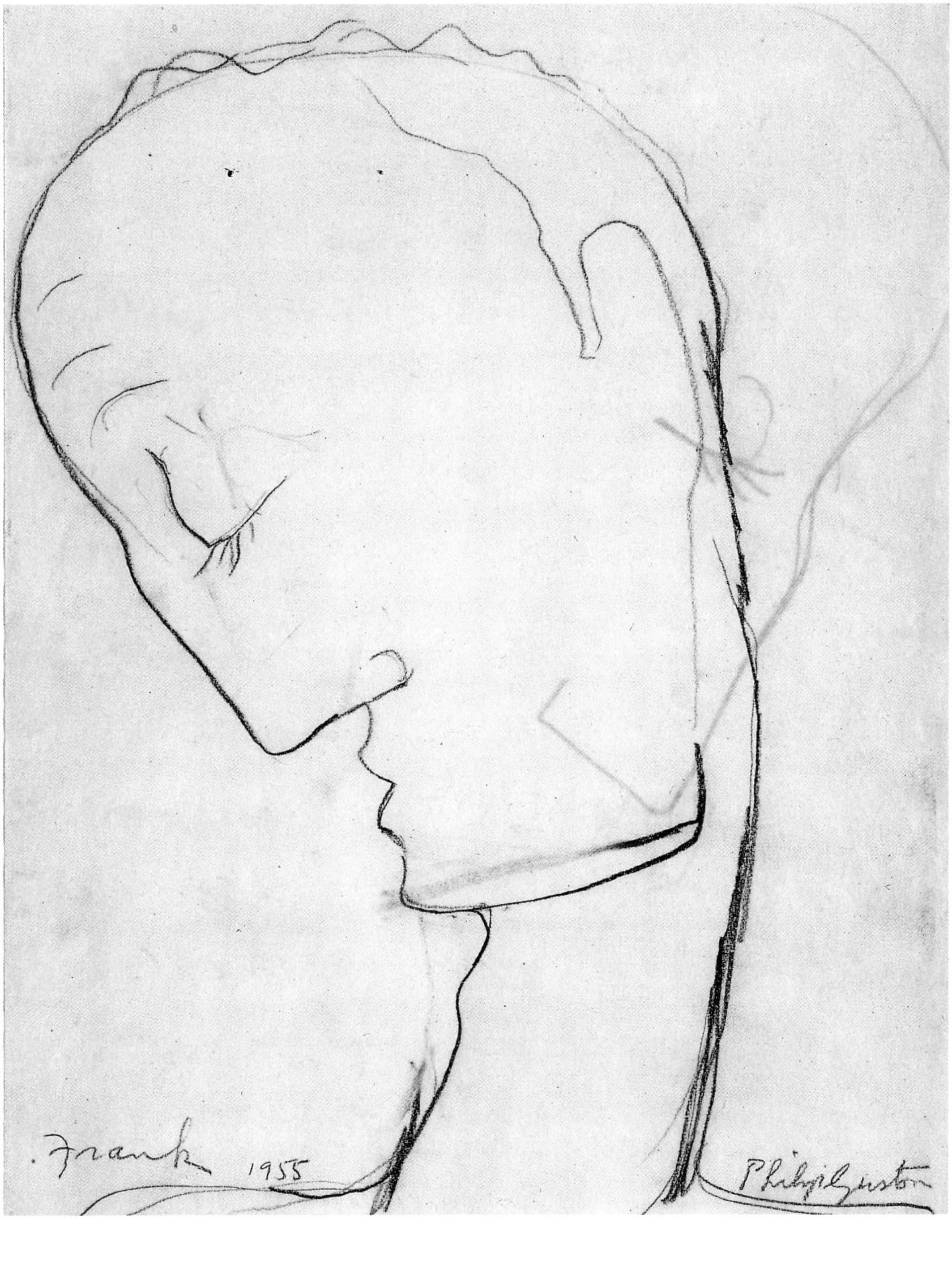

Philip Guston

Frank, 1955

Why I am not a painter

As a literary figure, O'Hara is usually said to be a member of the New York School of poets, a group that has as its core O'Hara, John Ashbery, Kenneth Koch, and James Schuyler, with a number of other distinguished poets such as Edwin Denby, Kenward Elmslie, and Barbara Guest sometimes included. Others such as Bill Berkson, Ted Berrigan, Alice Notley, Ron Padgett, and Tony Towle followed a little later. The idea of a "New York School" of poets began as a light-hearted imitation of the New York School of painting, a term that was itself initially a parody of the Schools of Florence, Paris, and so on. None of the poets involved saw themselves as a group in any sense beyond a group of friends, and Ashbery himself lived in Paris for most of the period during which the "School" might be said to have been most active.[14]

The New York School is thus a loose concept at best. Its central characteristics might be said to be an informality of both tone and structure, an idiomatic lack of pretension, and a self-conscious, often playful, spontaneity. Today it is impossible to read the work of Ashbery and O'Hara without feeling the enormous differences of style, intent, technique, and sensibility that separate the two poets. Indeed, as Marjorie Perloff has written,

> what we might call "criticism based on movement affiliation" is bound, sooner or later, to give way to a historical and literary reshuffling of the deck. Beckett the "absurdist" becomes Beckett the Anglo-Irish heir to Yeats and Joyce. Frank O'Hara, the "New York School Abstract Expressionist poet" becomes O'Hara, the oppositional gay American poet in the line of Whitman.[15]

As each wave of more or less facile characterizations emerges and recedes, what is left behind by such historical sifting (we hope) are the individual voices of the poets. It is precisely the specificity of O'Hara's poetry (much criticized at the time as "gossipy" or diaristic) that gives his voice such a distinct presence today. His language always tended toward the vernacular and the casual, in marked contrast to what Kenneth Rexroth called the "dreadful posturings"[16] of the poetry mainstream. O'Hara wanted to be able to pull his poetry right out of the life he was actually living, not cobble it together as labored allegory. "Lord! spare us from any more Fisher kings!" he sighed.[17] Instead, as Ashbery put it,

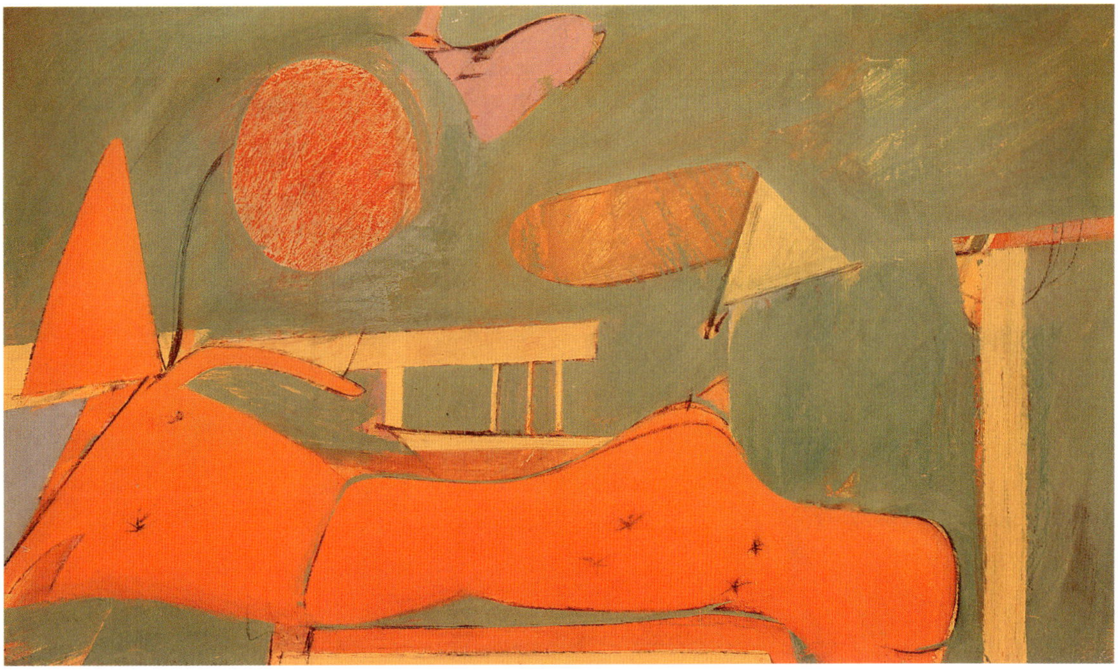

"O'Hara grabs for the end product—the delight—and hands it over, raw and palpitating."[18]

Of all the so-called New York School poets, it is unquestionably O'Hara who had the closest relationship with the painters for whom the term New York School has now become canonical, despite differences between the work of, say, Willem de Kooning and Barnett Newman that are at least as wide as those between O'Hara and Ashbery. O'Hara wrote the first monograph on Jackson Pollock (in 1959), he was a close friend of de Kooning and Franz Kline, and he organized The Museum of Modern Art retrospective of Robert Motherwell's work in 1965. One of his simplest and most affecting poems, "Radio," is written in praise of a de Kooning painting he owned at one time, *Summer Couch* (1943).

Well, I have my beautiful de Kooning
to aspire to. I think it has an orange
bed in it, more than the ear can hold[19]

These relationships with the giant figures of Abstract Expressionism remained the foundation of his career as a curator, even as he developed less reverential relationships with a younger generation of artists.

O'Hara's poem, "Why I Am Not a Painter," elucidates the differences between the practice of painting and that of poetry even as it subtly suggests some parallels.

Willem de Kooning, **Summer Couch**, 1943
Oil on board, 36 x 51 inches, Private Collection

I am not a painter, I am a poet.
Why? I think I would rather be
a painter, but I am not. Well,

for instance, Mike Goldberg
is starting a painting. I drop in.
"Sit down and have a drink" he
says. I drink; we drink. I look
up. "You have SARDINES in it."
"Yes, it needed something there."
"Oh." I go and the days go by
and I drop in again. The painting
is going on, and I go, and the days
go by. I drop in. The painting is
finished. "Where's SARDINES?"
All that's left is just
letters, "It was too much," Mike says.

But me? One day I am thinking of
a color: orange. I write a line
about orange. Pretty soon it is a
whole page of words, not lines.
Then another page. There should be
so much more, not of orange, of
words, of how terrible orange is
and life. Days go by. It is even in
prose, I am a real poet. My poem
is finished and I haven't mentioned
orange yet. It's twelve poems, I call
it ORANGES. And one day in a gallery
I see Mike's painting, called SARDINES.

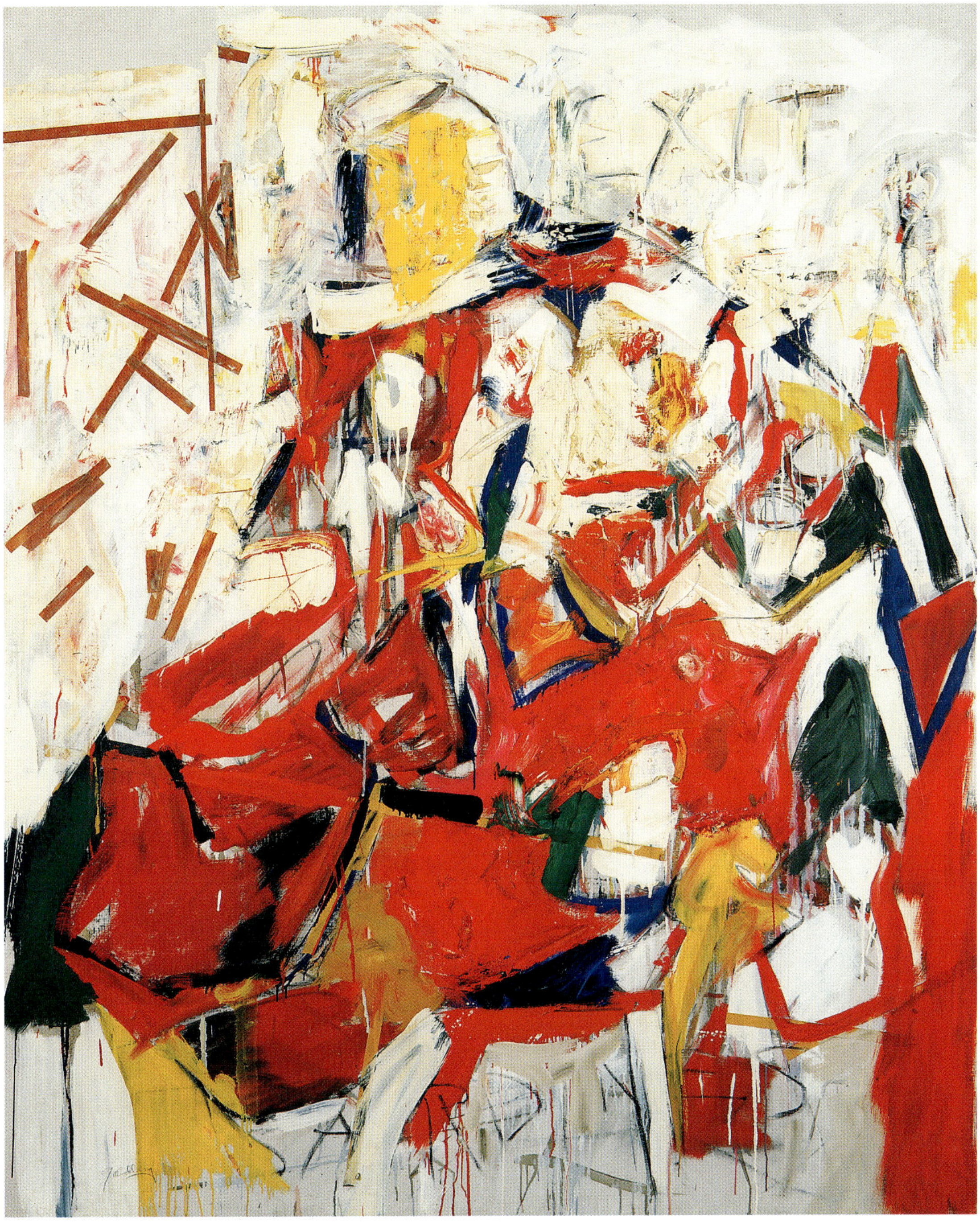

Michael Goldberg

Sardines, 1955

The poem evokes downtown artistic life in the mid-fifties, with the poet-critic regularly dropping by the studios of his friends. It is the kind of scene that would later be the stuff of myth-making, but in the poem there is only a workmanlike attention to the mechanics of creation and a shared enthusiasm for them. There is sociable drinking, there is the artist's laconic but friendly resistance to interpretation, and, most of all, there is the sense of work steadily progressing, almost with a life of its own, as the "days go by." And this is true for both the painter and the poet. Both men present themselves as engaged in a kind of dialogue with their work, a process in which they intervene without being able to exercise complete control. Goldberg's painting seems to speak to him, even as O'Hara's poem cycle tries to run away.

Beyond this sense of a simultaneous, parallel, and continuing process, O'Hara's poem sets up a complex web of comparisons and distinctions between the two practices. Goldberg can insert a word, "sardines," into his painting, but then he can smash that word into fragments, retaining it as a whole only in his title. "Exit" actually remains more prominent, although that too may be a fragment. Words for him are visual elements at least as much as they are signifiers of particular objects. O'Hara, symmetrically, begins with a color, orange, although, as he says, he never uses the word itself. Just as Goldberg breaks his word down into letters, O'Hara's poem devolves from "a line / about orange" into a "whole page of words, not lines." Lines here can stand for both conventional poetic structure, with which the poet can break ("It is even in / prose"), and the linearity of a painter's gesture, the purity of which he cannot reach, tied as he remains to the specificity of language. "Not lines" thus represents simultaneously a rebellion against literature and a failure to attain true independence from representation. For O'Hara, even if he never mentions orange, it retains its "terrible" quality as a word as well as a color.

While O'Hara sought out relationships between the paintings he loved and his work as a poet, he remained aware that any such connection would always be problematic. He denied that any of his poems, even sprawling explorations of spontaneity such as "Second Avenue," were abstract in any meaningful way, even if others saw them so. Allen Ginsberg, for example, called such "long meaningless poems" exercises in "freedom of composition"[20] and thus comparable to abstraction in art, but O'Hara himself saw Willem de Kooning's women in "Second Avenue." In fact O'Hara remained consistently interested in issues of representation in painting, even in an era when abstraction dominated. He was one of relatively few critics of the period, for example, to see that even for Pollock, representation remained an urgent issue. "The crisis of figurative as opposed to non-figurative art pursued him throughout his life,"[21] O'Hara wrote in 1959, when Pollock's achievement was all but universally taken to be purely abstract. And he knew that poetry would always be unable to completely break the chains of representation. Ashbery has emphasized that,

> artists like de Kooning, Franz Kline, Motherwell, Pollock—were free to be free in their painting in a way that most people felt was impossible for poetry. So I think we learned a lot from them at that time, and also from composers like John Cage and Morton Feldman, but the lessons were merely an abstract truth—something like Be yourself—rather than a practical one—in other words, nobody ever thought he would scatter words over a page the way Pollock scattered his drips.[22]

The work of Stéphane Mallarmé and the Dada poets notwithstanding, words always retain elements of representation. O'Hara never made any very serious attempt to pursue an experimental practice that would have taken him outside language as a referential system. He accepted that his poetry—any poetry—could never achieve the direct immediacy in itself of a brushstroke across a piece of canvas.

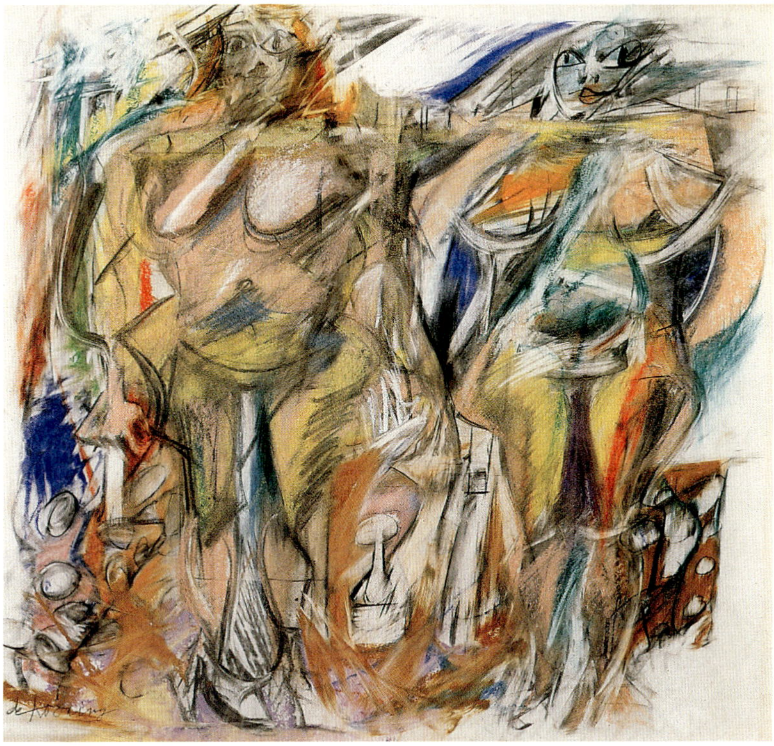

Willem de Kooning

Two Women with Still Life, 1952

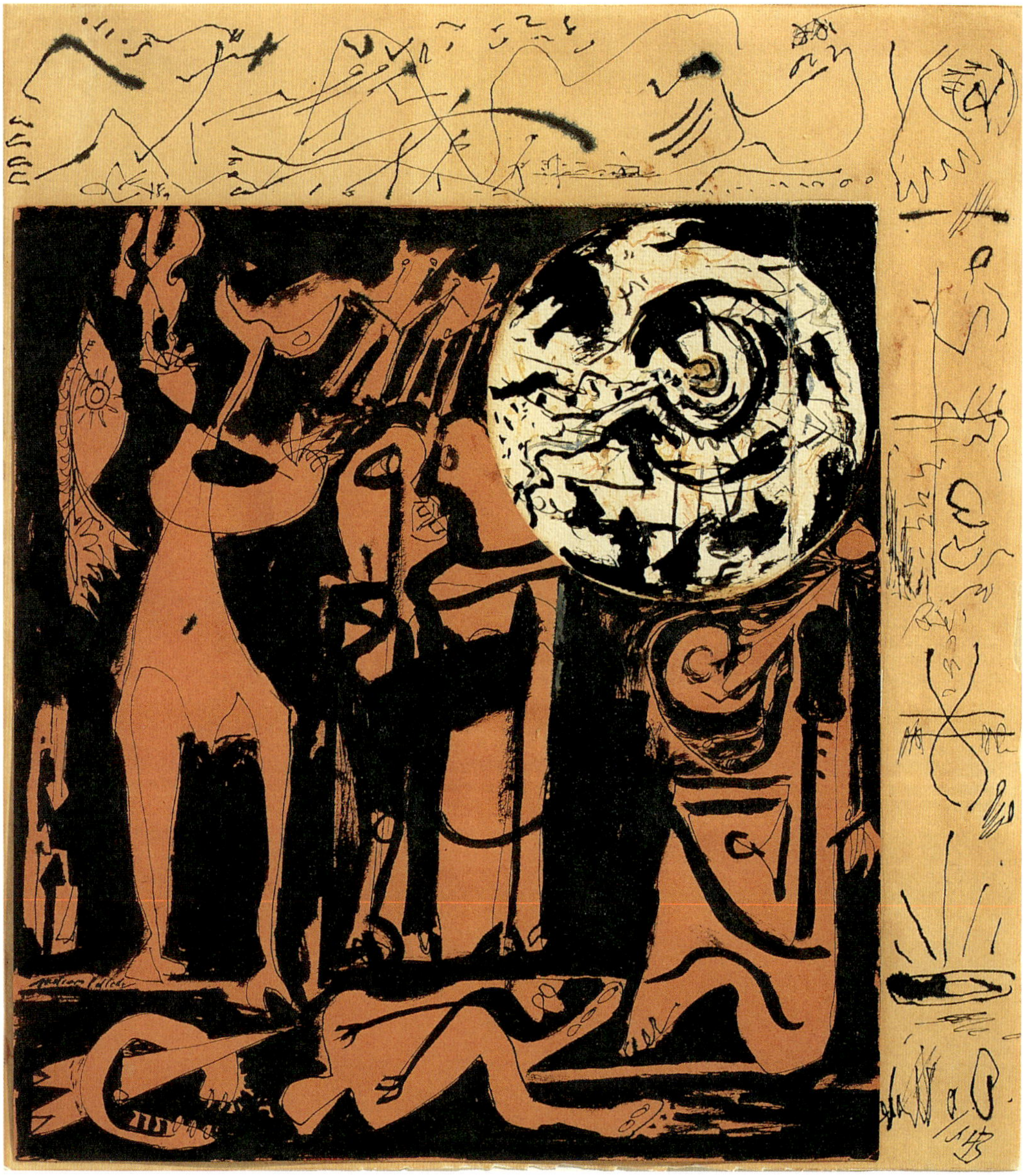

Jackson Pollock

Untitled, 1943

Everything suddenly

If there is a true point of contact between New York School painting and O'Hara's poetry, it is to be found less in the painters' pursuit of untrammelled access to the realms of the unconscious—O'Hara was above all self-conscious—than in the idea of the spontaneous. "Like Pollock," Ashbery wrote, "O'Hara demonstrates that the act of creation and the finished creation are the same."[23] He could produce wonderful poems in a single sitting, most famously "Poem (Lana Turner has collapsed!)," which he wrote on the Staten Island Ferry on the way to a reading with Robert Lowell:

> **I have been to lots of parties**
> **and acted perfectly disgraceful**
> **but I never actually collapsed**
> **oh Lana Turner we love you get up**

He was also capable of writing poems in bars or at parties, and often did so. Kenneth Koch vividly recalls him sitting typing in the middle of a crowded party. "Whatever was going through his head was precious. Frank was trying to run faster than ordinary consciousness."[24] This fecundity impressed painters who were struggling to produce. "All the artists I knew at the time were vaguely constipated," Goldberg recalls. "The favorite refrain of the period was 'Ain't it hard, gee ain't it hard.'"[25]

O'Hara's apparent casualness did not conceal his great learning, and he regularly dazzled his friends with the range of his knowledge. For O'Hara, however, the goal was never to flaunt his erudition, but rather to submerge its deeper content in the embrace of the quotidian; to write always in the now of a particular time and place. Where the first generation of New York School painters often sought an overt profundity, O'Hara strove to preserve in his writing the spontaneity and lightness of touch of his speech. "I don't believe in reworking—too much" he told Edward Lucie-Smith. "And what really makes me happy is when something just falls into place as if it were a conversation or something."[26] As Koch has convincingly argued, "The speed and accidental aspect of his writing are not carelessness but are essential to what the poems are about: the will to catch what is there while it is really there and still taking place."[27] Or as Bill Berkson put it, "It is not that he lacked selectivity or discrimination, but rather that his poems grew out of a process of natural selection—discrimination conjoining civility of attention—so that any particle of experience quick enough to get fixed in his busy consciousness earned its point of relevance."[28]

For O'Hara what was really there was always filtered through his relationships with other people. Although his poetry is highly personal, it is rarely confessional, a common trope in poetry both then and now. He complained, for example, that Lowell had "a confessional manner which [lets him] get away with things that are really just plain bad but you're supposed to be interested because he's supposed to be so upset."[29] O'Hara was certainly not opposed to the expression of emotion, only to emotional effects that he felt were obtained too easily, too cheaply. In this he could find common ground with the painters among whom he moved, who prized authenticity above all else. He rarely fell into the sentimental or self-indulgent. O'Hara was self-consciously a man of his time, for whom self-pity was something that had to be risen above. The dark, semi-apocalyptic mood that had characterized forties culture was dissipating and giving way to a new optimism about the present and the future. It is hard now to recapture the sense of supreme self-confidence that American culture had in the late fifties and early sixties. John F. Kennedy's election at the beginning of the sixties brought to the presidency a man in some ways very similar to O'Hara in background: a Harvard-educated Irish Catholic who had served in the Navy during the war. What is more, his administration seemed to look favorably on the arts. Jackie Kennedy visited the Tibor de Nagy Gallery, an event that O'Hara celebrated in a poem.[30] Among artists, critics, and poets, it was implicitly agreed that New York was simply the new center of the cultural world. O'Hara loved the rough, agitated, constantly surprising buzz of the city. "I can't even enjoy a blade of grass unless I know there's a subway handy, or a record store or some other sign that people do not totally *regret* life."[31] In many ways he has become *the* poet of New York City. Part of the success of his vision of New York is that, while it is intensely romantic, it is not *too* romantic. The hot dog stands and car repair places attracted him as much as or even more than the shining skyscrapers.

Is it dirty
does it look dirty
that's what you think of in the city

does it just seem dirty
that's what you think of in the city
you don't refuse to breathe do you[32]

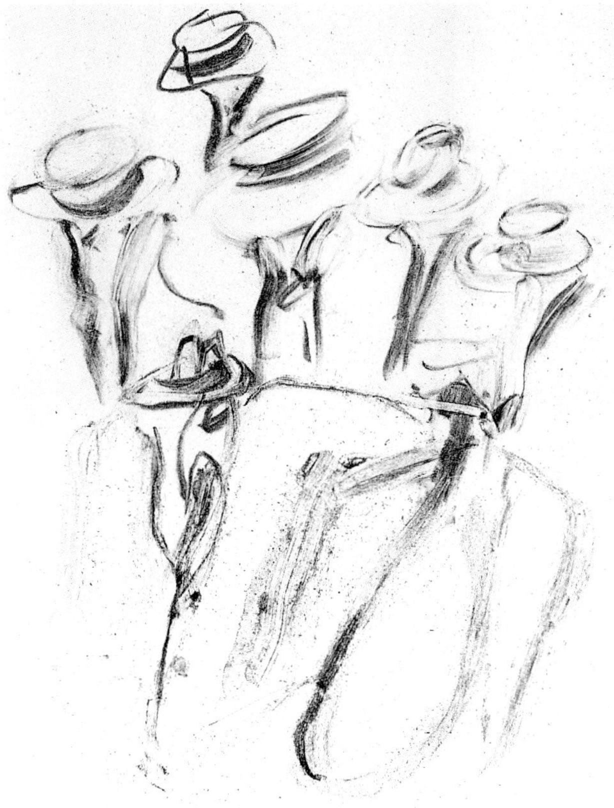

Ode to Willem de Kooning

1

Beyond the sunrise
where the black begins
                                        an enormous city
                                        is sending up its shutters

and just before the last lapse of nerve which I am already sorry for,
that friends describe as "just this once" in a temporary hell, I hope

I try to seize upon greatness
which is available to me
                                        through generosity and
                                        lavishness of spirit, yours

not to be inimitably weak
and picturesque, my self
                                        but to be standing clearly
                                        alone in the orange wind

while our days tumble and rant through Gotham and the Easter narrows
and I have not the courage to convict myself of cowardice or care

for now a long history slinks over the sill, of patent absurdities
and the fathomless miseries of a small person upset by personality

and I look to the flags
in your eyes as they go up
                                        on the enormous walls
                                        as the brave must always ascend

into the air, always the musts
like banderillas dangling

and jingling jewel-like amidst the red drops on the shoulders of men
who lead us not forward or backward, but on as we must go on

                                        out into the mesmerized world
                                        of inanimate voices like traffic

noises, hewing a clearing
in the crowded abyss of the West

"Ode to Willem de Kooning" (1957),
illustrated by Willem de Kooning,
from **In Memory of My Feelings**, 1967

Now there is only one man I love to kiss when he is unshaven, Heterosexuality! you are inexorably approaching. (How discourage her?)

St. Serapion, I wrap myself in the robes of your whiteness which is like midnight in Dostoevsky. How am I to become a legend, my dear? I've tried love, but that hides you in the bosom of another and I am always springing forth from it like the lotus—the ecstasy of always bursting forth! (but one must not be distracted by it!) or like a hyacinth, "to keep the filth of life away," yes, there, even in the heart, where the filth is pumped in and slanders and pollutes and determines. I will my will, though I may become famous for a mysterious vacancy in that department, that greenhouse.

Destroy yourself, if you don't know!

It is easy to be beautiful; it is difficult to appear so. I admire you, beloved, for the trap you've set. It's like a final chapter no one reads because the plot is over.

"Fanny Brown is run away—scampered off with a Cornet of Horse; I do love that little Minx, & hope She may be happy, tho' She has vexed me by this Exploit a little too. —Poor silly Cecchina! or F: B: as we used to call her.—I wish She had a good Whipping and 10,000 pounds." —Mrs. Thrale.

I've got to get out of here. I choose a piece of shawl and my dirtiest suntans. I'll be back, I'll re-emerge, defeated, from the valley; you don't want me to go where you go, so I go where you don't want me to. It's only afternoon, there's a lot ahead. There won't be any mail downstairs. Turning, I spit in the lock and the knob turns.

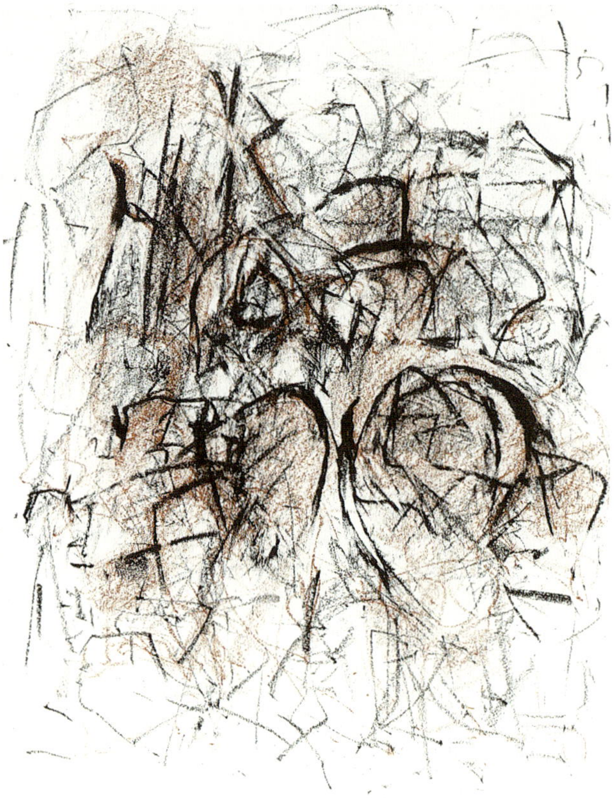

"Meditations in an Emergency" (1954),
illustrated by Joan Mitchell,
from **In Memory of My Feelings**, 1967

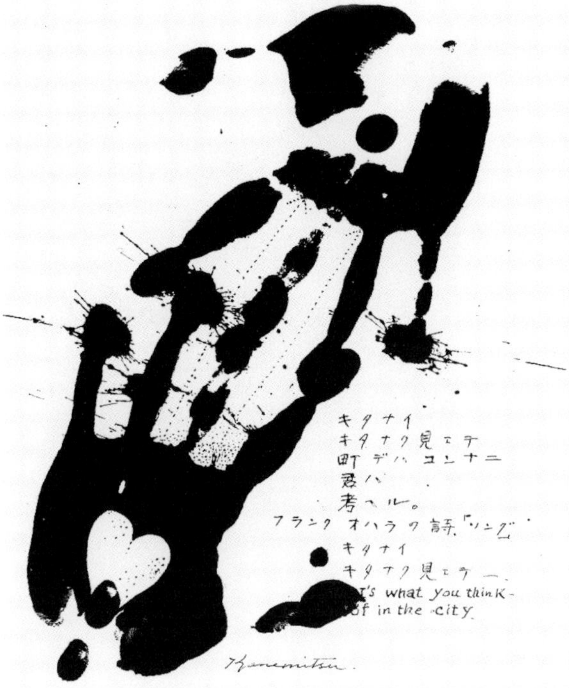

Song

Is it dirty
does it look dirty
that's what you think of in the city

does it just seem dirty
that's what you think of in the city
you don't refuse to breathe do you

someone comes along with a very bad character
he seems attractive. is he really. yes. very
he's attractive as his character is bad. is it. yes

that's what you think of in the city
run your finger along your no-moss mind
that's not a thought that's soot

and you take a lot of dirt off someone
is the character less bad. no. it improves constantly
you don't refuse to breathe do you

"Song" (1959),
illustrated by Mike Kanemitsu,
from **In Memory of My Feelings**, 1967

Sleeping on the Wing

Perhaps it is to avoid some great sadness,
as in a Restoration tragedy the hero cries "Sleep!
O for a long sound sleep and so forget it!"
that one flies, soaring above the shoreless city,
veering upward from the pavement as a pigeon
does when a car honks or a door slams, the door
of dreams, life perpetuated in parti-colored loves
and beautiful lies all in different languages.

Fear drops away too, like the cement, and you
are over the Atlantic. Where is Spain? where is
who? The Civil War was fought to free the slaves,
was it? A sudden down-draught reminds you of gravity
and your position in respect to human love. But
here is where the gods are, speculating, bemused.
Once you are helpless, you are free, can you believe
that? Never to waken to the sad struggle of a face?
to travel always over some impersonal vastness,
to be out of, forever, neither in nor for!

The eyes roll asleep as if turned by the wind
and the lids flutter open slightly like a wing.
The world is an iceberg, so much is invisible!
and was and is, and yet the form, it may be sleeping
too. Those features etched in the ice of someone
loved who died, you are a sculptor dreaming of space
and speed, your hand alone could have done this.

Curiosity, the passionate hand of desire. Dead,
or sleeping? Is there speed enough? And, swooping,
you relinquish all that you have made your own,
the kingdom of your self sailing, for you must awake
and breathe your warmth in this beloved image
whether it's dead or merely disappearing,
as space is disappearing and your singularity.

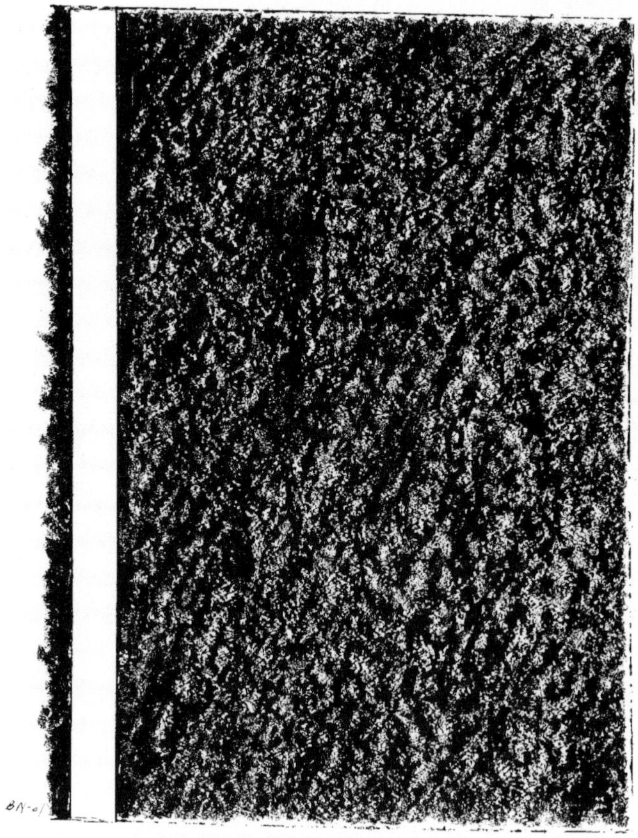

"Sleeping on the Wing" (1955),
illustrated by Barnett Newman,
from **In Memory of My Feelings**, 1967

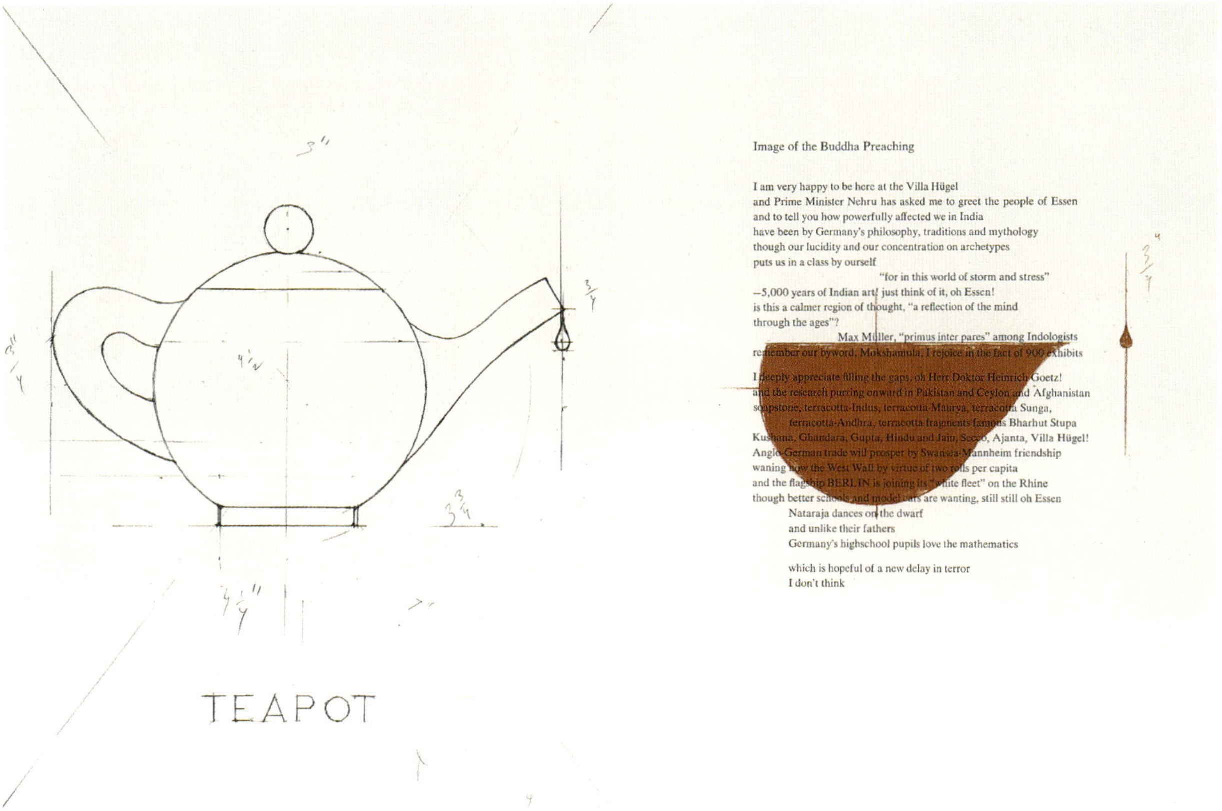

Image of the Buddha Preaching

I am very happy to be here at the Villa Hügel
and Prime Minister Nehru has asked me to greet the people of Essen
and to tell you how powerfully affected we in India
have been by Germany's philosophy, traditions and mythology
though our lucidity and our concentration on archetypes
puts us in a class by ourself
"for in this world of storm and stress"
–5,000 years of Indian art! just think of it, oh Essen!
is this a calmer region of thought, "a reflection of the mind
through the ages"?
Max Müller, "primus inter pares" among Indologists
remember our byword, Mokshamula, I rejoice in the fact of 900 exhibits

I deeply appreciate filling the gaps, oh Herr Doktor Heinrich Goetz!
and the research purring onward in Pakistan and Ceylon and Afghanistan
soapstone, terracotta-Indus, terracotta-Maurya, terracotta Sunga,
terracotta-Andhra, terracotta fragments famous Bharhut Stupa
Kushana, Ghandara, Gupta, Hindu and Jain, Secco, Ajanta, Villa Hügel!
Anglo-German trade will prosper by Swansea-Mannheim friendship
waning now the West Wall by virtue of two rolls per capita
and the flagship BERLIN is joining its "white fleet" on the Rhine
though better schools and model cars are wanting, still still oh Essen
Nataraja dances on the dwarf
and unlike their fathers
Germany's highschool pupils love the mathematics

which is hopeful of a new delay in terror
I don't think

"Image of the Buddha Preaching" (1959),
illustrated by Claes Oldenburg,
from **In Memory of My Feelings**, 1967

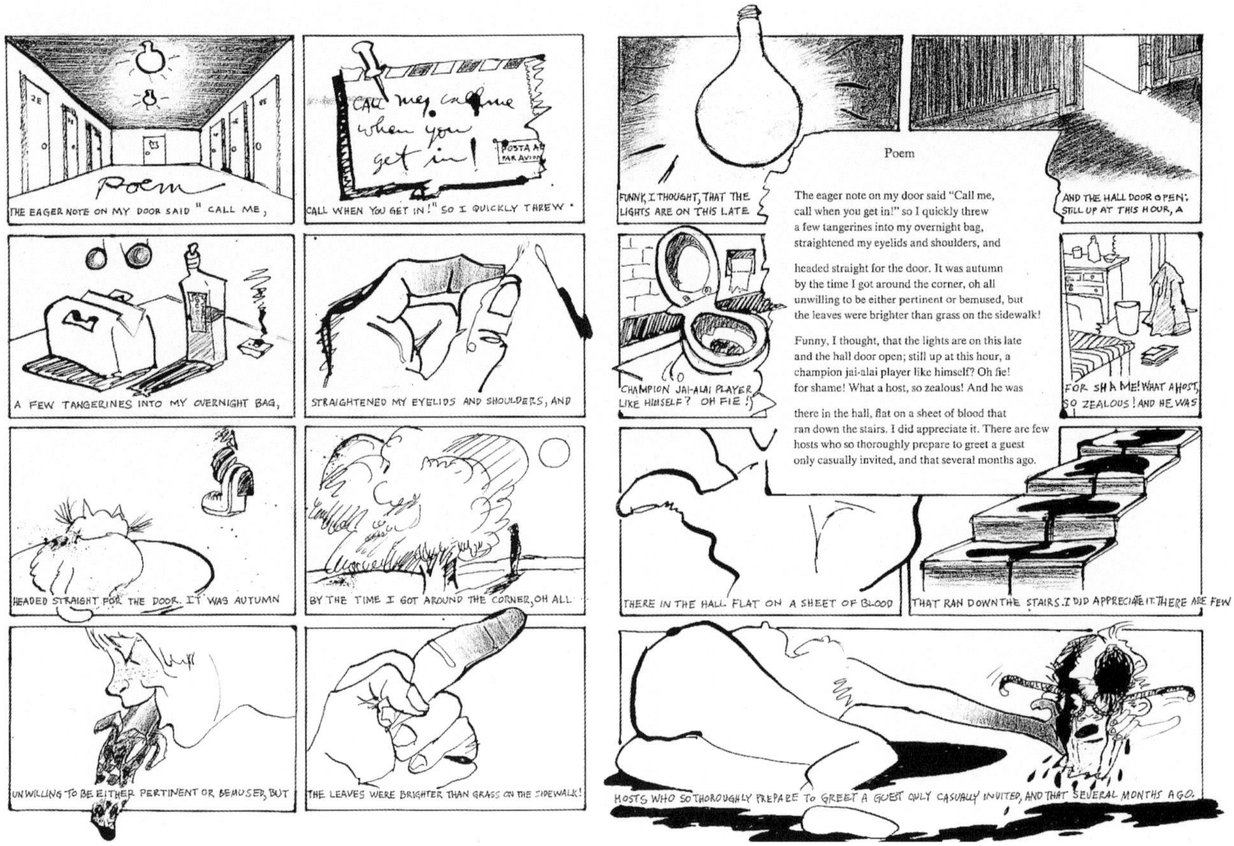

"Poem (The eager note. . .)" (1950),
illustrated by Alfred Leslie,
from **In Memory of My Feelings**, 1967

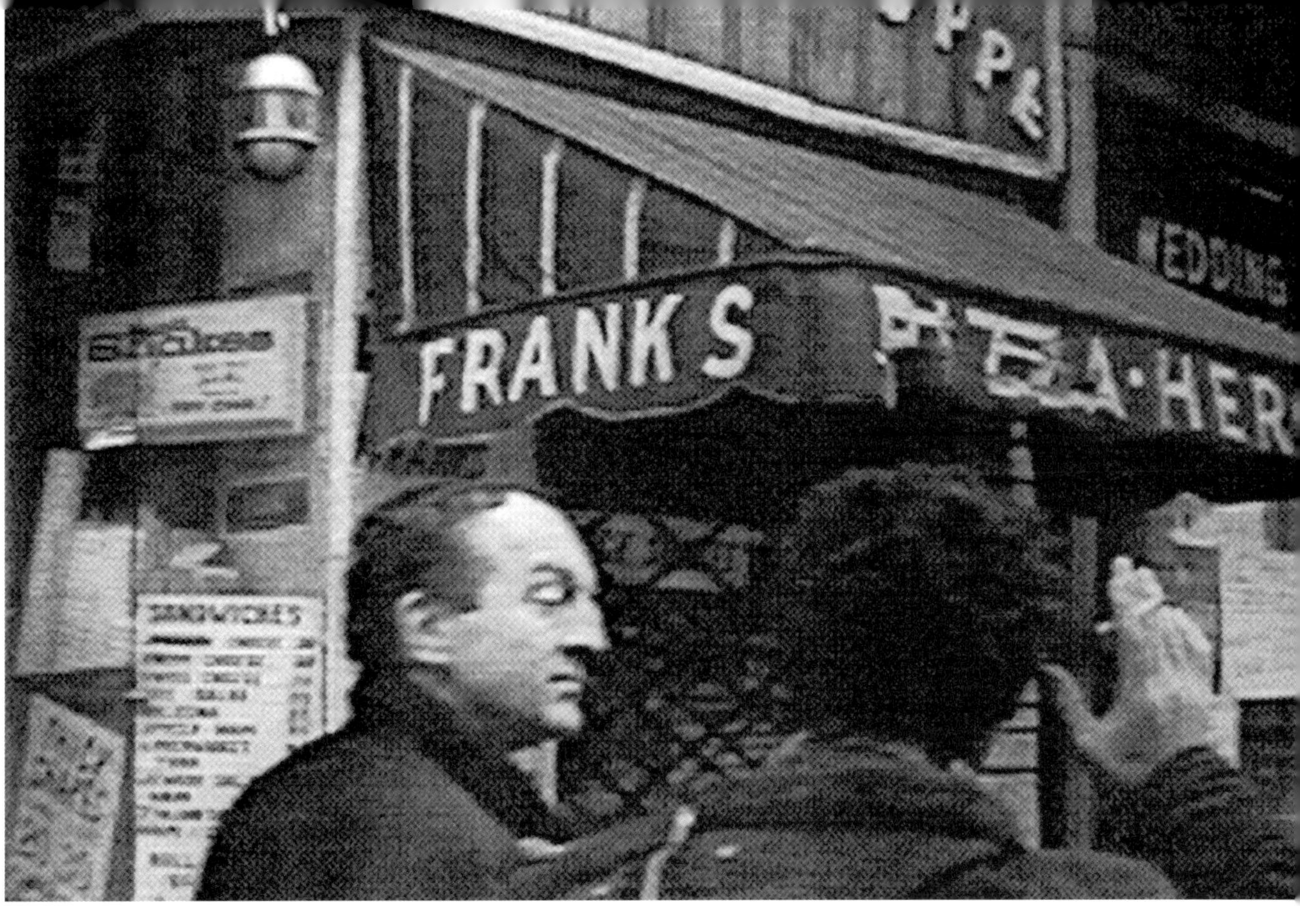

still from
USA Poetry: Frank O'Hara, 1966

This love for the filth of the city was matched by a hostility to the country. "I'm not a pastoral type any more," he wrote. "I hate the country and its bells and its photographs."[33] The unchanging rhythm of church bells and the frozen passage into the past of old photographs form an unwelcome counterpart to the ever-changing clamor of the city, the constantly evolving present in which O'Hara wants to live. The city can even be seen as the *new* nature, superseding the old rather than simply obliterating it. "A woman stepping off a bus may afford a greater insight into nature than the hills outside Rome, for nature has not stood still since Shelley's day."[34] He welcomed the changing fabric of the city, the construction workers continually transforming the urban landscape. His friend William Weaver was with him one day as some old brownstones were being demolished. "I said, in the usual clichéd way, 'Oh what a pity they're tearing down those brownstones.' Frank said, 'Oh no, that's the way New York is. You have to just keep tearing it down and building it up.'"[35] O'Hara's new nature is a kaleidoscope of individual moments that flow into and out of his consciousness, and his New York is both grimy and glamorous.

It's my lunch hour, so I go
for a walk among the hum-colored
cabs. First, down the sidewalk
where laborers feed their dirty
glistening torsos sandwiches
and Coca-Cola, with yellow helmets
on. They protect them from falling
bricks, I guess. Then onto the
avenue where skirts are flipping
above heels and blow up over
grates. The sun is hot, but the
cabs stir up the air.[36]

In the evening there were cocktail parties and dinners. Jane Freilicher's *Early New York Evening* (1953-54) shows us the view from her studio as the sun starts to go down over the city. O'Hara was a constant presence here, and this downtown view gives us the dirty but alluring city he loved.

In a moving "Poem Read at Joan Mitchell's" (1957), but addressed to Freilicher on the occasion of her marriage, O'Hara called up the city they all shared:

Tonight you probably walked over here from Bethune Street
down Greenwich Avenue with its sneaky little bars and the Women's Detention House,
across 8th Street, by the acres of books and pillows and shoes and
illuminating lampshades,
past Cooper Union where we heard the piece by Mortie Feldman with "The
Stars and Stripes Forever" in it
and the Sagamore's terrific "coffee and, Andy," meaning "with a cheese
Danish"—
did you spit on your index fingers and rub the CEDAR's neon circle for
luck?
did you give a kind thought, hurrying, to Alger Hiss?[37]

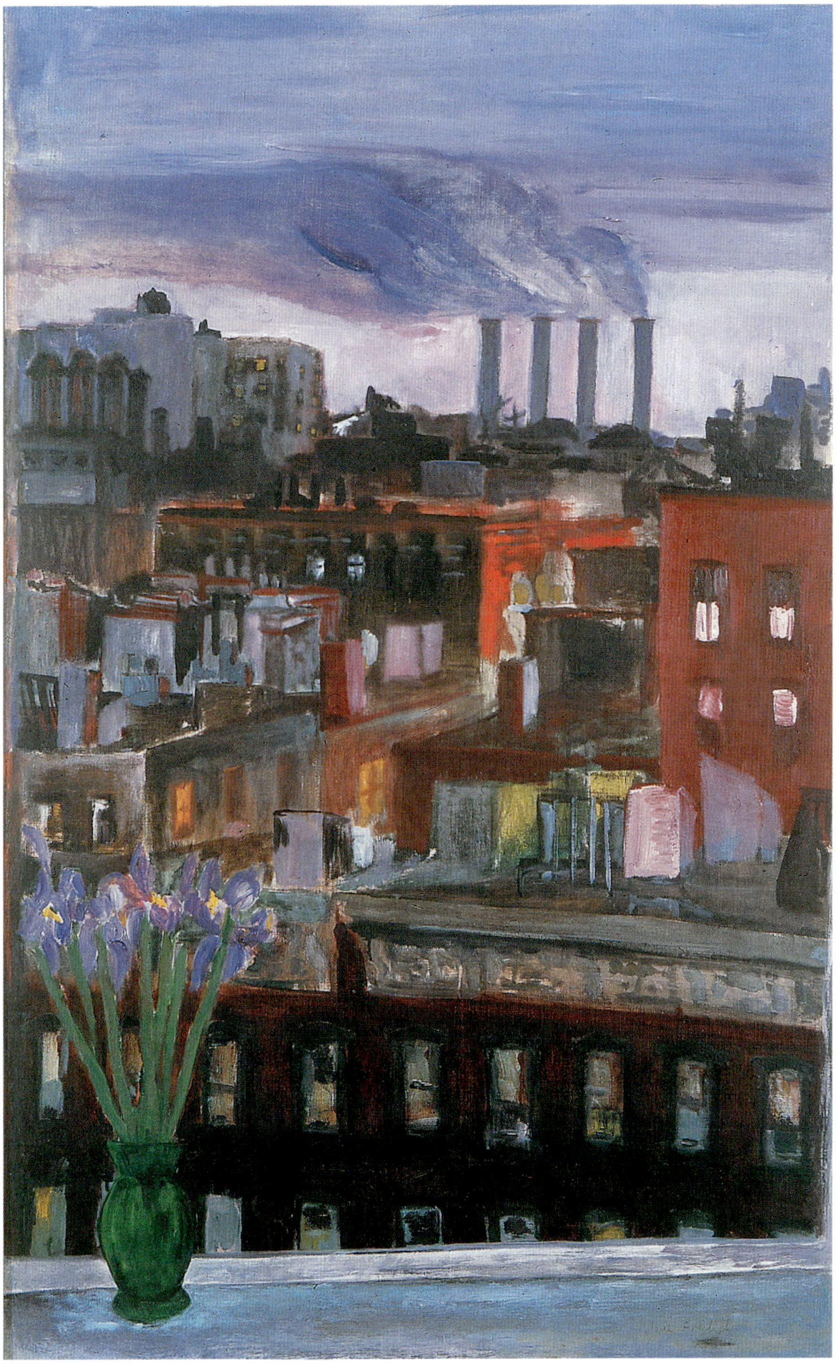

Jane Freilicher

Early New York Evening, 1953-54

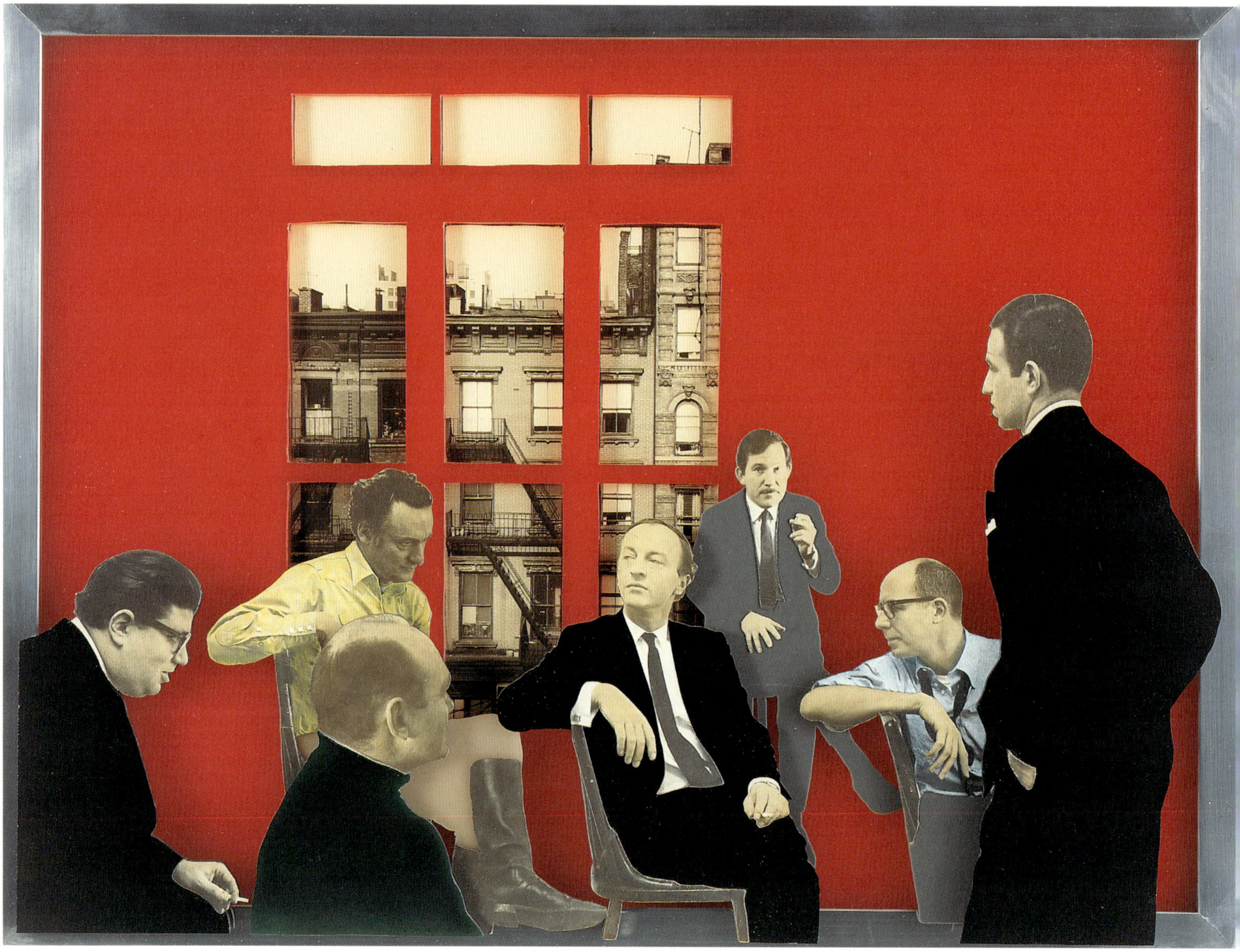

Howard Kanovitz

The New Yorkers, 1967

This kind of evocation, verging on invocation, demonstrates the perfect pitch for the telling detail that O'Hara brought to his walks down the streets of the city. "Attention was Frank's gift and his requirement," Bill Berkson wrote. "You might say it was his message."[38] But his attention was not simply a matter of close observation. The details are always acutely personal, specific to particular individuals, in this case Jane Freilicher.

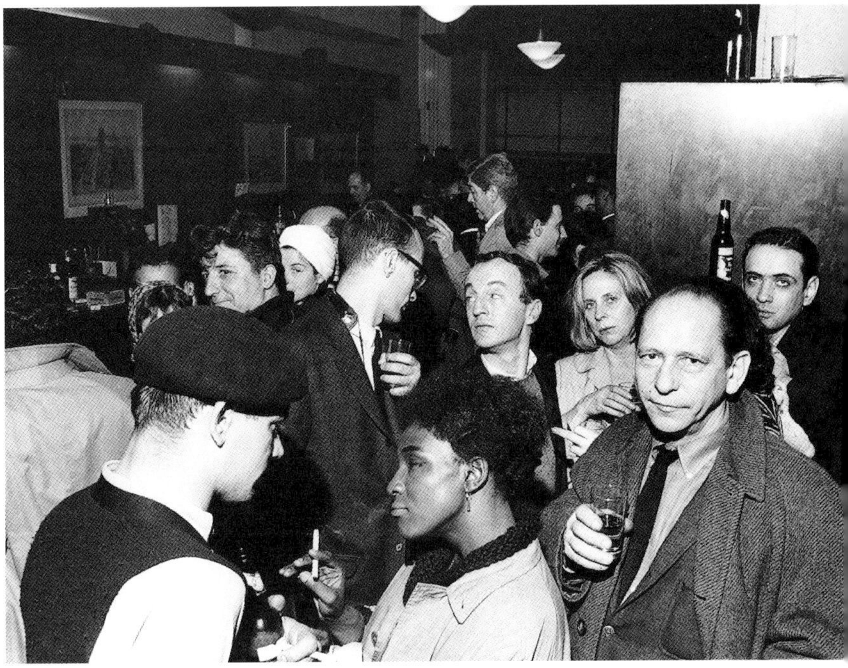

If Freilicher's *Early New York Evening* evokes a moment of calm before the evening begins and before O'Hara had risen to real prominence, Howard Kanovitz's *The New Yorkers* (1967) shows us O'Hara in full flight, an urbane sophisticate exulting in brilliant conversation. O'Hara's poetry begins in the middle of real lives, casually dropping names as if they were as familiar to the reader as to the poet. While the informality of the tone can at first seem baffling, as a reader one is quickly drawn into O'Hara's world, access to which is surprisingly easy to obtain. He simply *assumes* that people will be interested enough to find their way in, as he himself had quickly found his way into the worlds of avant-garde painting and poetry after he came to New York. The invitation is open for those who care to accept it. O'Hara is confident that it will be taken up.

Barbara Guest remembers being in Paris with O'Hara in the summer of 1960. She had identified the location of the "bateau-lavoir" building where Picasso and many other artists had had their studios in the early years of the century. But O'Hara didn't care; he wouldn't even go inside. "'Barbara,' he said, 'that was their history and it doesn't interest me. What does interest me is ours, and we're making it now.'"[39] That sense of riding the wave of the present can be felt in much of O'Hara's best poetry; the urgency of his need to be right there, right now. As Marjorie Perloff has written, "O'Hara loves the *motion* picture, *action* painting, and all forms of dance—art forms that capture the *present* rather than the

Fred W. McDarrah
Closing of the Cedar Bar, March 30, 1963. Jack Micheline (left) at the bar, Frank O'Hara and Barbara Guest (center), Allan Kaplan (right), and sculptor Abram Schlemowitz (foreground), 1963

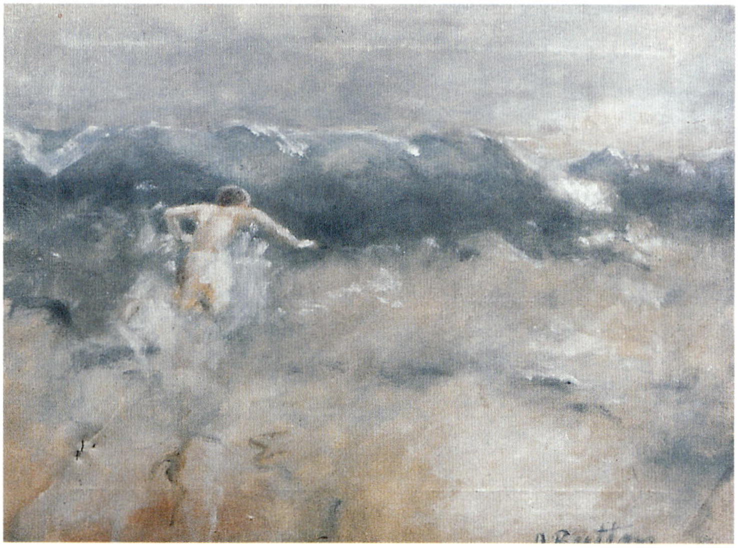

past, the present in all its chaotic splendor."[40] His poetry is strewn with markers of precise dates and times that add precision to his emotions.

It is 12:20 in New York a Friday
three days after Bastille day, yes
it is 1959 and I go get a shoeshine
because I will get off the 4:19 in Easthampton
at 7:15 and then go straight to dinner[41]

At any moment, the whole world that surrounds him and through which he moves can suddenly come into the sharpest focus, and it is necessary to be absolutely in that moment. At lunchtime in midtown Manhattan on a hot summer day, "Everything / suddenly honks: it is 12:40 of / a Thursday."[42]

Such intensity of living always carries with it the fear, actually the certain knowledge, that at any moment it could all come to an end, and this too is part of what drives O'Hara's writing.

There's nothing more beautiful
than knowing something is going
to be over[43]

Until it is over, life is to be lived with style, but also with an intense emotional commitment to each moment as it passes.

John Button's portrait of the dancer Vincent Warren, with whom O'Hara had a passionate affair, shows him stretched upward in a pose that can be held only briefly. It is a perfectly balanced visual representation of an image that will inevitably pass away in another second or two, but which approaches perfection while it lasts. Its very ephemerality makes it all the more urgent to grasp. Its counterpart is Button's portrait of O'Hara diving into a wave. The tension is resolved, as the poet flies headlong into the ever-changing crest of the present.

John Button
Swimmer, c. 1956

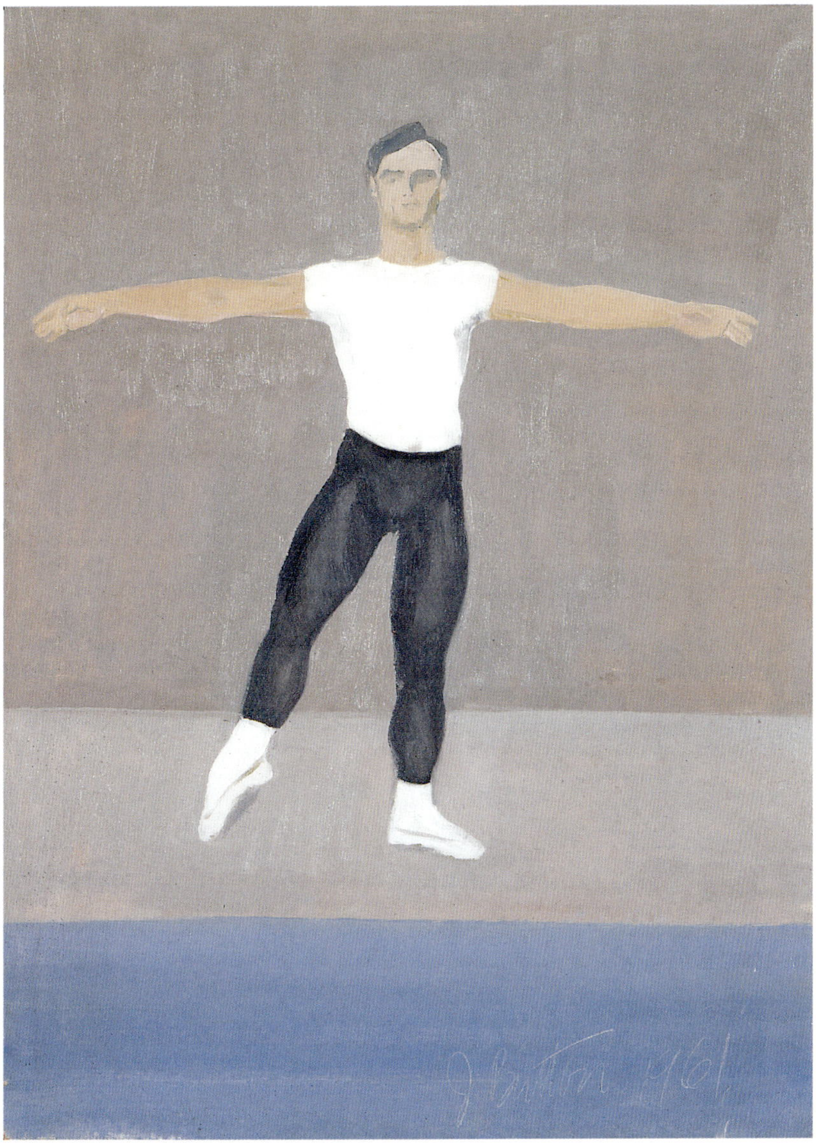

John Button

The Dancer, 1961

Poetry was declining

From his earliest days in New York, O'Hara had found among painters a congenial milieu that constituted both an audience for his poetry and a model of avant-garde practice. "I think the *example* of certain of the Abstract Expressionists in particular and then later other artists in New York and in Europe gave me the feeling that one should work harder and should really try to do something... that one should go further."[44] This sense of a shared community was reciprocal. "The poets were the only ones who wrote serious criticism of our work,"[45] Mike Goldberg recalls. The overlapping circles of the still small but increasingly confident New York avant-garde extended to the worlds of dance, theater, and music as well as to poetry and painting. "When John Cage had his first concerts," O'Hara remembered, "everybody went because they had to know about it, whether they were bored or they weren't bored, they felt like it was important to know what John Cage thought, or did, or sounded like."[46] This small enclave of the pre-Pop art world in New York is often said to have comprised no more than three hundred people. "The community was much smaller in those days," Goldberg observed. "Downtown was a place where everyone was active. No one had any money. Age differences didn't matter: everybody you cared to know was available to you."[47]

The Club, the artists' discussion society, was a focal point of the scene, and O'Hara quickly became a regular. As Dore Ashton describes it,

> the dialogue took place within a heterogenous and shifting population of impatient individualists whose only assumption was that something unusual was happening. When public sessions were held, everyone turned up expecting chaotic, excited, and often ridiculous exchanges among recognized antagonists, and they revelled in talk itself as a mode of self-affirmation.[48]

This was just the kind of environment in which a brilliant talker like O'Hara could shine, and he quickly became prominent there. In March of 1952, he led a discussion on abstract painting with a group of artists who had become his close friends: Jane Freilicher, Grace Hartigan, Alfred Leslie, Joan Mitchell, and Larry Rivers. A month later he led a panel on "The Image in Poetry and Painting," and a little later appeared in an evening devoted to

"New Poets" with John Ashbery, Barbara Guest, and James Schuyler.[49] "The painters were the only generous audience for our poetry," O'Hara said, "and most of us read first publicly in art galleries or at The Club. The literary establishment cared about as much for our work as the Frick cared for Pollock and de Kooning."[50]

A key figure in the intersection between art and poetry, and also a fixture at The Club, was the editor of *Art News,* Thomas Hess, who engaged a number of poets as writers for the magazine. Hess was in broad sympathy with O'Hara's taste for the emotional, the gestural, and the individual, and in 1953 he hired him as an editorial associate. This not only gave O'Hara a more public status as an art critic, it also enabled him to quit his job at the front desk of The Museum of Modern Art, a position he had originally taken in order to see the museum's Matisse exhibition on a daily basis.

That same year, the Tibor de Nagy Gallery published O'Hara's poem cycle "Oranges," referred to in "Why I Am Not a Painter." John Bernard Myers, the gallery's director, was a tireless promoter both of poets and of figurative painters. The publication was a mimeographed booklet produced to accompany an exhibition of twelve paintings, also "Oranges," by Grace Hartigan. Each of the one hundred copies of the booklet has an original oil sketch by Hartigan for its cover. O'Hara and Hartigan had become very close, seeing each other or speaking by phone every day, and O'Hara dedicated many poems to her, including "Second Avenue" and "In Memory of My Feelings." When Hartigan told O'Hara that she wanted to paint "a lot of something" he replied with his usual insouciance, "How about oranges? I have a dozen."[51] The resulting paintings stand at the crossroads of abstraction and representation, recognizable figures half-submerged in a broad gestural field. This ambiguity is

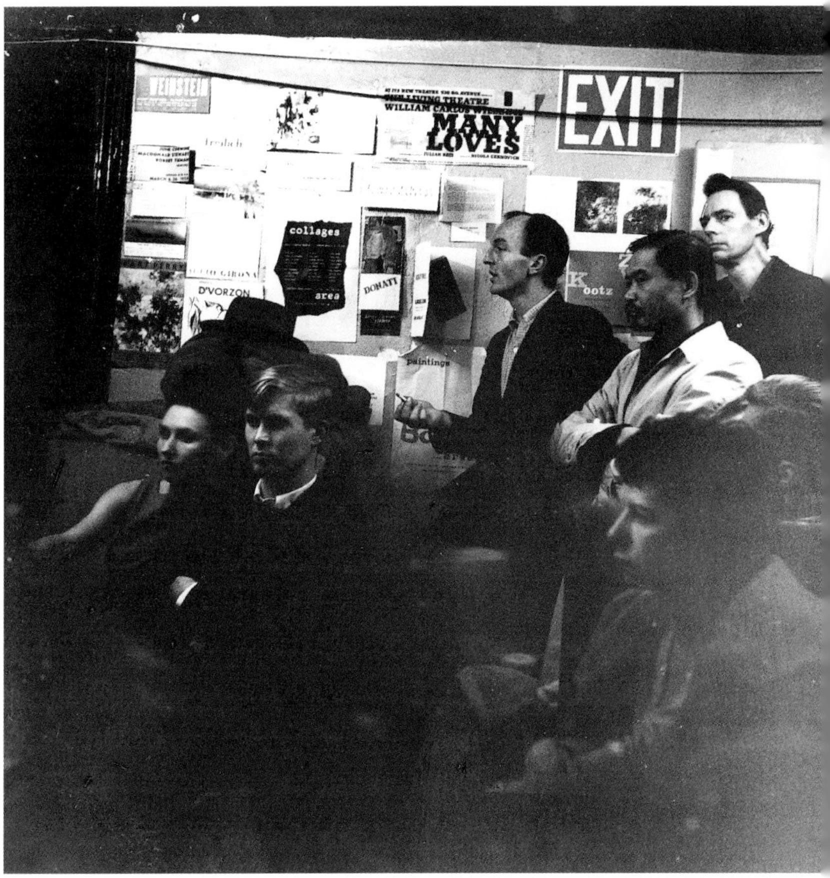

Fred W. McDarrah
Club panel discussion, March 20, 1959. Left to right: Lucia Dlugoszewski and Joseph LeSueur (seated); Frank O'Hara, Mike Kanemitsu, and Ronald Bladen (standing); and Golda Lewis (seated, foreground)

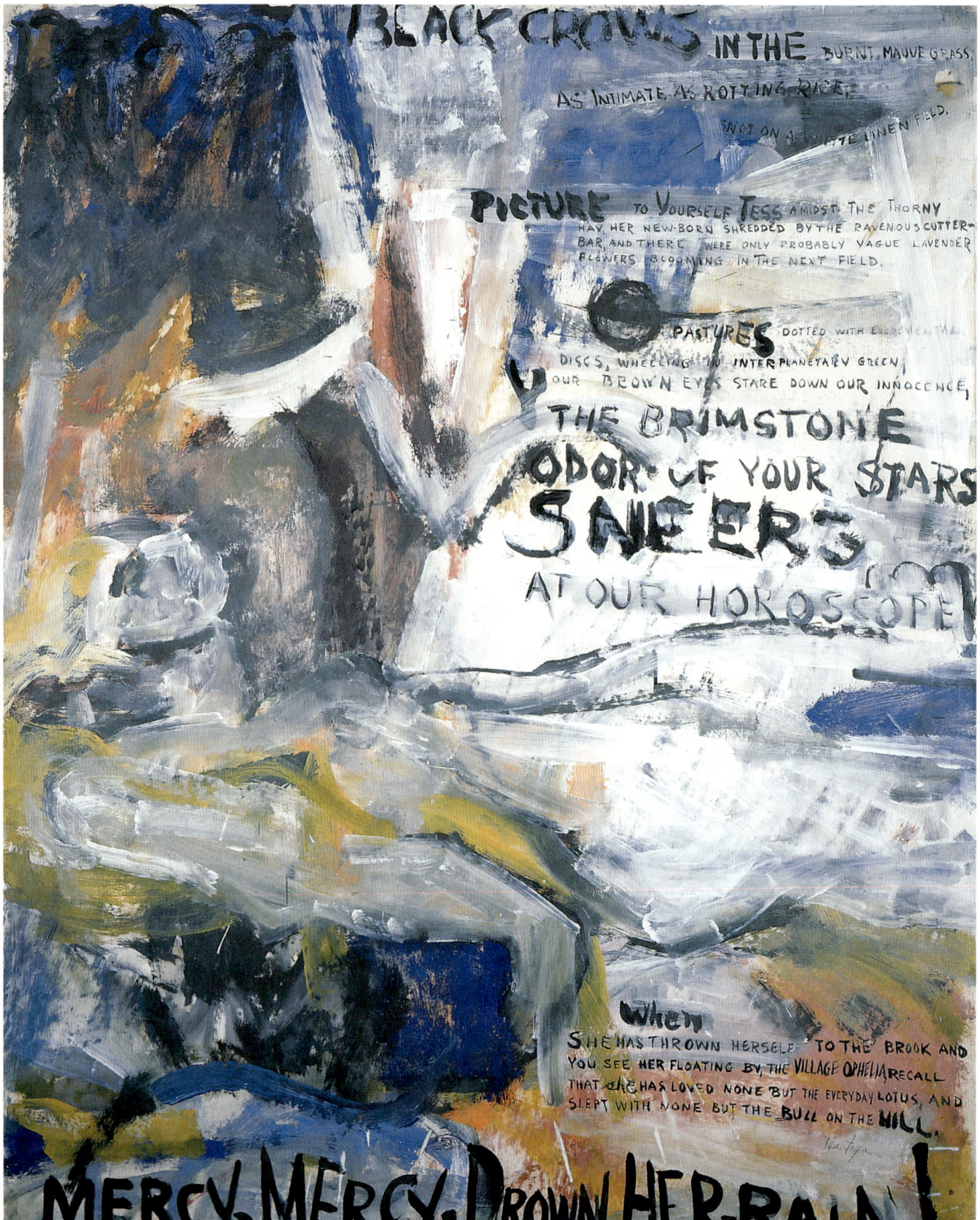

Grace Hartigan

Oranges No. 1, 1952

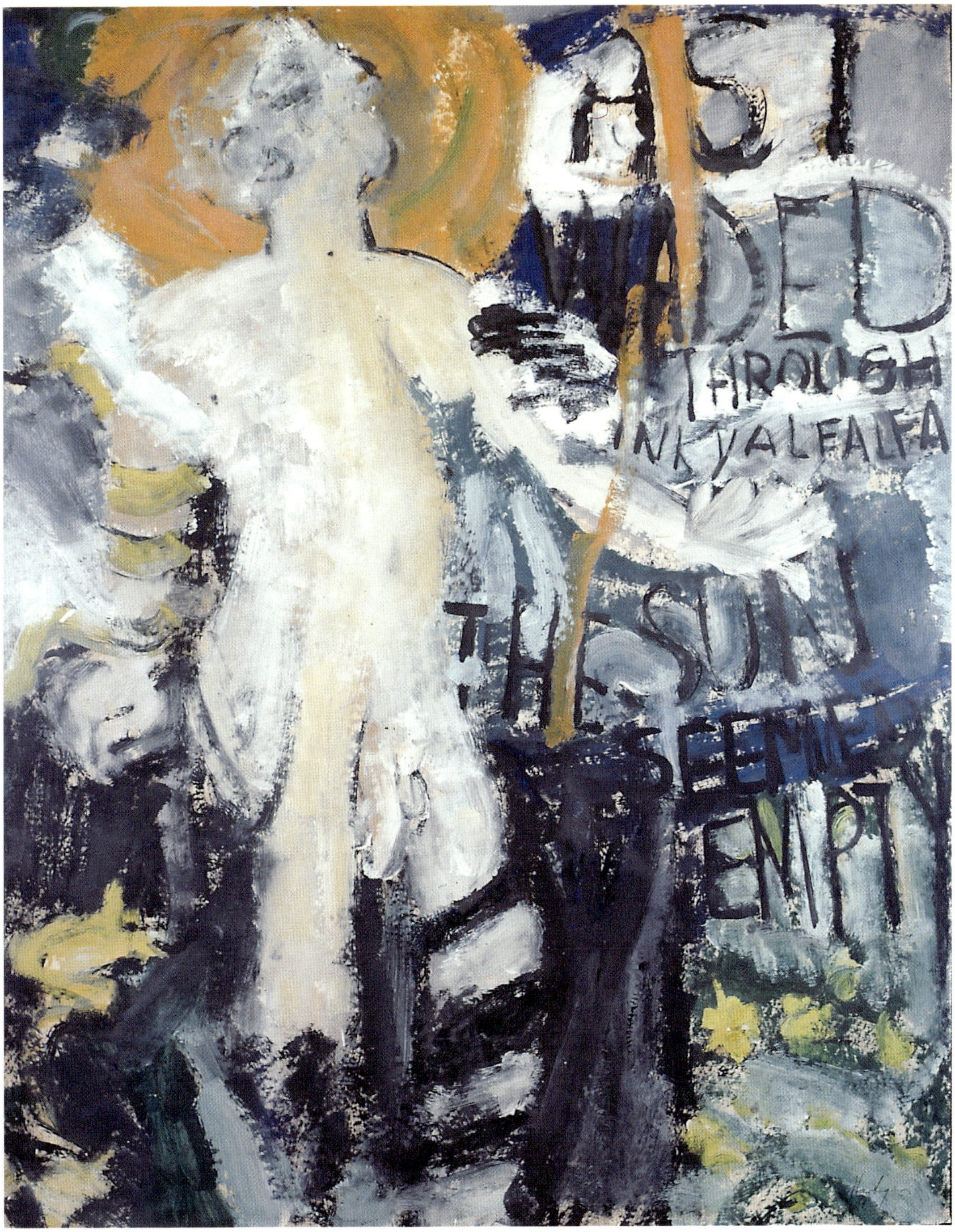

Grace Hartigan

Oranges No. 7, 1952

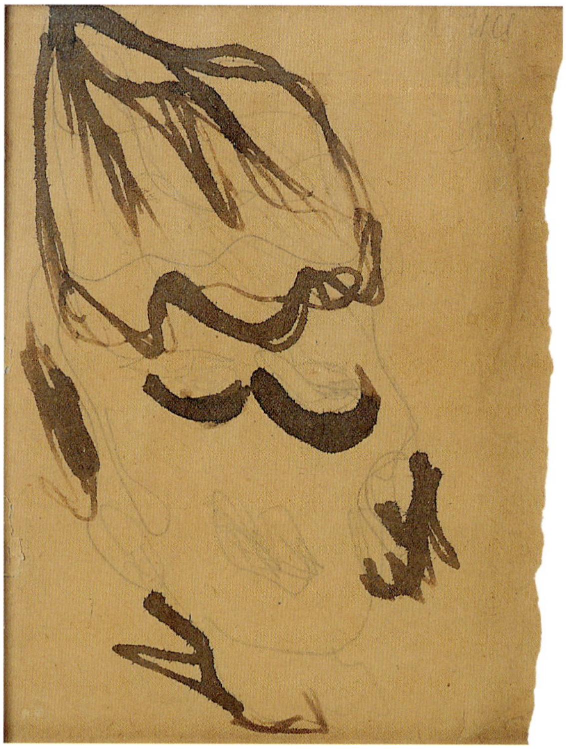

heightened by Hartigan's painterly renderings of O'Hara's poems. The words march unevenly but decisively across the paper, heightening the emotional tone even as they contribute to a flattening out of the surface itself.

O'Hara's "Oranges" still bear the traces of a somewhat overheated and ill-digested Surrealism, but the constant vacillation between the beautiful and the disgusting forms an effective counterpoint to the tortured and sexually charged figures of the paintings. The cycle concludes: "O my posterity! This is the miracle: that our elegant invention the natural world redeems by filth." It is a fitting summation for Hartigan's struggle for expression in paint, torn as she was between the pure invention of abstraction and her desire to represent the texture of the world around her.

O'Hara did make a few drawings and collages himself, and he would sometimes pick up a brush to amuse himself in the studio of a painter friend, but he was in no doubt that his real talent was in poetry. "I've gotten very discouraged when I've tried to paint," he told Edward Lucie-Smith, "and the harder I've tried the more muddy it gets. I don't really know how to resolve my own ideas in the medium and get anything that satisfies me really."[52] In the spirit of the overlapping and cross-pollinating downtown scene, however, O'Hara was ready for all kinds of collaborative projects with artists he admired.

Frank O'Hara
Fabrizio del Dongo, c. 1962

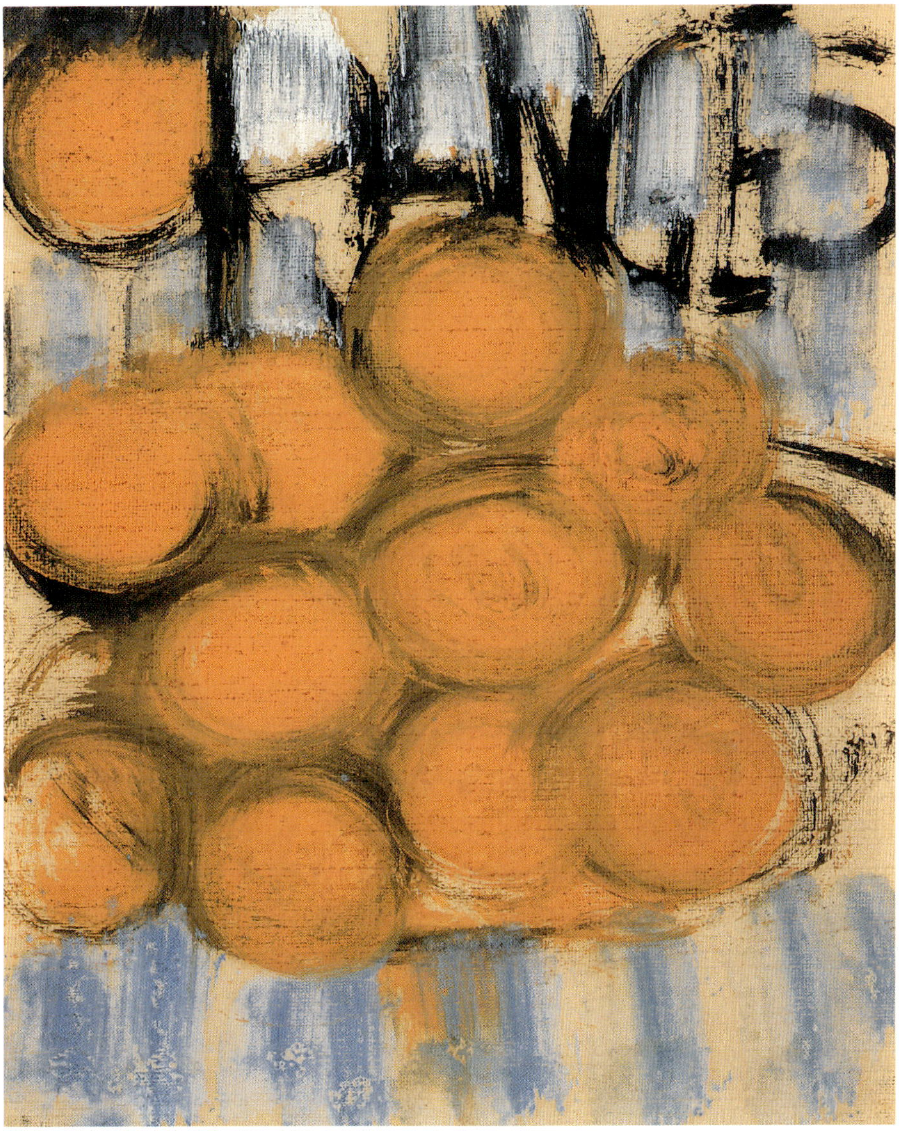

Grace Hartigan,
cover for **Oranges** by Frank O'Hara, 1953

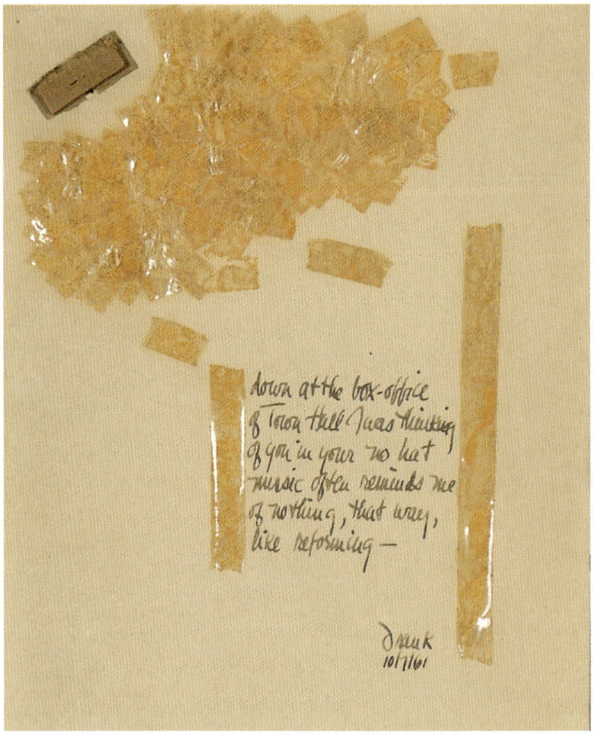

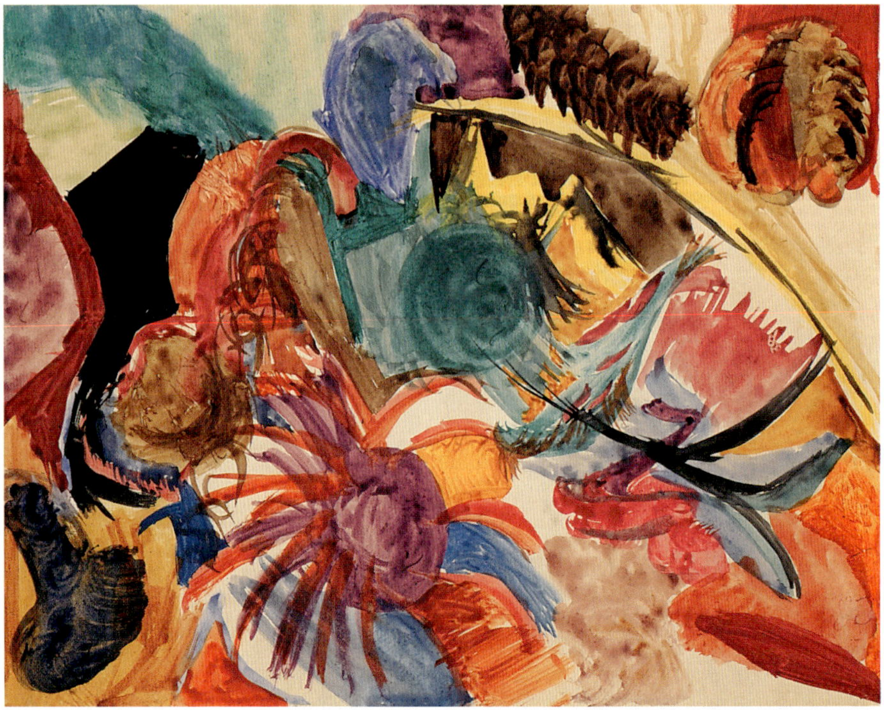

Frank O'Hara
Untitled ("Down at the Box Office"), 1961

Frank O'Hara
Untitled, c. 1957

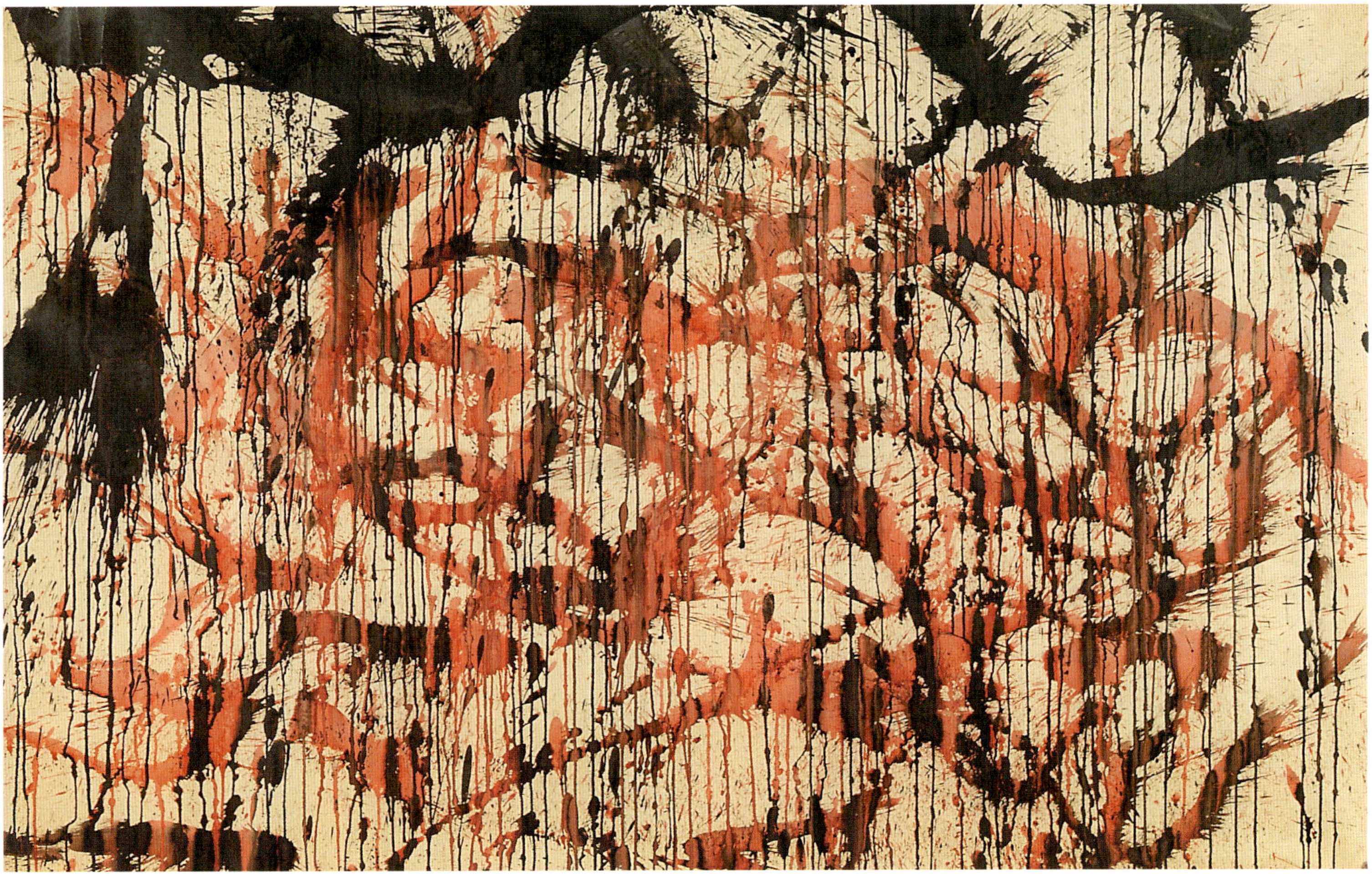

Norman Bluhm
Backdrop sketch for *Loves Labor*,
a play by Frank O'Hara, 1958

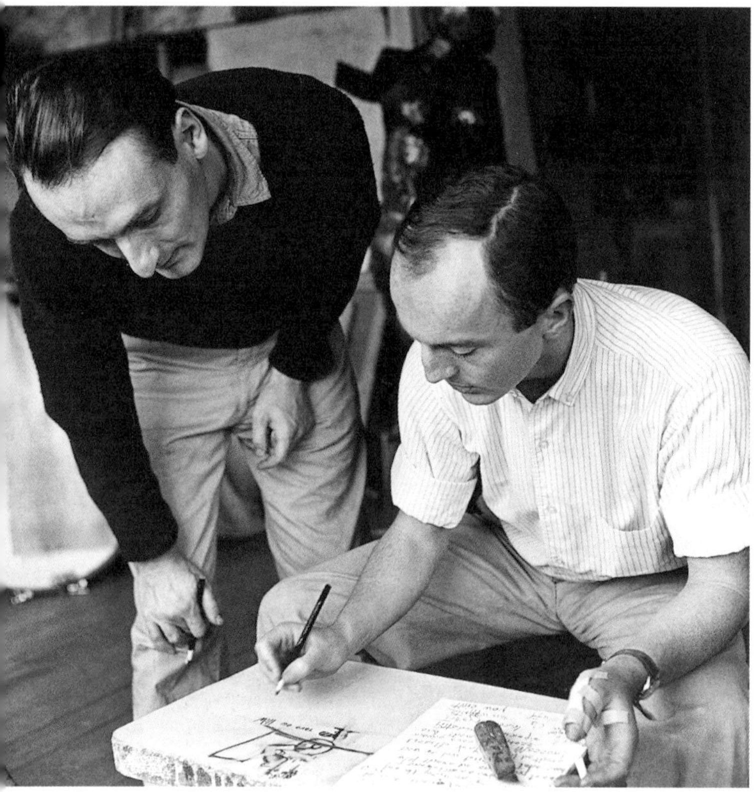

In 1950, O'Hara met Larry Rivers at a cocktail party thrown by John Ashbery. Their mutual attraction was instantaneous. As O'Hara recalled the meeting, "I thought he was crazy and he thought I was even crazier. I was very shy, which he thought was intelligence; he was garrulous, which I assumed was brilliance—and on such misinterpretations, thank heavens, many a friendship is based."[53] Rivers, said O'Hara, was "rather like a demented telephone. Nobody knew whether they wanted it in the library, the kitchen, or the toilet, but it was electric."[54] Of course, Rivers began to appear in O'Hara's poetry, and the two collaborated on various texts, including the sarcastic set of rules for painters, "How to Proceed in the Arts" ("Later on, imitate yourself. After all, who do you love best?"[55]) and the play, *Kenneth Koch: A Tragedy.* (O'Hara's playwriting led to a number of collaborations with artists, on set designs and backdrops.)

In 1957, the two began a series of lithographs together, entitled *Stones*, which was the first project of Tatyana Grosman's Universal Limited Art Editions. Grosman visited Rivers at his studio in Southampton to explain what she wanted to do: "a book that would be a real fusion of poetry and art, a real collaboration, not just drawings to illustrate poems, and Larry listened, and then he called out, 'Hey, Frank!' And down the stairs came a young man in blue jeans. It was Frank O'Hara."[56] Despite the ad hoc nature of the project's inception, O'Hara took it very seriously. The complexity of the lithographic process militated against complete spontaneity. Most strikingly, he had to learn how to write backwards on stones that would print in reverse. It was, however, a true collaboration, as O'Hara stressed: "We worked on the stones together. He did not work on the stone if I wasn't there and I didn't work on the stone if he wasn't there to see what I was doing."[57] Hans Namuth's photographs capture the intensity of the process, and the closeness of the working relationship as the two responded to each other's contributions.

Hans Namuth
Frank O'Hara and Larry Rivers at work on **Stones**, 1958

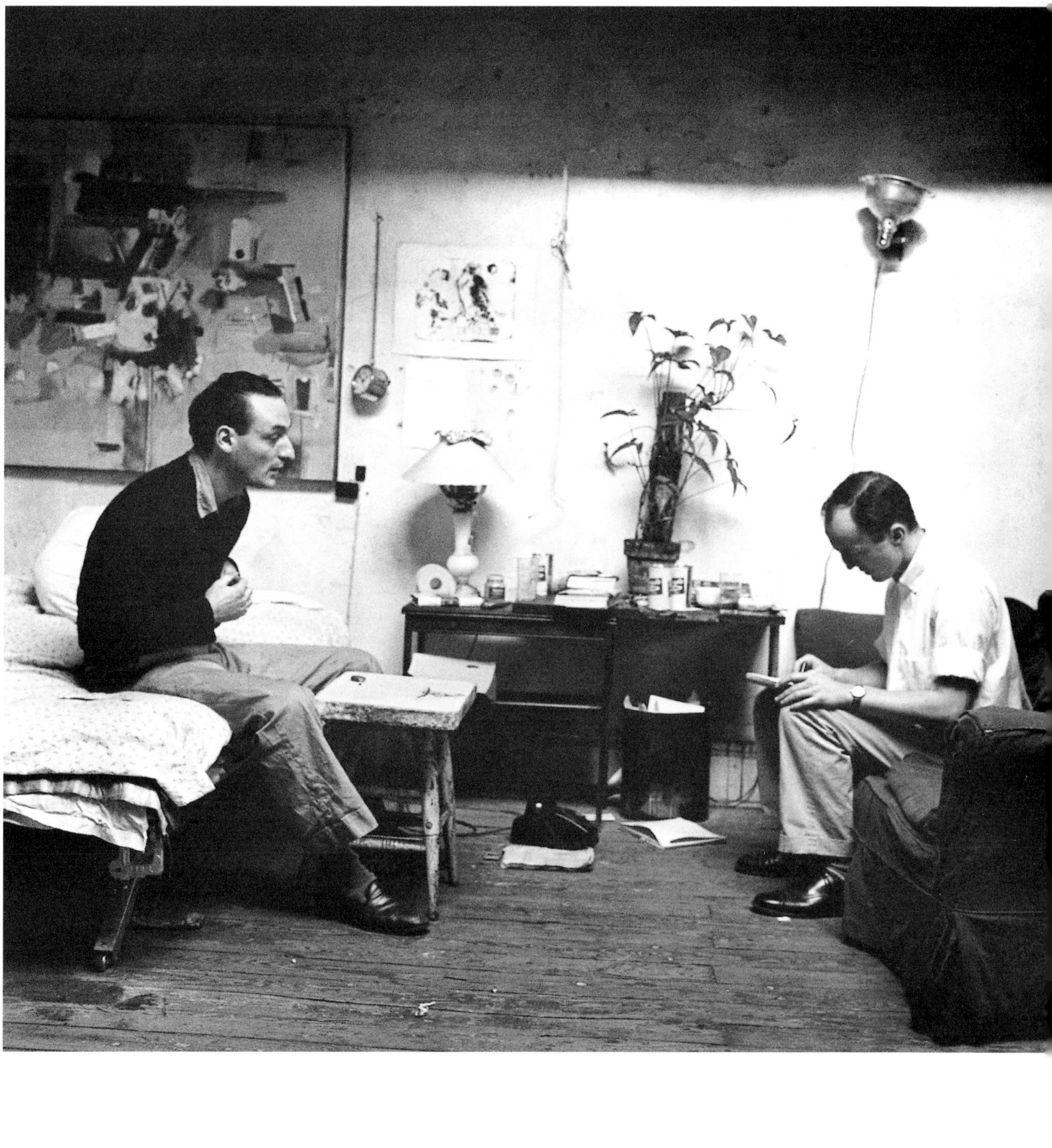

Hans Namuth

Frank O'Hara and Larry Rivers at work on **Stones**, 1958

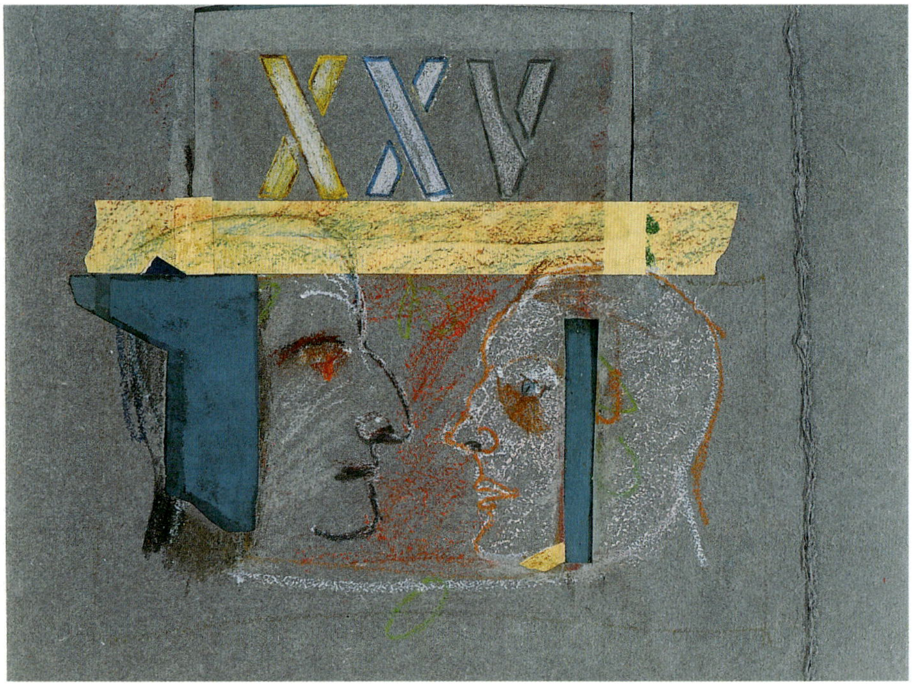

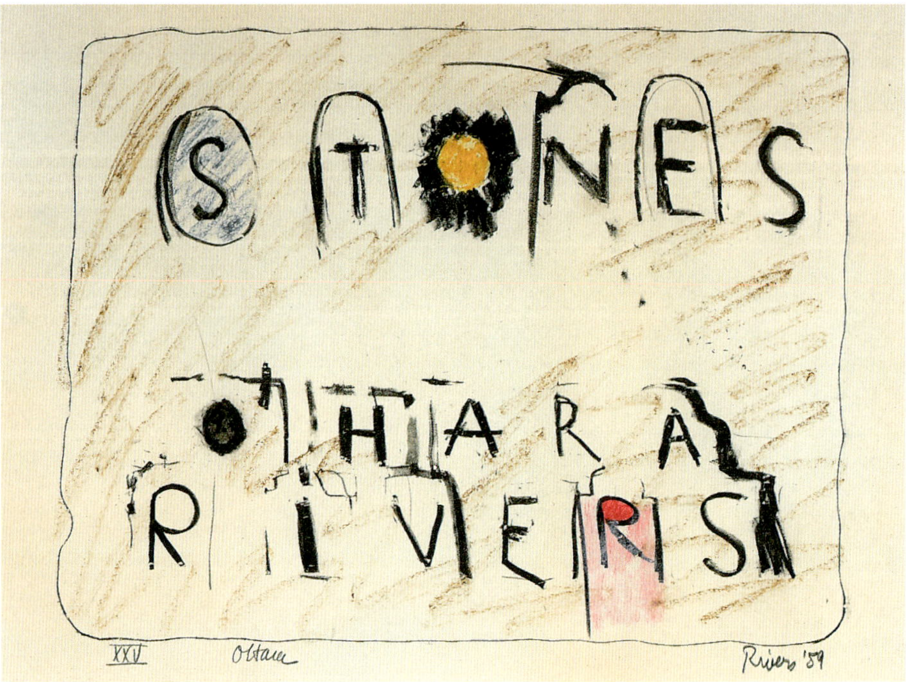

Larry Rivers and Frank O'Hara

Stones: Inner Folder, 1957-60

Stones: Title Page, 1959

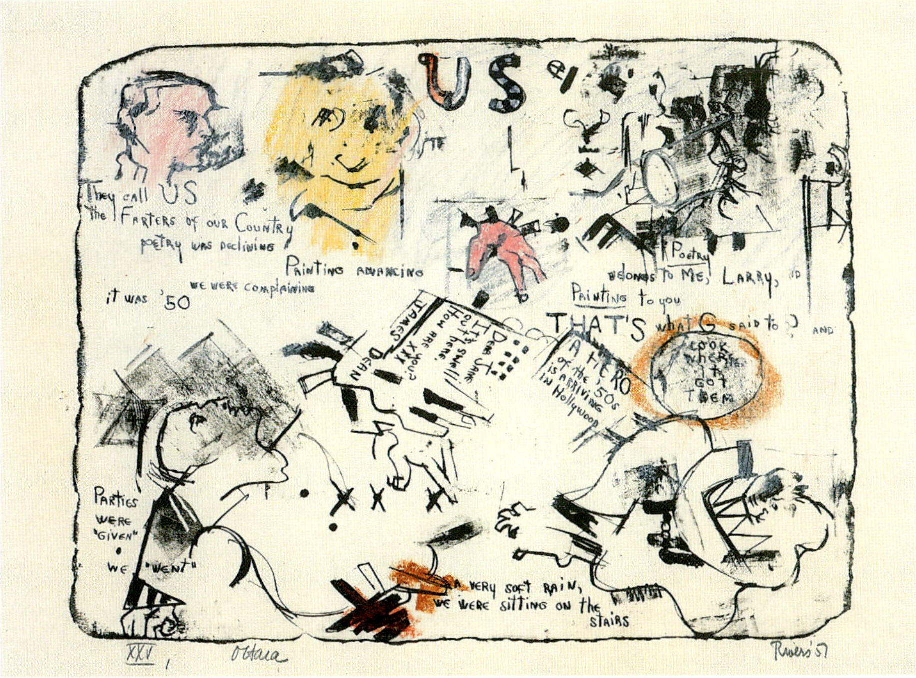

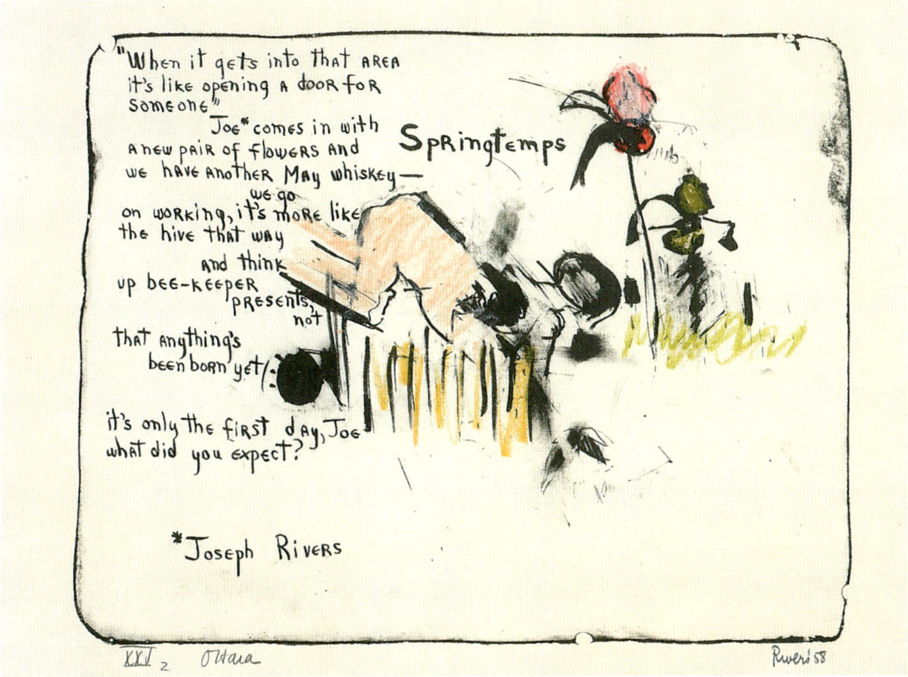

Stones: US, 1957

Stones: Springtemps, 1958

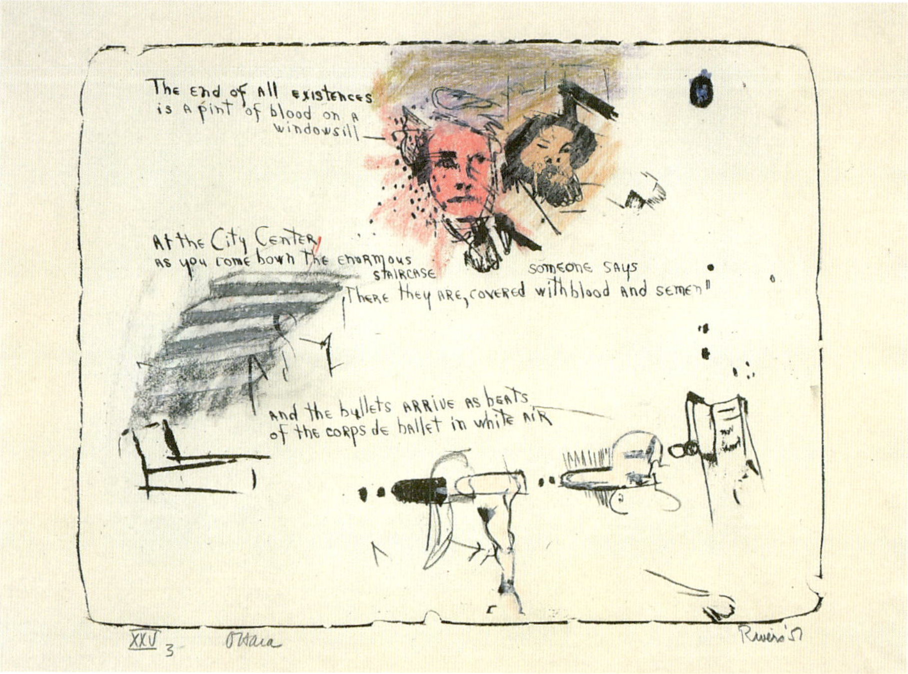

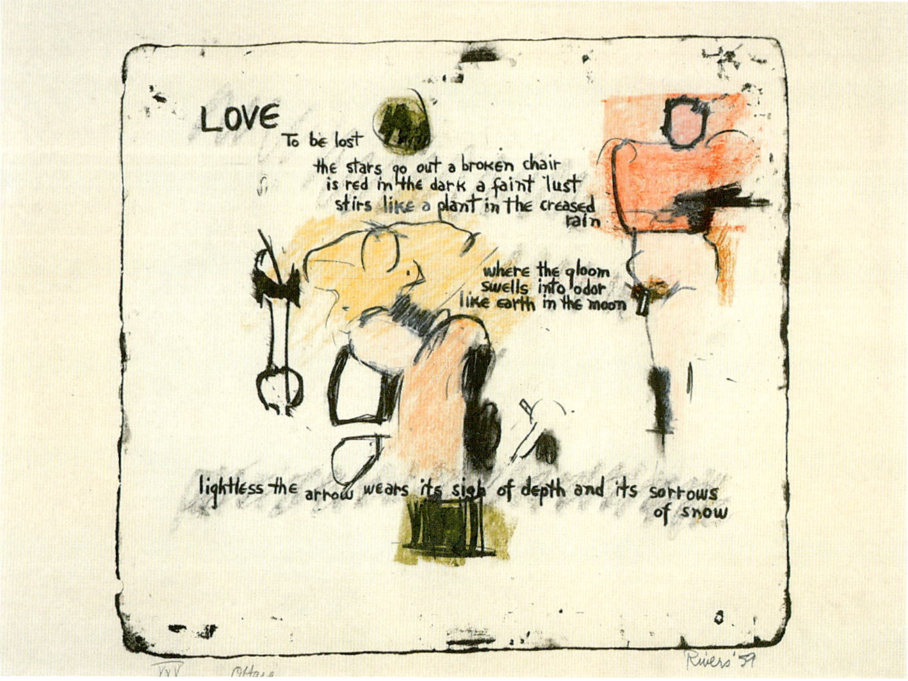

Larry Rivers and Frank O'Hara

Stones: The End of All Existences, 1957

Stones: Love, 1958

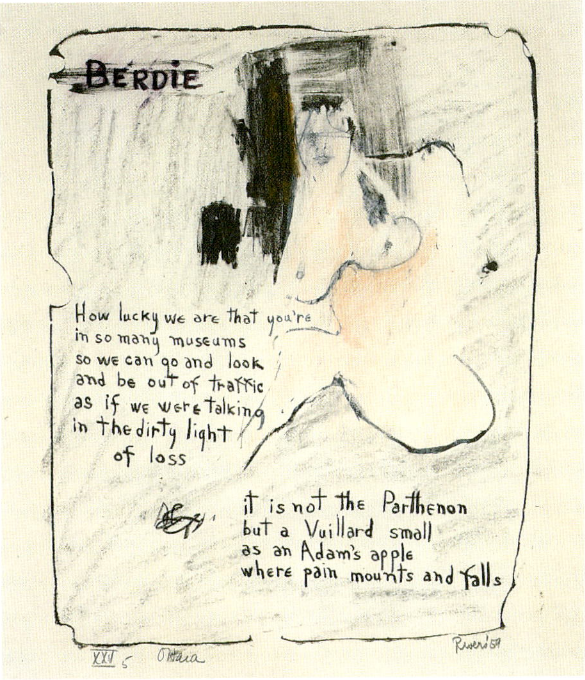

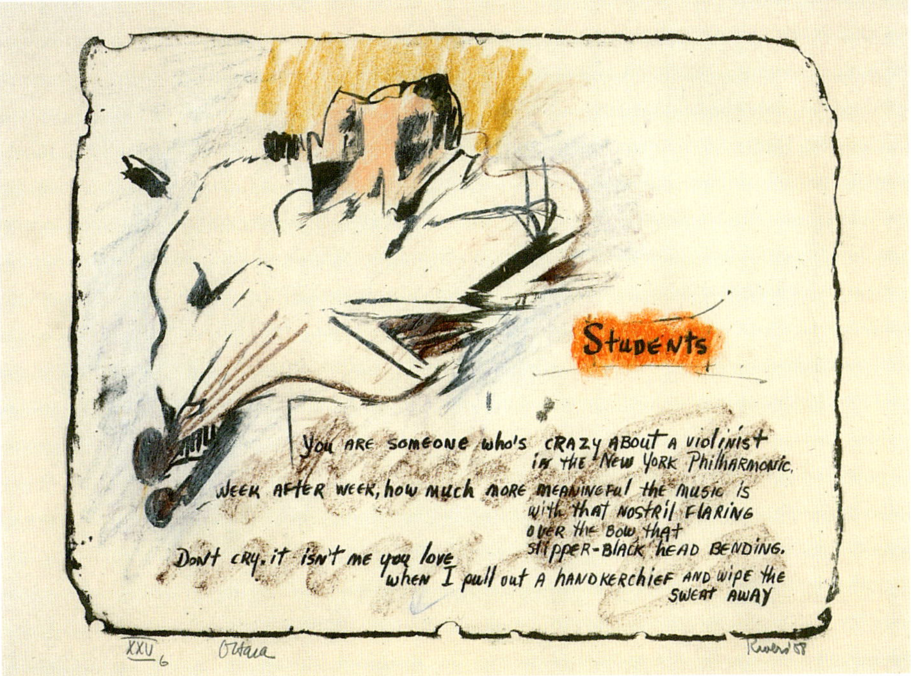

Stones: Berdie, 1959

Stones: Students, 1958

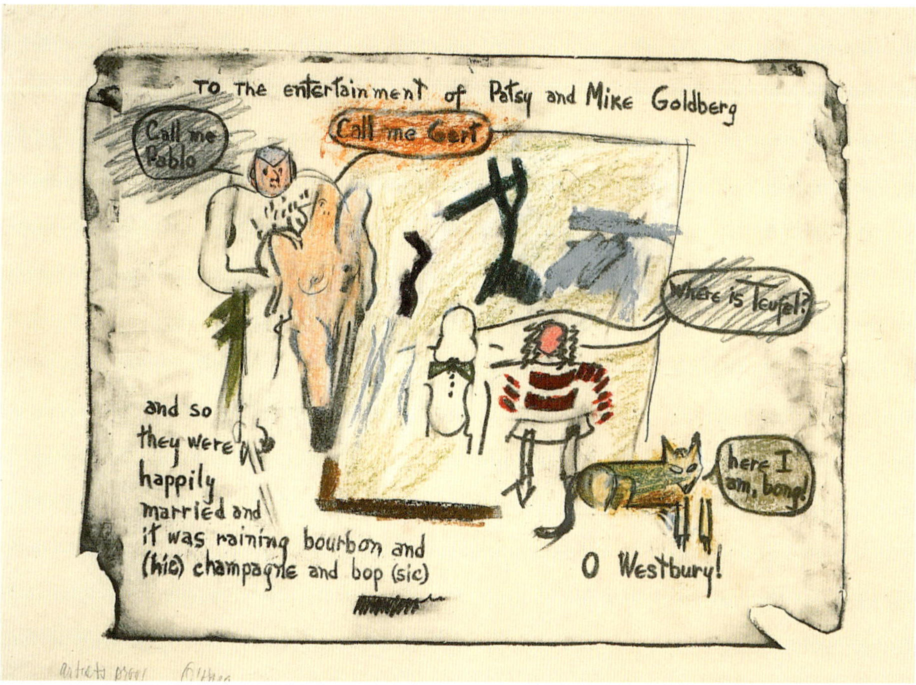

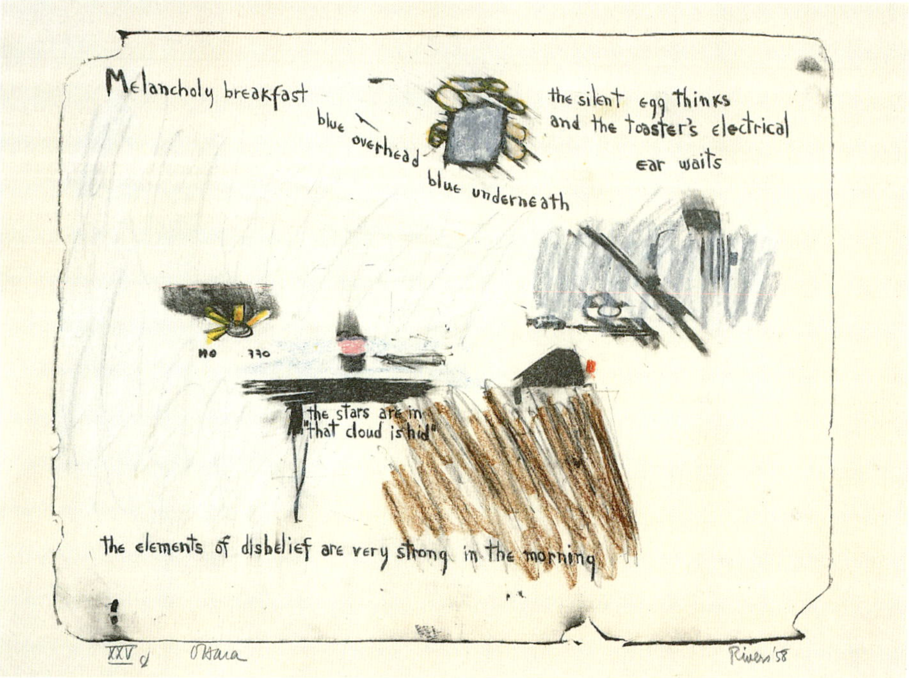

Larry Rivers and Frank O'Hara

Stones: To the Entertainment of Patsy and Mike Goldberg, 1958

Stones: Melancholy Breakfast, 1958

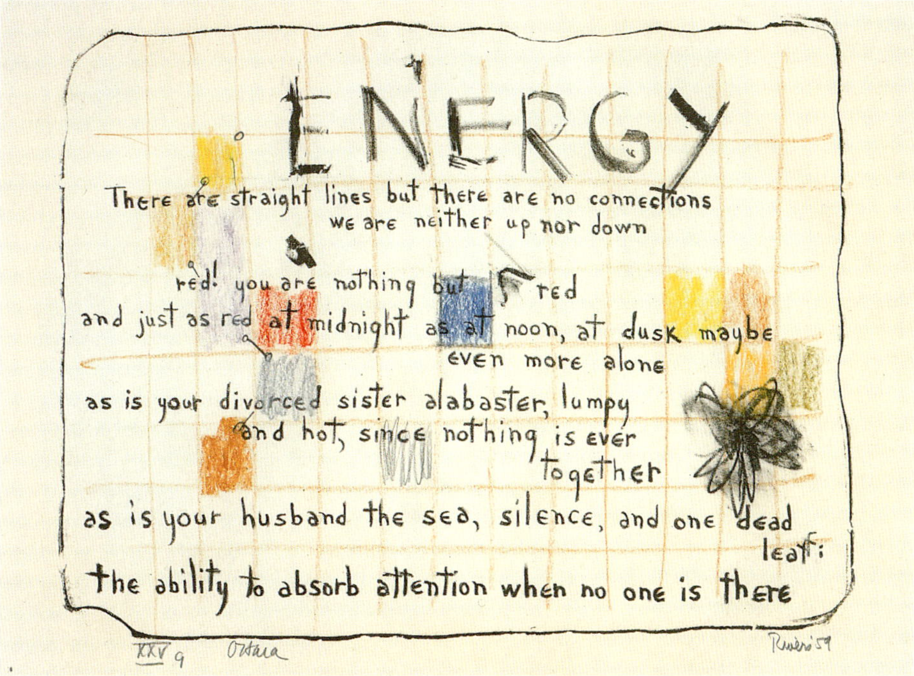

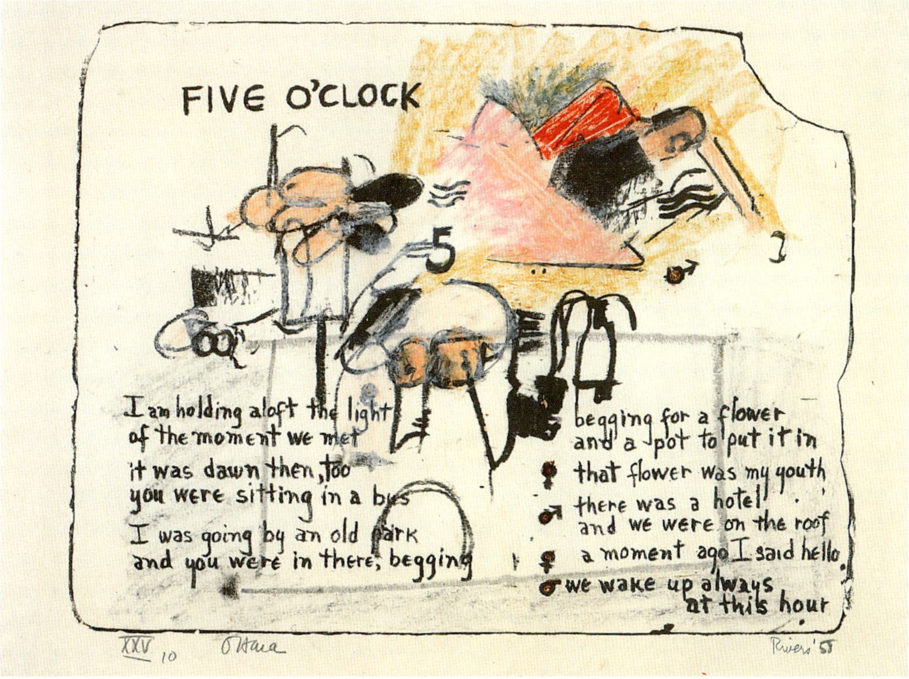

Stones: Energy, 1959

Stones: Five O'Clock, 1958

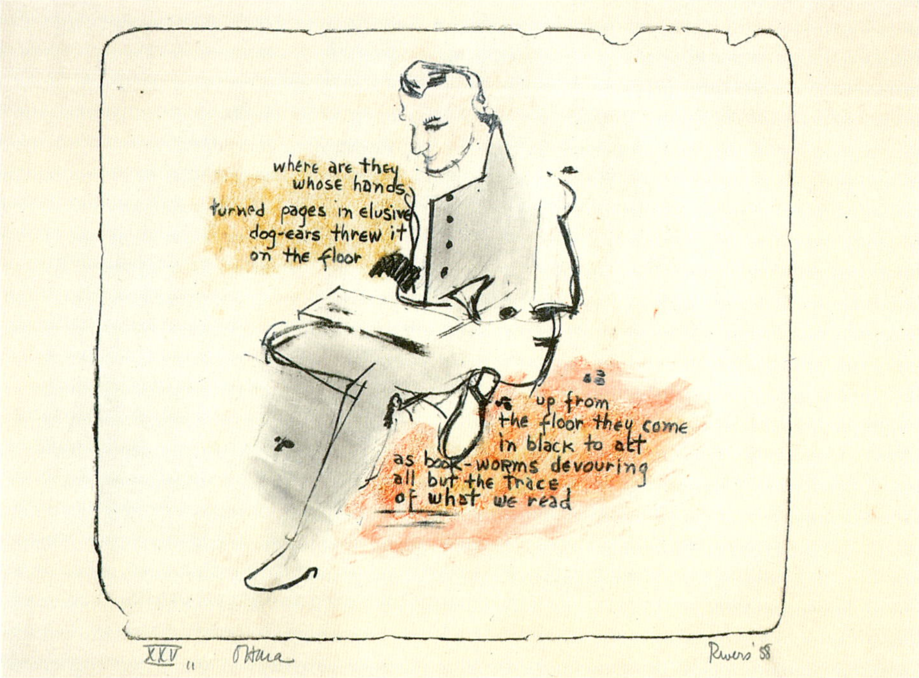

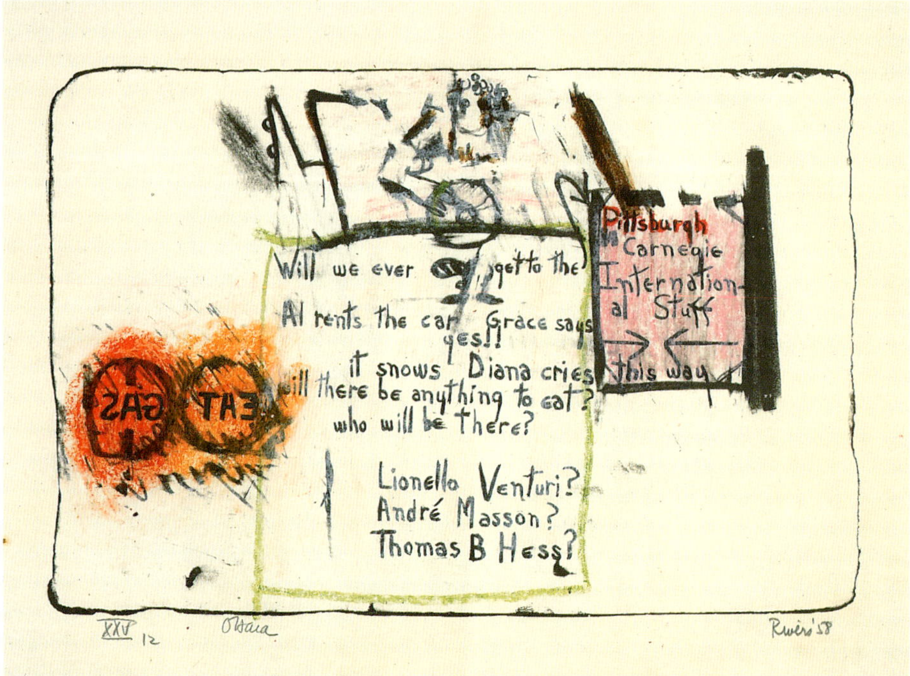

Larry Rivers and Frank O'Hara

Stones: Where Are They, 1958

Stones: Will We Ever Get, 1958

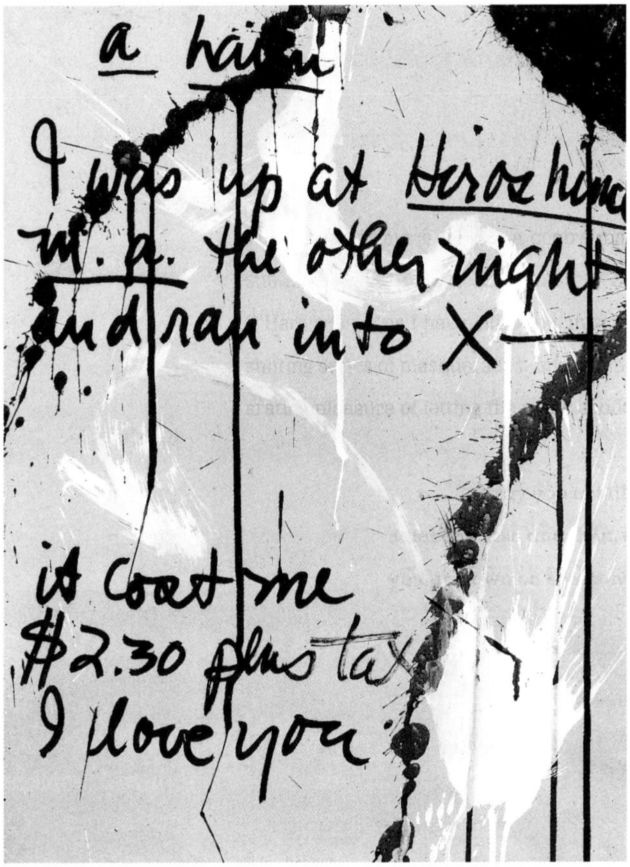

O'Hara's texts sometimes look back with a trace of nostalgia:

poetry was declining
Painting advancing
we were complaining
it was '50

Rivers's "groovy little images"[58] match that sense of lightness, the free-floating figures echoing the unpredictable action of memory. Although the enterprise itself was clearly in a French tradition, and includes specific references to Rimbaud, Verlaine, and Picasso, O'Hara's voice in these works has shed its earlier "decadent" and Surrealist pretensions in favor of a more informal, personal, even conversational tone.

In 1955, the painter Norman Bluhm returned to New York from Paris, and quickly became part of O'Hara's circle. Joe LeSueur recalls his striking presence:

> Clad in somber colors, with a scarf around his neck, his long black hair in artful disarray, a de rigueur Gauloise dangling from his lips, spewing a

Norman Bluhm and Frank O'Hara
A Haiku, 1960

rough American slang spiked with a Gallic patois like nobody else spoke, with grand words like politesse and geste tossed in for good measure.[59]

One rainy Sunday in October of 1960, O'Hara visited Bluhm in his studio on Park Avenue South, as he often did. As they talked they listened to a Prokofiev piano sonata on the radio. Bluhm had sheets of cheap paper tacked up around the studio, and at a certain point he picked up a brush to illustrate a point he was making about the music. O'Hara stood up and wrote a word or two on the sheet. A different kind of collaboration was suddenly underway, more spontaneous and unrehearsed than the prints he had made with Rivers. "Right away, we decided to do some more," Bluhm remembers. Soon twenty-six sheets were being worked on at once. "Each one was different. Frank would write something on a sheet of paper while I was in another part of the studio, making a gesture on the paper. It was all instantaneous, like a conversation between friends. Quick and playful."[60]

The series combines Bluhm's powerful brushstrokes with O'Hara's loose and increasingly calligraphic writing. Sometimes Bluhm will strike through O'Hara's words, or O'Hara will write right through one of Bluhm's splashy gestures. At other times the painting and the writing follow each other's lines in a spontaneously choreographed *pas de deux.* In *Hand,* for example, O'Hara's text wraps itself around the fingers of Bluhm's roughly grasping hand:

> **You eat all the time**
> **you even know how to use**
> **chopsticks**
> **so why don't you write me**
> **a letter**

and then ending in the thumb: "forget it."

These works are perhaps the closest O'Hara ever came to fusing the spontaneity of his poetry with the spontaneity of abstract painting, and the results retain, after forty years, the excitement of true improvisation, a collaboration carried out as a witty and engaged conversation, without thought of exhibition or even other viewers.

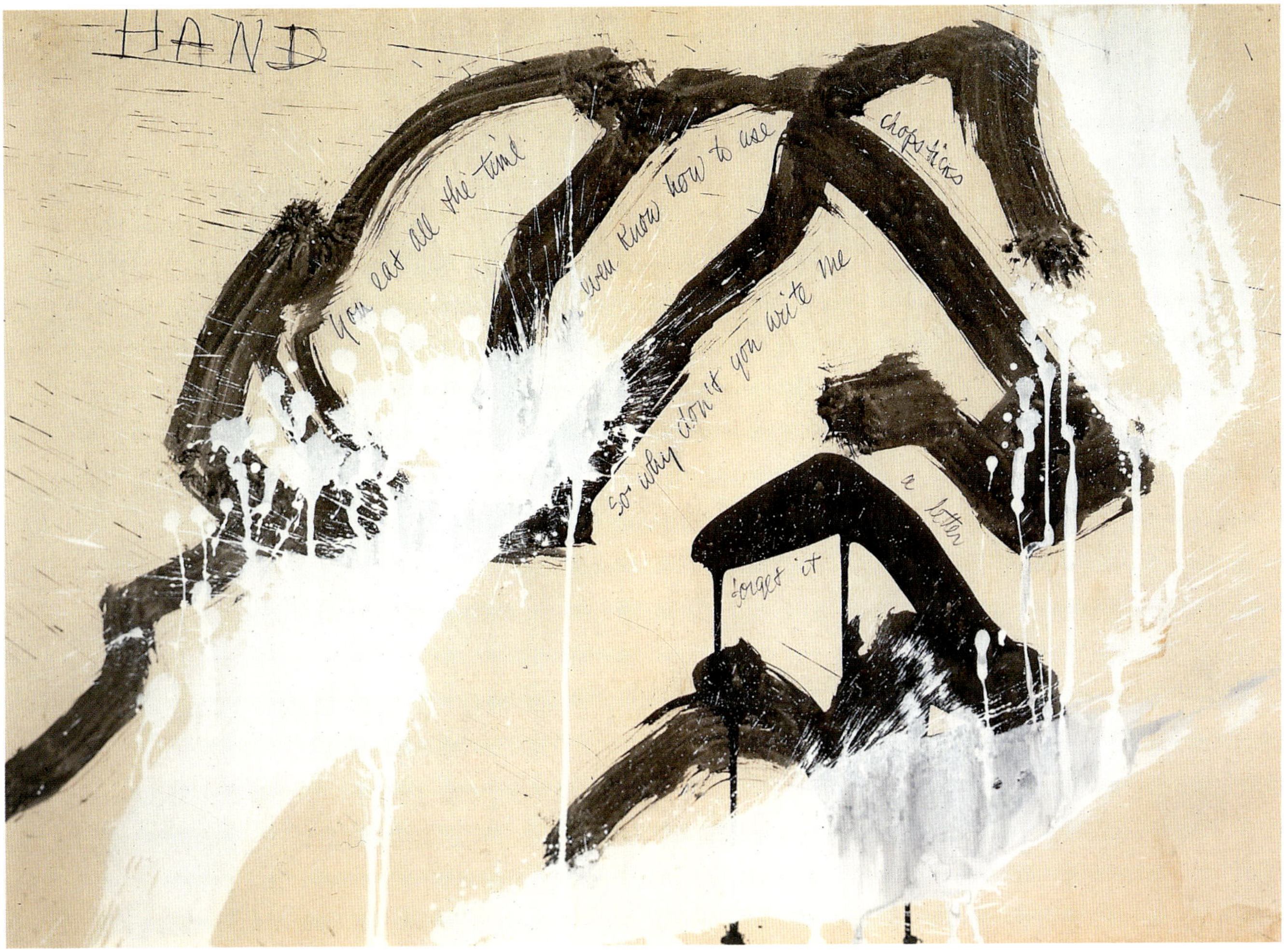

Norman Bluhm and Frank O'Hara

Hand, 1960

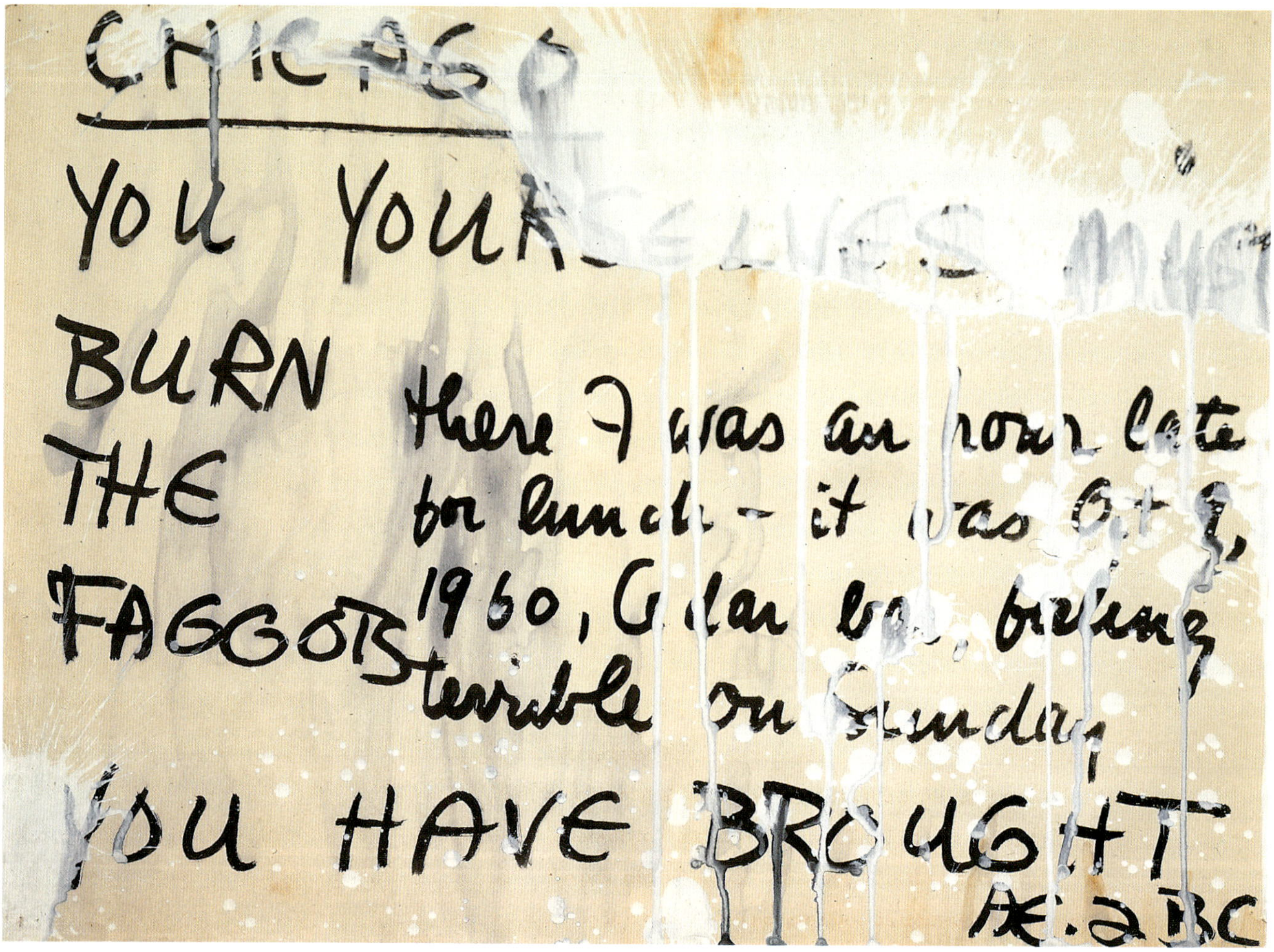

Norman Bluhm and Frank O'Hara

Chicago, 1960

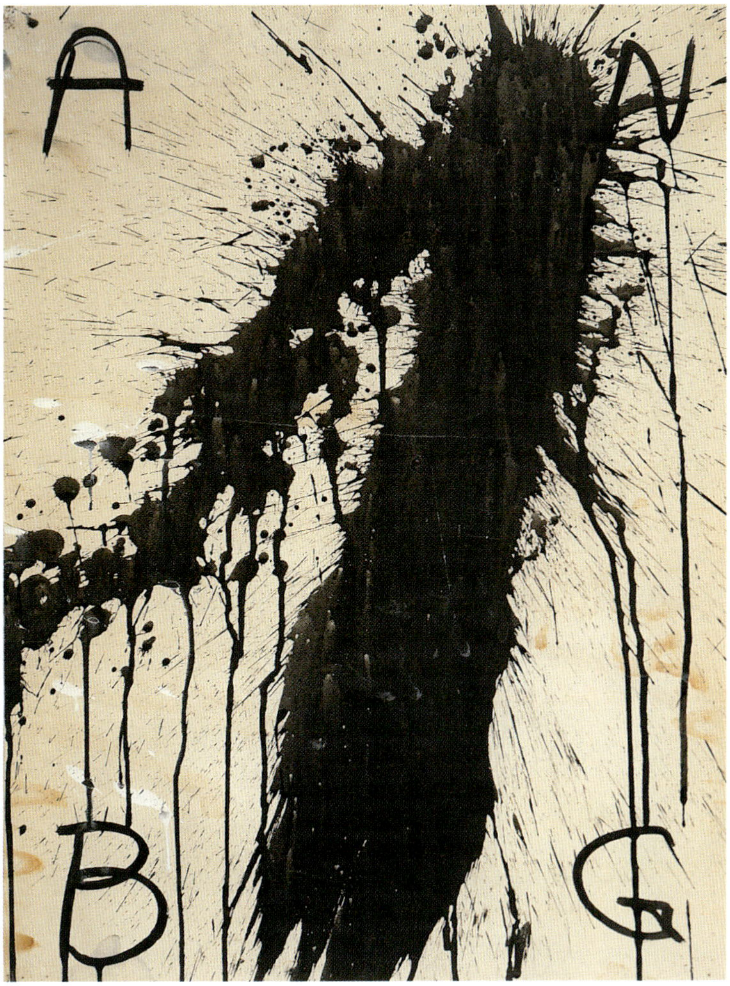

Bang, 1960

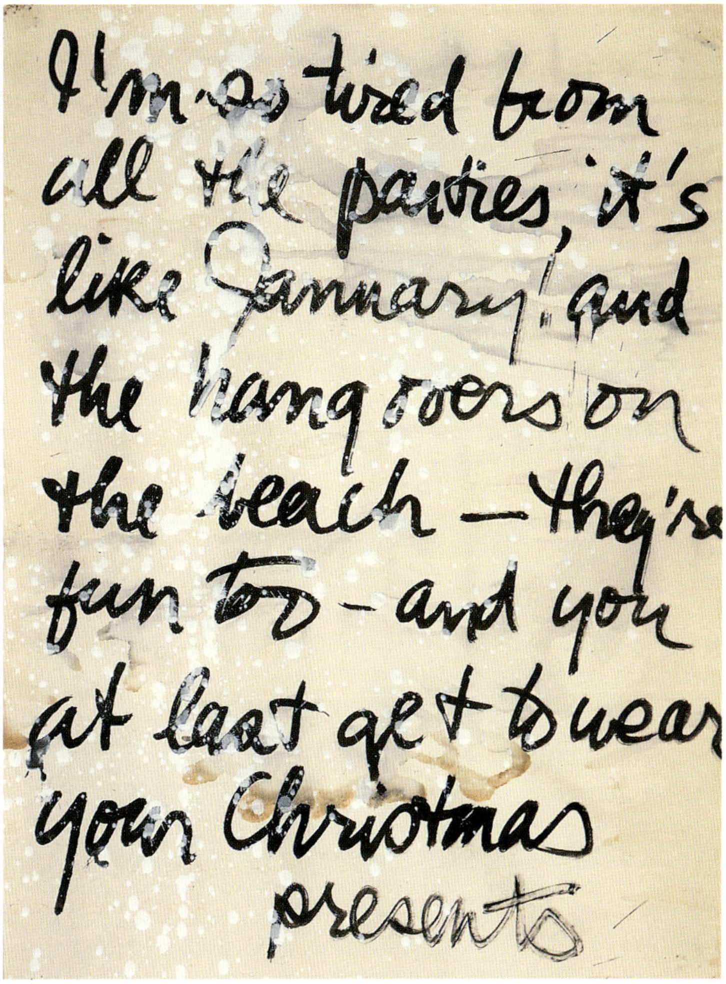

I'm So Tired, 1960

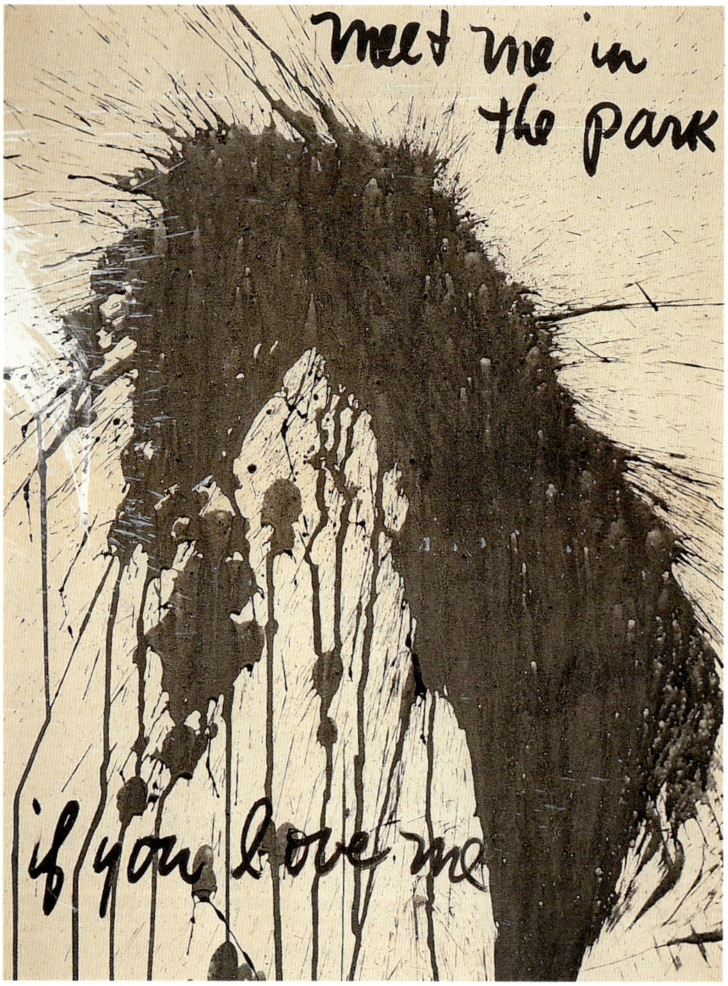

Norman Bluhm and Frank O'Hara

Meet Me In The Park, 1960

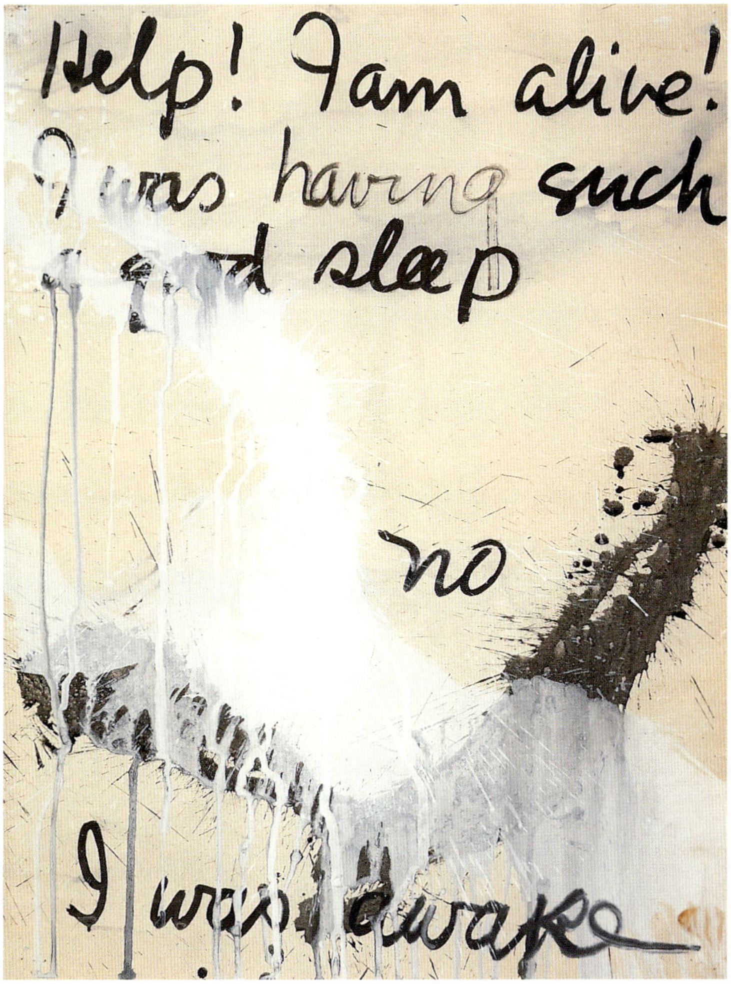

Help! I am Alive!, 1960

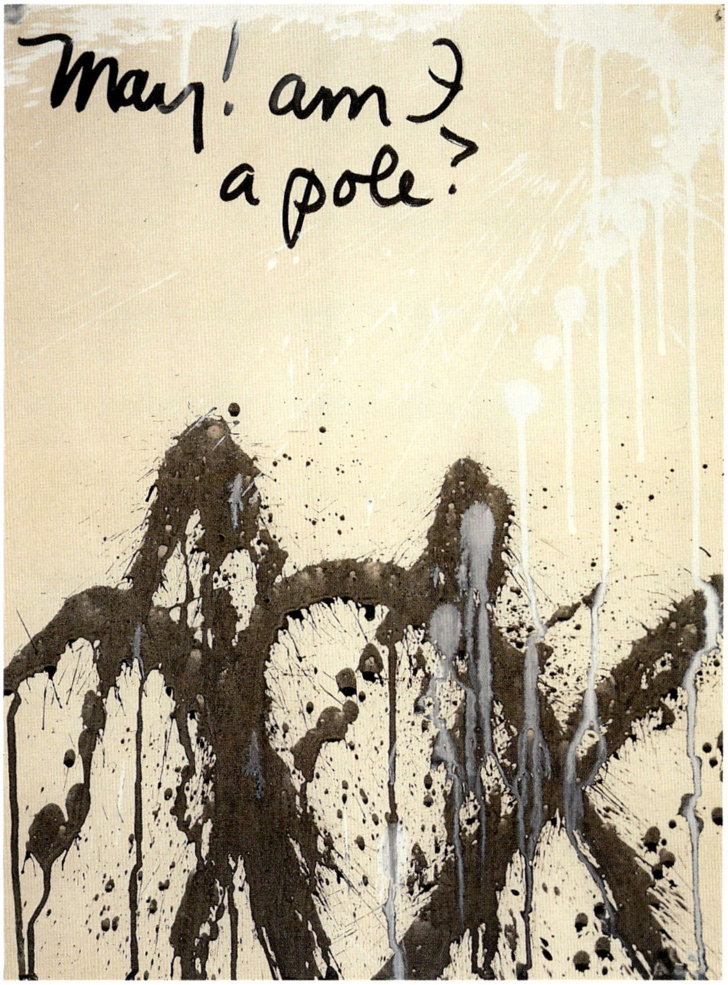

May!, 1960

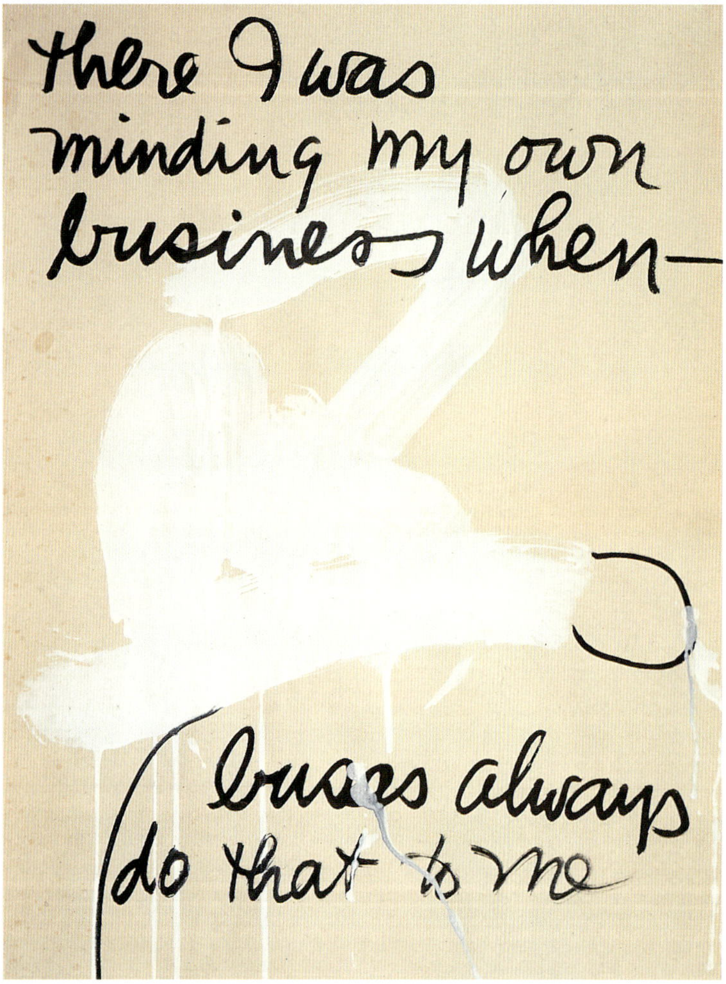

Norman Bluhm and Frank O'Hara

There I Was, 1960

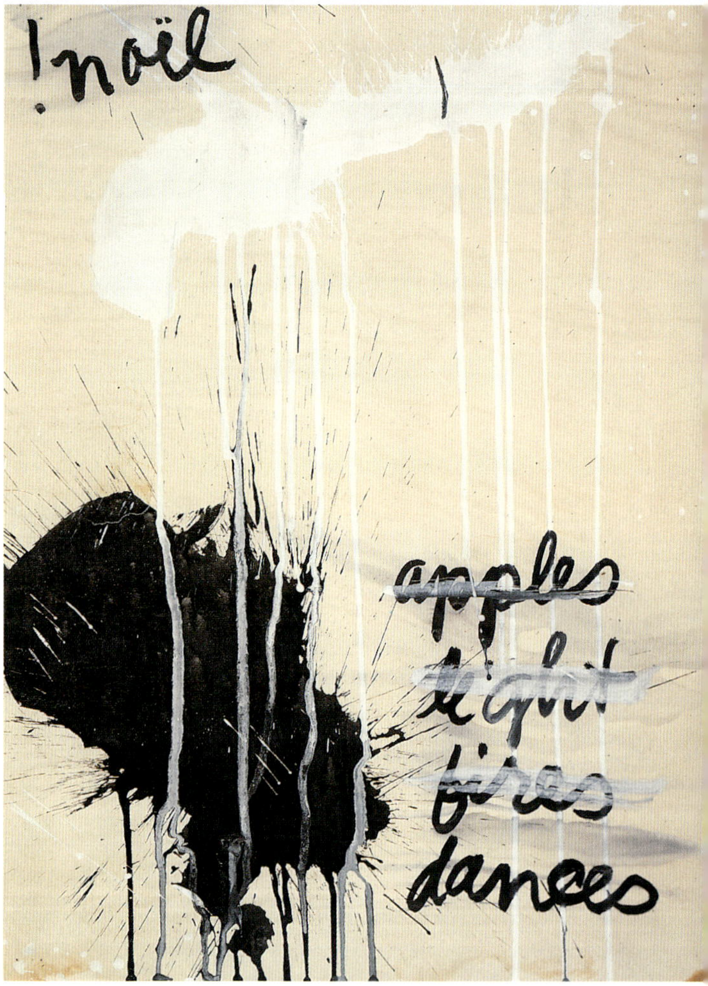

Noël, 1960

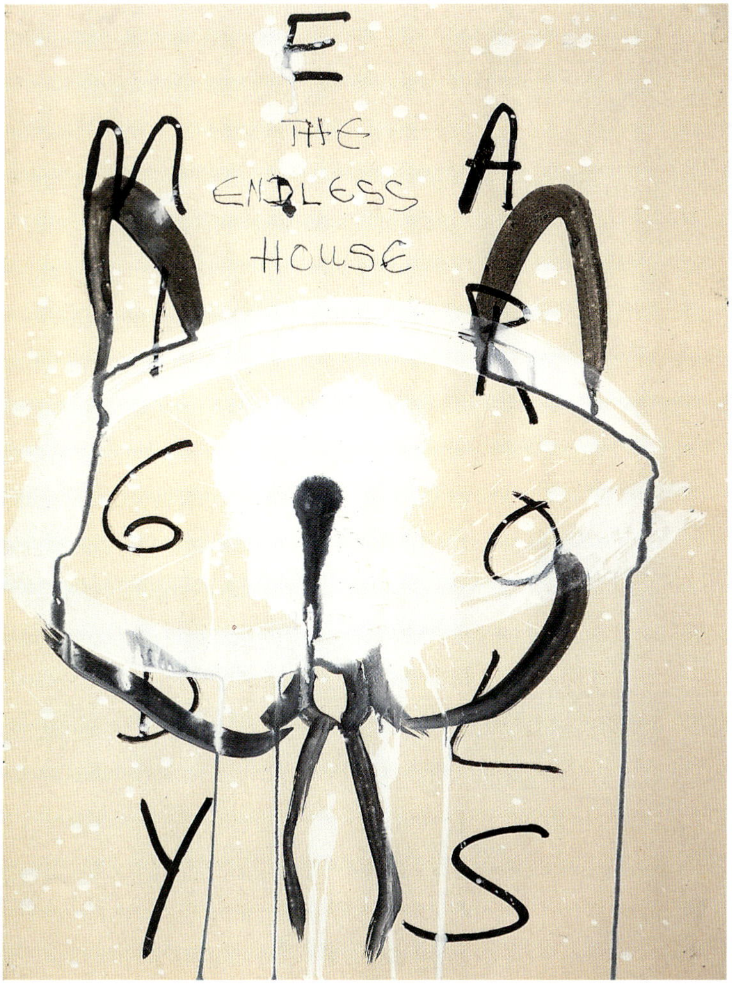

The Endless House, 1960

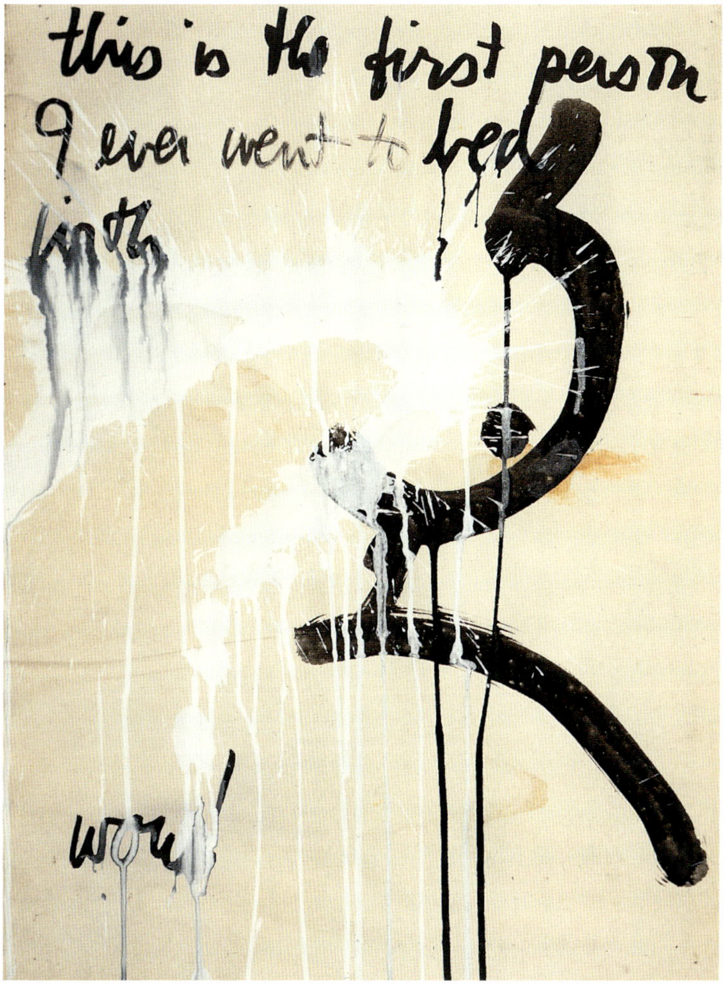

This Is The First, 1960

With Michael Goldberg, O'Hara was able to collaborate in a variety of ways. Their *Odes* (1960) combine O'Hara's poetry with Goldberg's gestural markings, coming together most completely in the "Ode on Necrophilia." The process began with O'Hara's loosely written version of the poem, over which Goldberg improvised. To Richard Miller of the Tiber Press, publisher of the book, O'Hara wrote an amusing poem that invokes the difficulties of getting bohemian artists like Goldberg to meet their deadlines, as well as demonstrating that O'Hara could rhyme when he wanted to.

Where is Mike Goldberg? I don't know,
he may be in the Village far below
or lounging on Tenth Street with the gang
of early-morning painters (before noon)
as they discuss the geste or jest
of action painting, whether it's Yang
or Yin and related to the sun or moon

Maybe he is living sketches of an ODE
ON SEX which I do not intend to write
in his abode or drinking bourbon in the light
of his be-placticked skylight. I will goad
him into Tibering and hope all's for the best[61]

The charismatic Goldberg was the subject of many poems. "Ode to Michael Goldberg ('s Birth and Other Births)" (1959) reduces O'Hara's own birth to burlesque:

I hardly ever think of June 27, 1926
when I came moaning into my mother's world
and tried to make it mine immediately
by screaming, sucking, urinating
and carrying on generally
it was quite a day

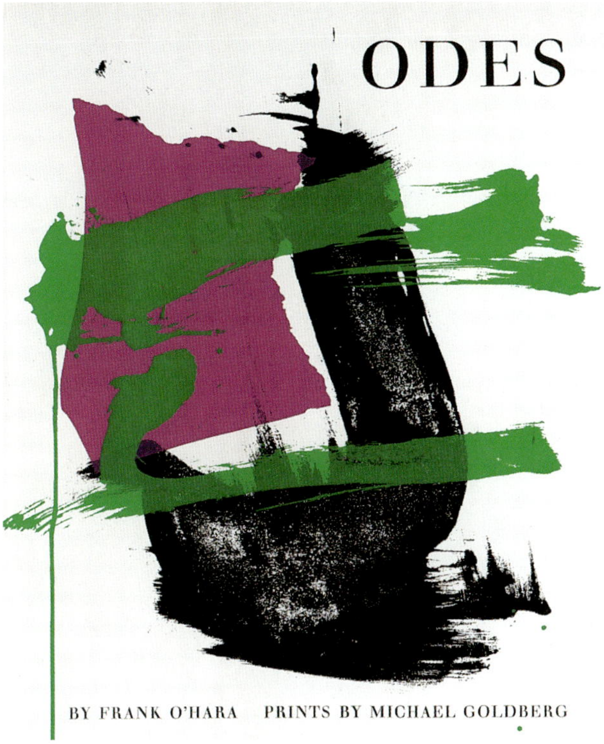

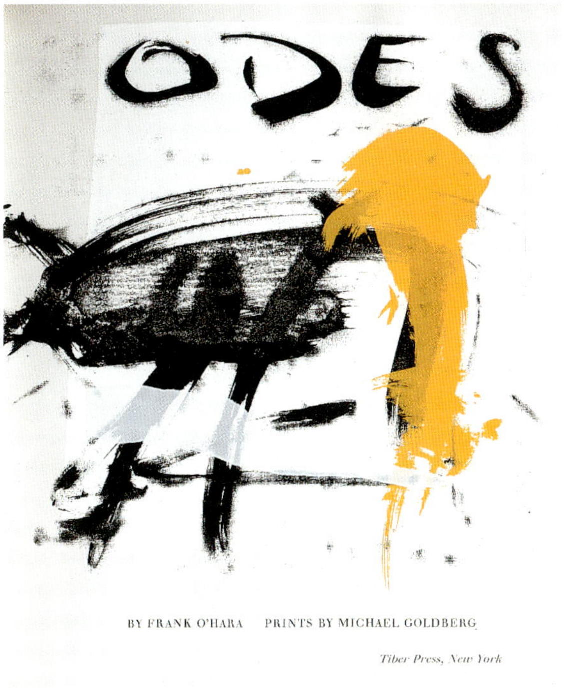

Michael Goldberg and Frank O'Hara
Cover and title page of **Odes,** 1960

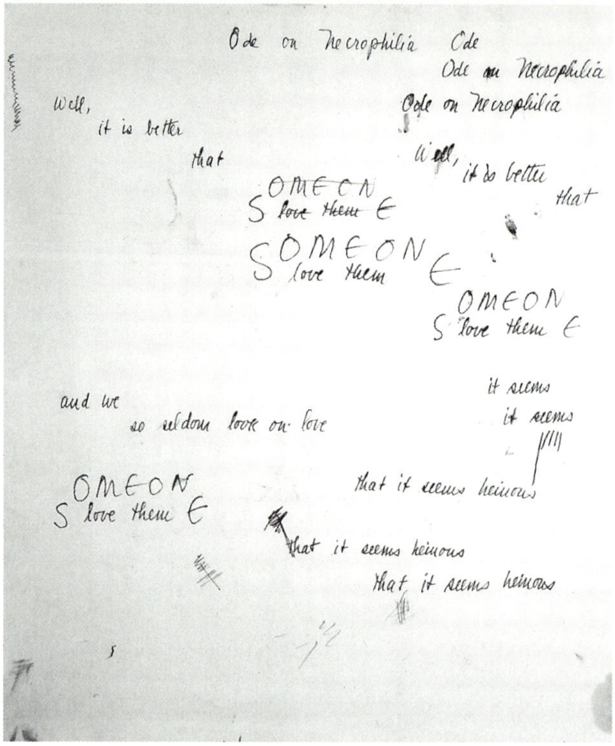

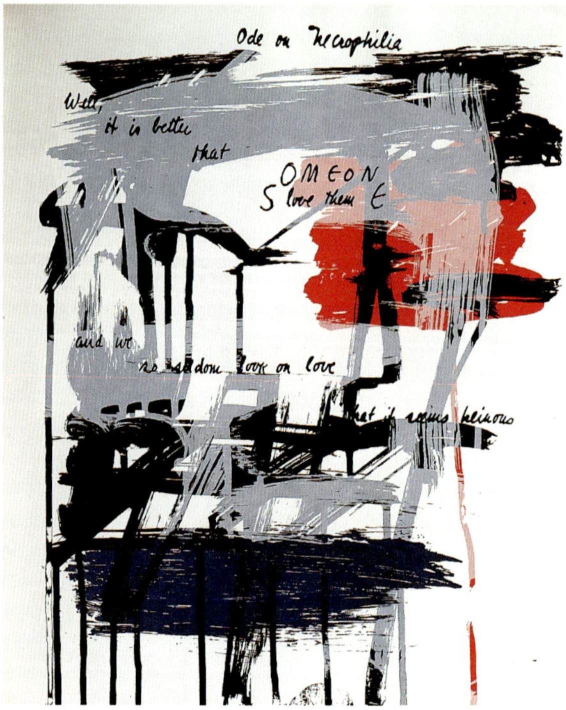

Frank O'Hara
Ode on Necrophilia, 1960

Michael Goldberg and Frank O'Hara
Ode on Necrophilia, 1960

but it also contains some of his most romantic images of his own childhood:

> **climbing the water tower I'd**
> **look out for hours in wind**
> **and the world seemed rounder**
> **and fiercer and I was happier**
> **because I wasn't scared of falling off**

Later, when O'Hara was traveling in Europe, Goldberg made a series of paintings on paper, "Dear Diary" (1962), that pick up their classicizing references from O'Hara's postcards and letters. The loosely sketched representational elements in these informal but elegant works are unusual for Goldberg, committed as he was to abstraction. His desire to mirror O'Hara's travels in paint reflects the closeness of their relationship.

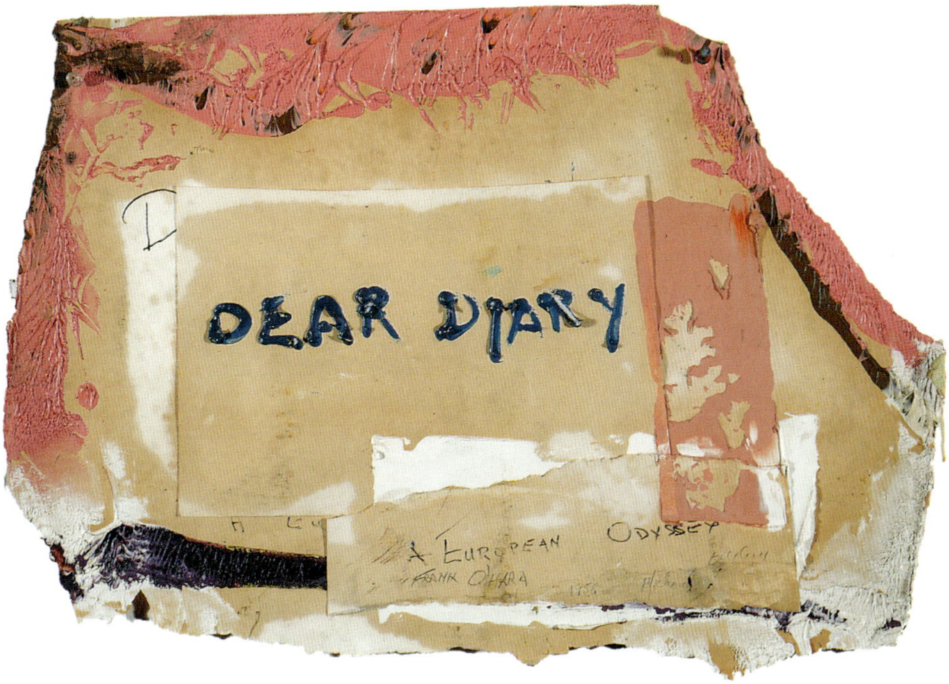

Michael Goldberg
Dear Diary, 1962

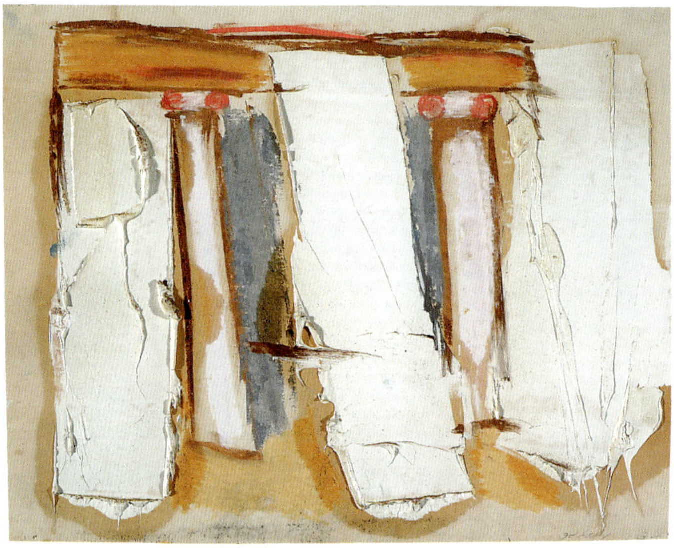

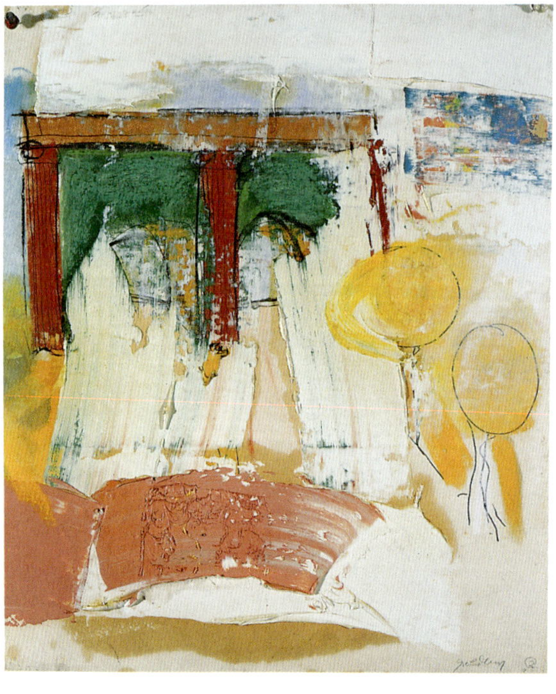

Michael Goldberg

Dear Diary, 1962

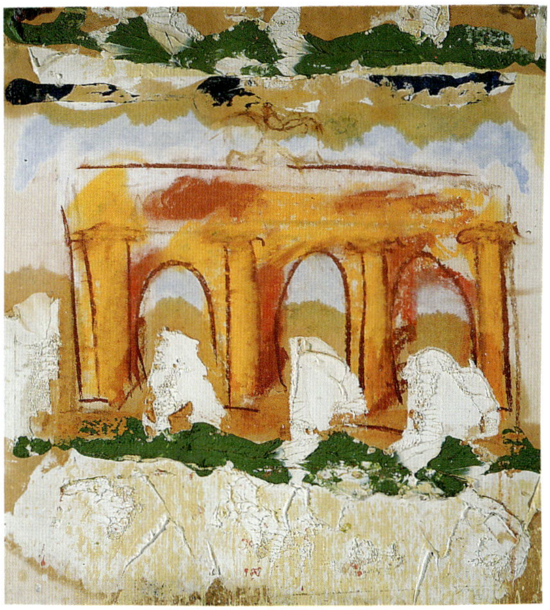

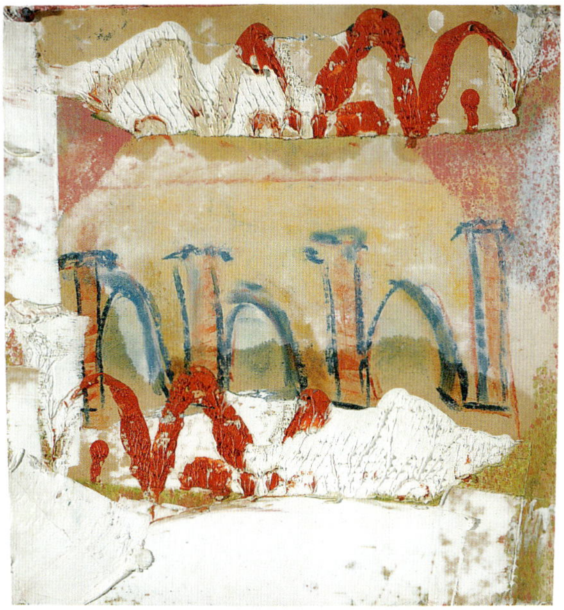

Dear Diary, 1962

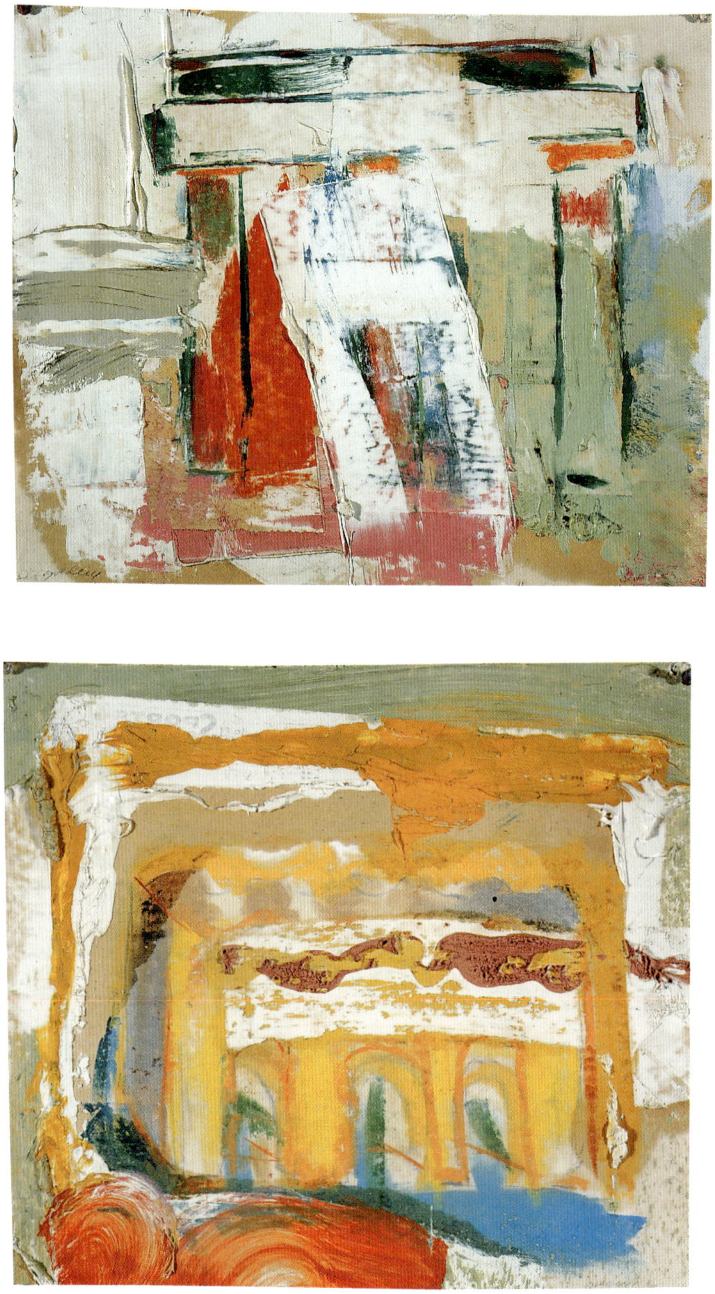

Michael Goldberg

Dear Diary, 1962

O'Hara's increasing visibility in the art world meant that even the artists of a slightly older generation became part of his milieu. In 1960, for example, Franz Kline made an etching that included O'Hara's "Poem (I will always love you)" in the poet's handwriting; not a true collaboration, perhaps, but certainly a mark of the increasing respect O'Hara was winning from a widening circle of artists. By 1965, when *Art in America* ran a portfolio of "Painters and Poets," the project's editor, Francine du Plessix, reported that O'Hara had been by far the most often named poet when the invited artists were asked with whom they wished to collaborate.[62]

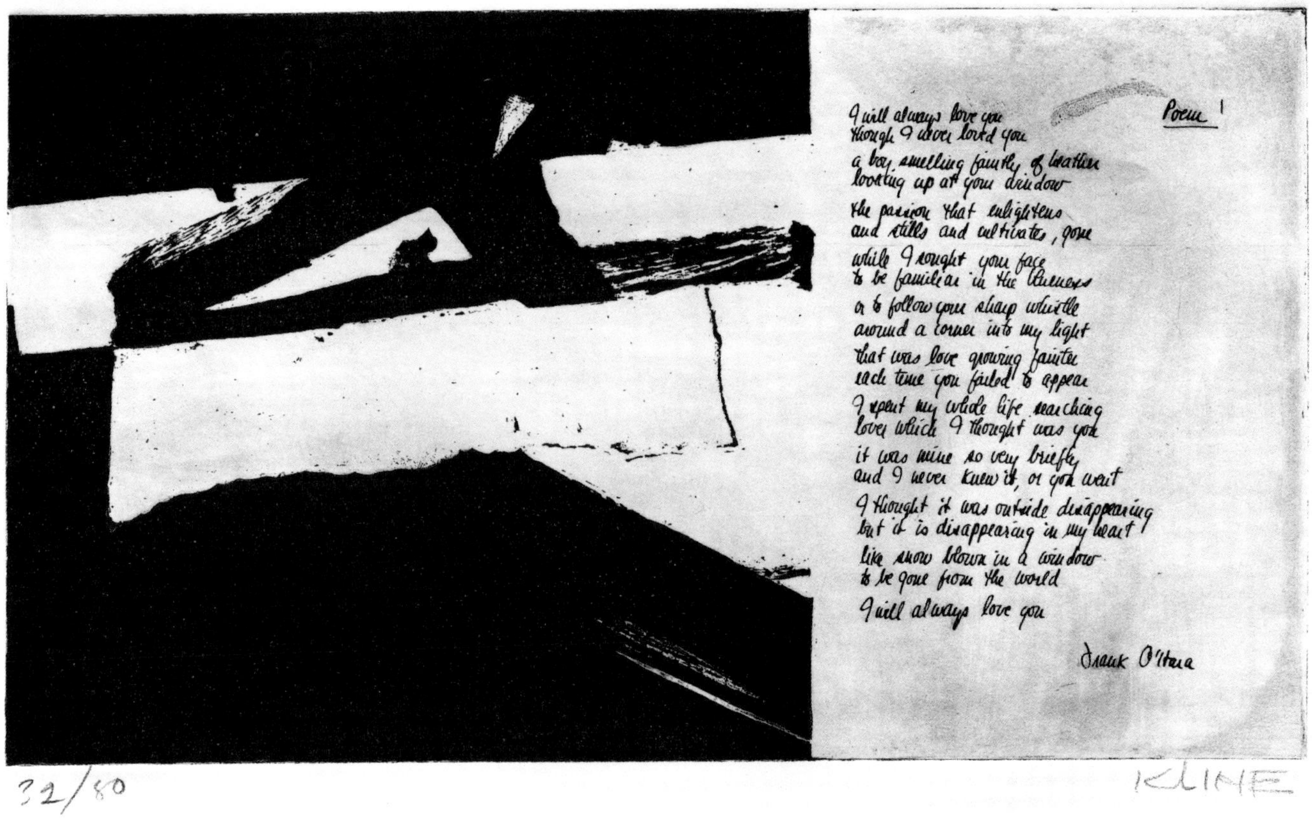

Franz Kline
Plate from **21 Etchings and Poems**, 1960

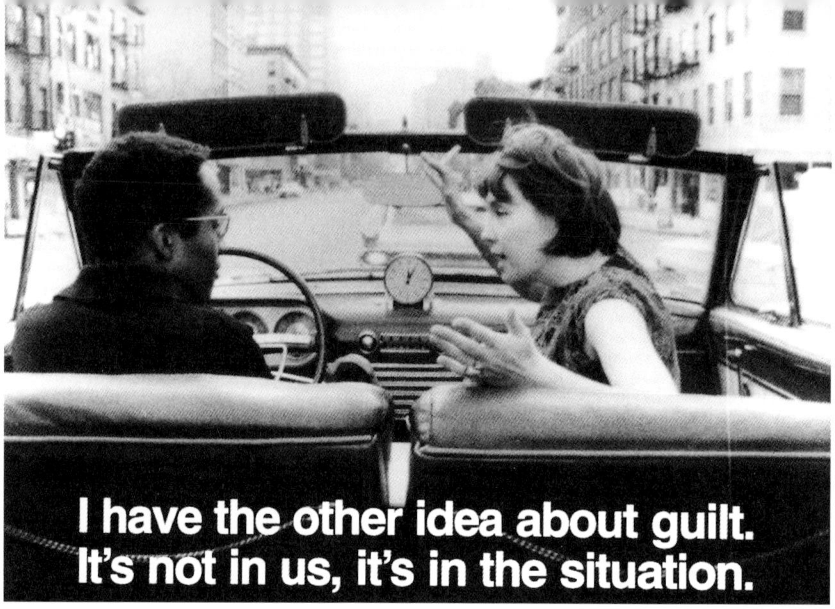

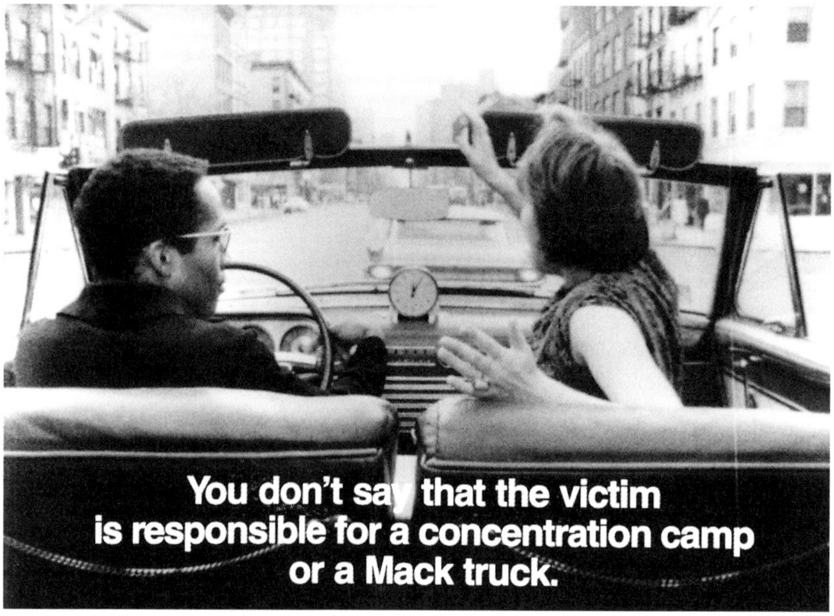

In 1964, O'Hara provided subtitles for Alfred Leslie's film, *The Last Clean Shirt.* The film shows a couple getting into a car and driving around Manhattan for about ten minutes, filmed from a stationary point of view in the back seat. The man (Richard White) remains silent, while the woman (Ruth Cazalet) jabbers incessantly and incomprehensibly (she is actually speaking Finnish doubletalk[63]). This sequence then repeats twice more, this time with subtitles by O'Hara that purport to be a translation of the woman's speech and of

Alfred Leslie
stills from **The Last Clean Shirt**, 1964

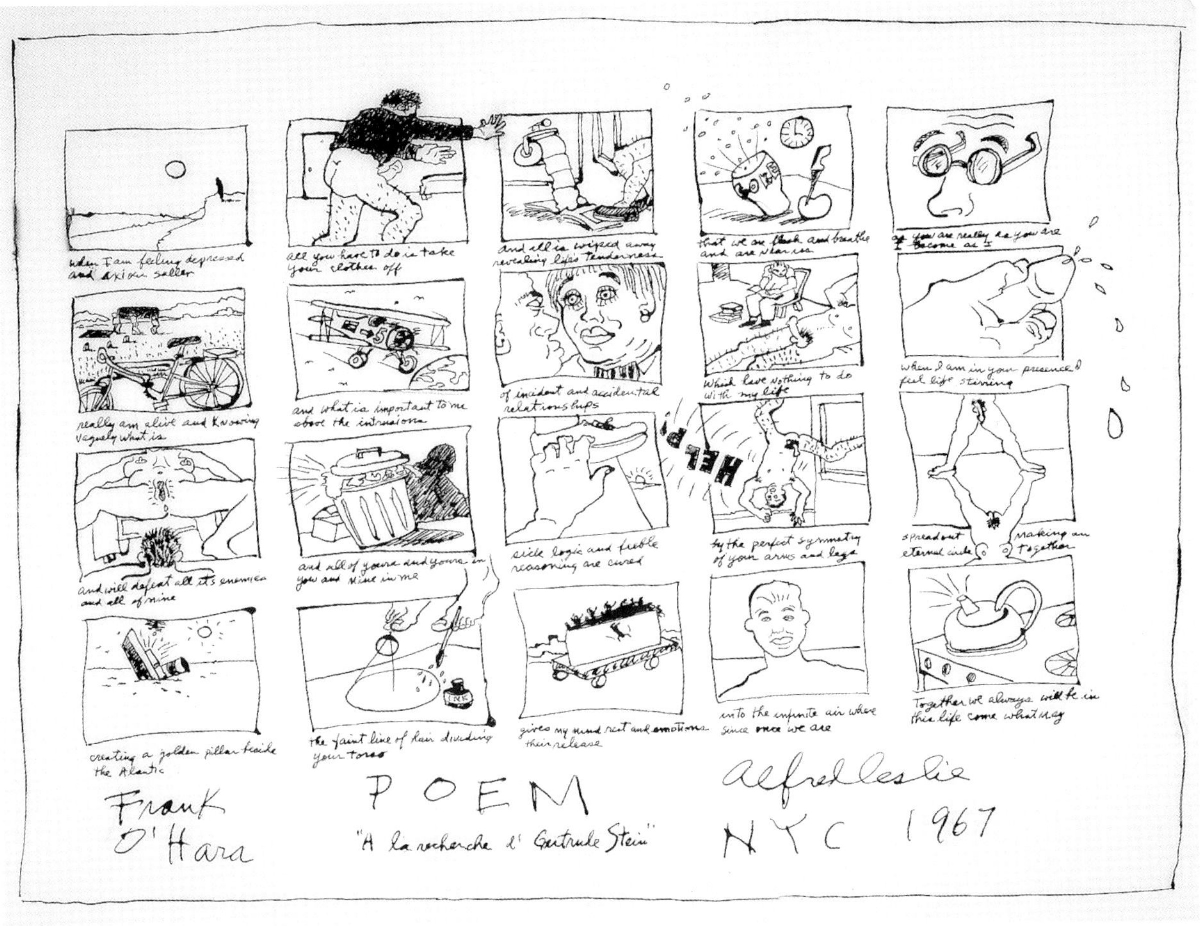

the man's thoughts. The film's long takes, repetition, attention to issues of language, and willingness to test the patience of its viewers anticipates many later experimental films. It provoked a near-riot when it was first shown in New York. O'Hara's subtitles are a stream of consciousness that echo the tropes of his poetry, moving from passing thoughts ("I just hope the rain won't..."; "if only more people looked like Jerry Leiber" [the well-known song-writers Leiber and Stoller provided the film's music]) to more profound feelings ("It's the nature of us all to want to be unconnected"), all accompanied by the car's steady passage through the streets of New York. This astonishing work, with its playful but uncompromising questioning of the very capability of language to communicate any authentic truth, hints at one direction O'Hara's continuing openness to new forms of collaboration might have led him had his life not been cut short. Leslie also storyboarded some of O'Hara's poems. These drawings were sketches for animated films that Leslie planned to make, a project that did not come to fruition.

Alfred Leslie
Poem "À la recherche d'Gertrude Stein", 1967

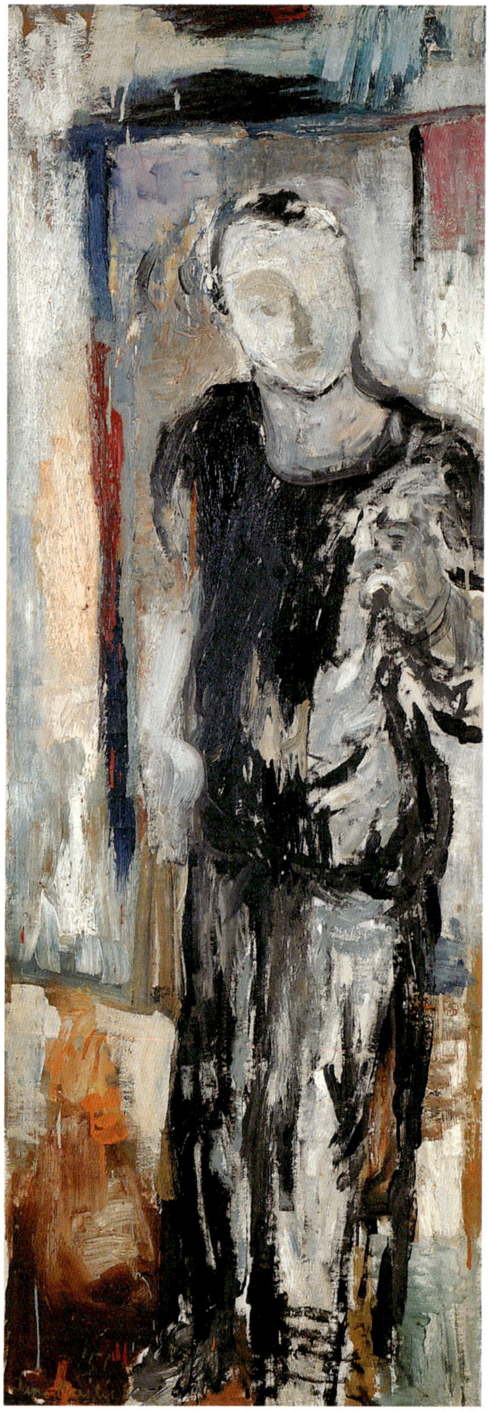

Jane Freilicher

Frank O'Hara, 1951

A little effortless and helpless

O'Hara's unlimited availability to his friends led to a number of superb portraits of him. The earliest of these is Jane Freilicher's of 1951. O'Hara was a constant visitor to her studio in his early years in New York, and she became a recurring presence in his poetry. Freilicher has never been well-known as a portrait painter, but this work succeeds completely in capturing the edgy poise of the young poet as he stands waiting in a doorway. As she describes the work,

> It is really a sketch painted from memory as he appeared characteristically in those days. . . with his dark fuzzy shetland sweater, no shirt, chino pants and tennis shoes—Ivy League but rather exotic and chic in the New York art world in those days.... However, my painting was just an attempt to capture a fleeting sense of his physical presence as he seemed, often, to be standing in the doorway of a room, one arm bent up at the elbow, his weight poised on the balls of his feet, maybe saying something funny or charming, proffering a drink or listening attentively, alert and delightful.[64]

Freilicher, like many painters in New York (especially those who remained interested in representation), had been enormously impressed by the Bonnard exhibition at The Museum of Modern Art in 1948.[65] O'Hara's comments on that artist offer a clue as to how he wanted to present himself: "It is simply a property of Bonnard's mature work, and one of its most fragile charms, to look slightly washed-out, to look what every sophisticated person let alone artist wants to look: a little 'down,' a little effortless and helpless."[66]

Rivers painted O'Hara's portrait repeatedly. The pattern of their relationship was typical of the way in which O'Hara ignored any distinction between professional admiration and personal intimacy. Portraits and various collaborations often followed. "I began doing portraits of Frank in the fall of '52," Rivers recalled. "That was after I'd slit my wrists over something. I phoned Frank, who happened to be in, and he came over and bandaged me up. Then we began seeing a lot more of each other and it was only natural for me to use him as a model. Sex we got into later, when I'd already started drawing and painting him." For Rivers, O'Hara's striking features made him an ideal subject: "He had blazing blue eyes, so if you were stuck you could always put a little blue to make the work more interesting. His widow's peak gave you a place to anchor the picture, and his broken nose was dramatic and easy to get." Even more than these visual qualities, however, O'Hara, unlike the usual, silent model, talked back during portrait sessions, continuing the kind of exchange between them that stimulated Rivers to push harder: "There was always a dialogue going on during our working sessions. He gave me feedback and made me feel what I was doing mattered, and after a while I found I needed him for my work. He was a great model. . . he even felt complimented that you asked him to."[67]

In 1954 Rivers painted the most striking of all his portraits of O'Hara. In this huge canvas O'Hara stands boldly in the center, stark naked except for his leather combat boots. As much as any artist in New York at that time, Rivers loved to measure himself against the old masters, and this painting is as ambitious as a portrait by Van Dyck or Rubens. Like their work, it shows a proud aristocrat, but in this case the subject is self-made, an aristocrat of the intellect who needs no trappings. Here O'Hara embodies bohemian New York in the fifties, supremely self-confident, unafraid to shock. Part of the shock, especially in 1954, is that this portrait is an unmistakably homoerotic work. The prominence of the penis and the rough trade suggestion of the boots leave no doubt about that. His arms are raised above his head, as if to emphasize his act of self-revelation. Rivers's lavish and loving brushwork is evidence of the obsessive looking at O'Hara's naked body over the months of sittings that the work took to realize. At the same time, however, the painting is an equally explicit attempt to take on (in both senses of that phrase: to assimilate and to challenge) the grand manner of nineteenth-century French Romantic painting. As O'Hara himself put it, "I think what Larry was trying to do was keep it from being academic. But at the same time getting into the ring with Géricault."[68] This telling remark gives an insight into the strategies of painters working in the crucible that was New York in the fifties. To be painting in the wake of the triumphal success of the first generation of New York School painters meant enormous pressure for artists to make the next breakthrough. The struggle was often expressed in the rhetoric of physical violence. Artists were always "getting in the ring with" their heroes.[69] Yet at the same time there was a pervasive sense of fatigue and frustration with the existing models.

Larry Rivers
O'Hara Nude with Boots, 1

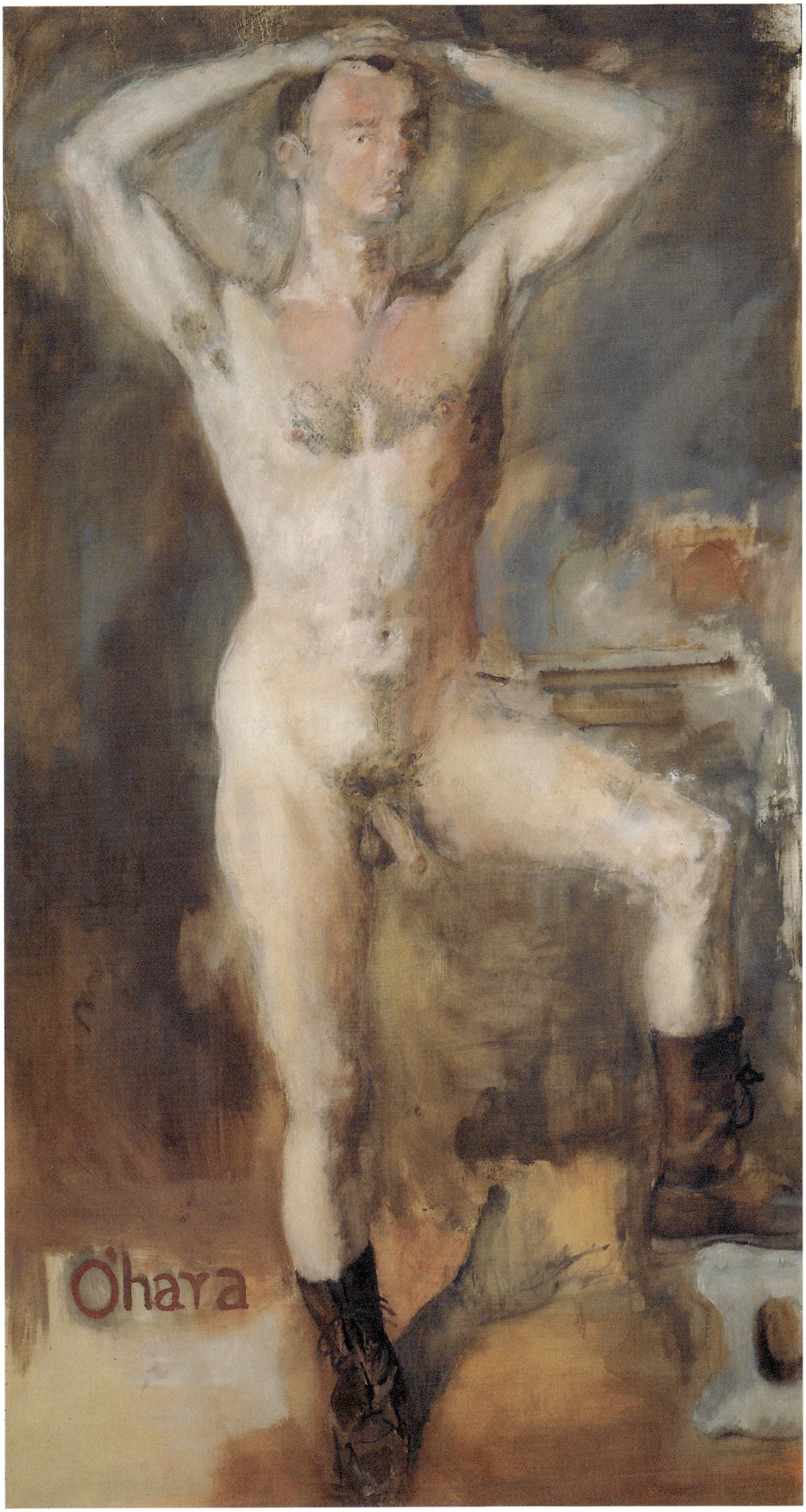
O'hara

One response was to step away from Abstract Expressionism and move towards work that was not then at the forefront of critical attention, even if that move might seem inexplicable or marginalizing. O'Hara felt that all artists made use of such a strategy to a greater or lesser extent, and he related it to his own constant struggle to stay fully engaged:

> The avant-garde has been made up, I think, completely, and all through history, with people who are *bored* by other people's ideas.... I think that if de Kooning says that what he really is interested in is Poussin; that's his way of not being bored with Kandinsky, or *by* Kandinsky. You see, when all the world is looking at Kandinsky, he suddenly says I think Ingres and Poussin are the real things to look at. Now it may only work for two years, but that doesn't matter in the life of the artist as long as it energizes him.[70]

When all the world is looking at de Kooning, it is surely equally necessary to turn one's attention elsewhere.

It is fascinating to discover that Fairfield Porter, another artist who continued to look back at older traditions, made several drawings of O'Hara as he posed for Rivers's grand portrait. These elegant sketches show an identical pose, but compared with Rivers's impassioned Romanticism, they pursue a classicism that does indeed suggest an interest in Ingres. The tone of Porter's own full-scale portrait of O'Hara of 1957 is quite different from Rivers's (mock?) heroic portrait. O'Hara reclines on a couch, as the surface of the painting becomes a field in which the richly patterned fabric has an importance almost equal to that of the sitter. O'Hara had written about Porter a few years earlier: "He has moved into an area of positive feeling for the painting where the ideas, the passions, the subjects do nothing other than identify his work, like handwriting—they have little to do with his main project which is apparently the perfect painting. And he is very close, at least, to his object."[71] The figure of O'Hara himself comes close here to becoming pure painting, notwithstanding the strong likeness that Porter delivers at the same time.

Alice Neel's two portraits of O'Hara from 1960 take German Expressionism as their inspiration, lingering as they do over every blemish on O'Hara's striking face. The first was relatively conventional, and it succeeds in conveying O'Hara's characteristic alertness (as well as his distinctive profile). It was painted over five sittings, and Neel described it as "a romantic falconlike profile with a bunch of lilacs."[72] Pamela Allara has suggested that

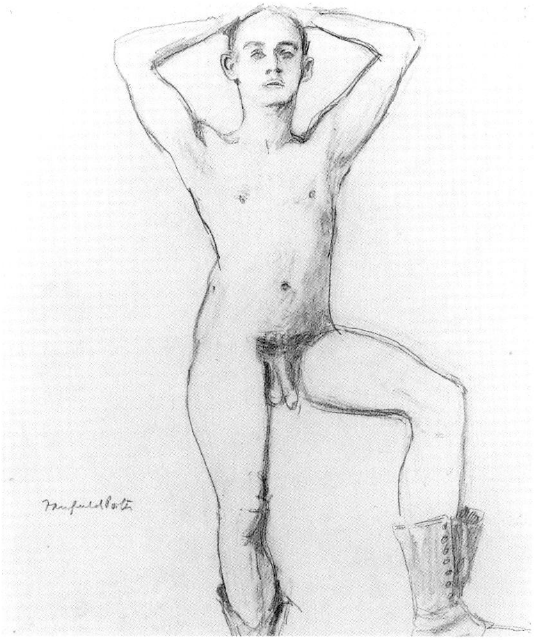

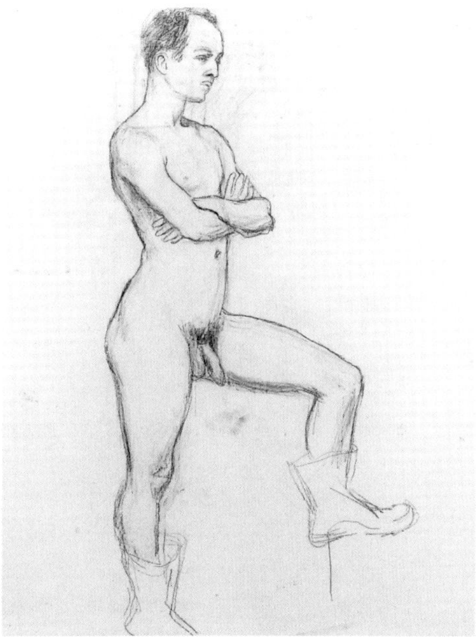

Fairfield Porter

Male Nude (Frank O'Hara), 1954

Untitled Male Nude (in Boots), 1954

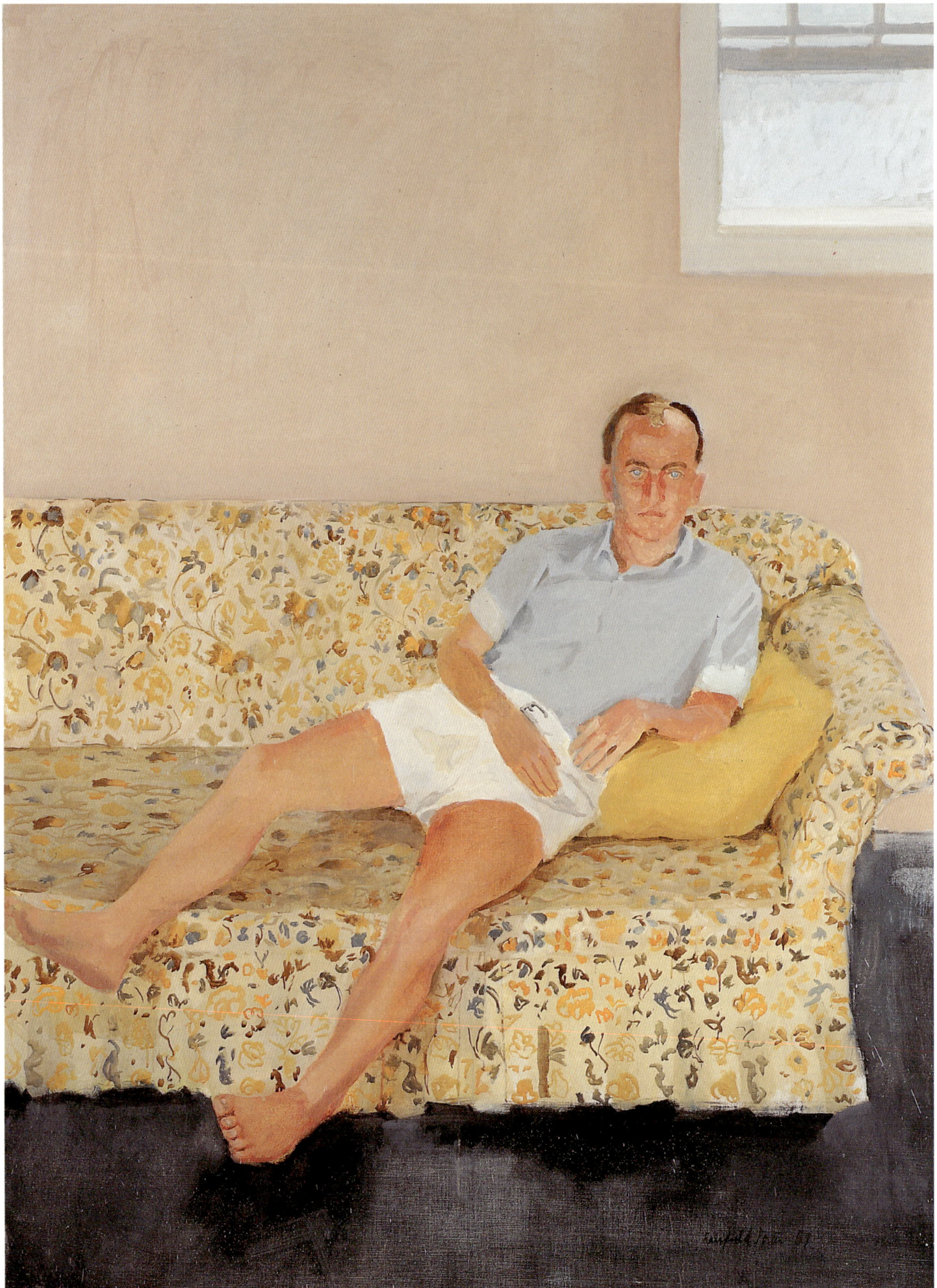

Fairfield Porter

Portrait of Frank O'Hara, 1957

Neel's desire to paint O'Hara was motivated not just by his striking appearance, but also by the desire to curry favor with an increasingly influential figure in the art world.[73] But the second portrait, *Frank O'Hara No. 2,* painted in a single day, hardly seems designed to flatter. It endows its dramatically lit sitter with a desperate quality reminiscent of portraits by Max Beckmann. "I started with the mouth. His teeth looked like tombstones; the lilacs had withered. When he saw the picture he said: 'My God! Those freckles! But the Fauves went that far.'"[74] The comment is charmingly revealing of O'Hara's personality: his horror at appearing in a grossly unflattering light is instantly superseded by an unequivocal acceptance of the artist's vision.

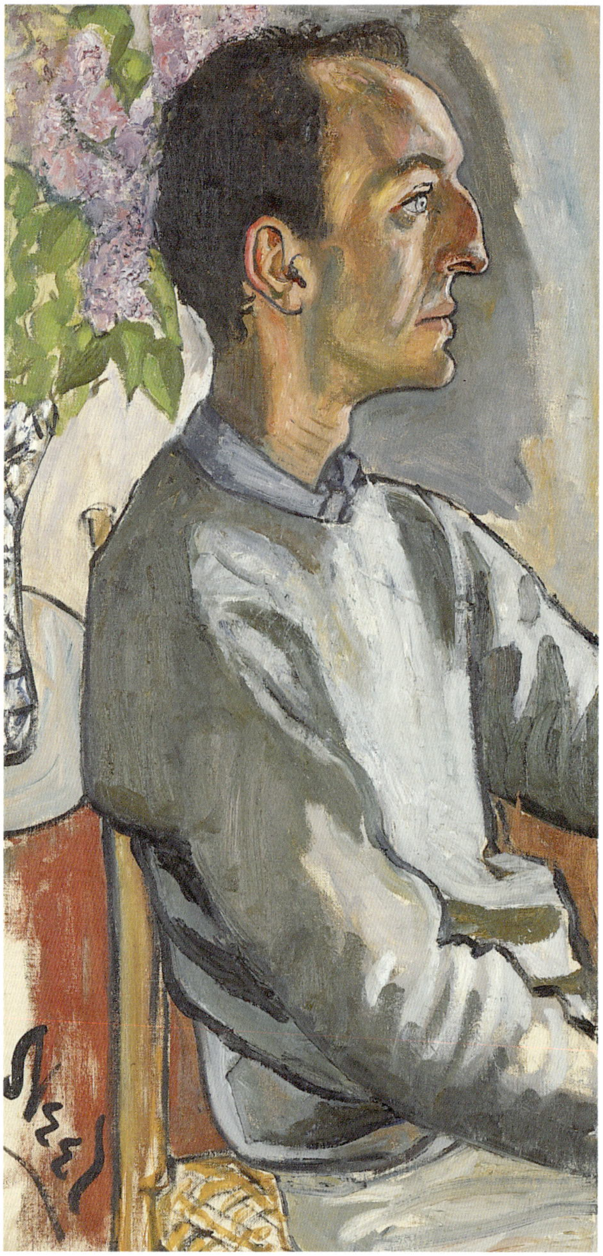

Alice Neel

Frank O'Hara, 1960

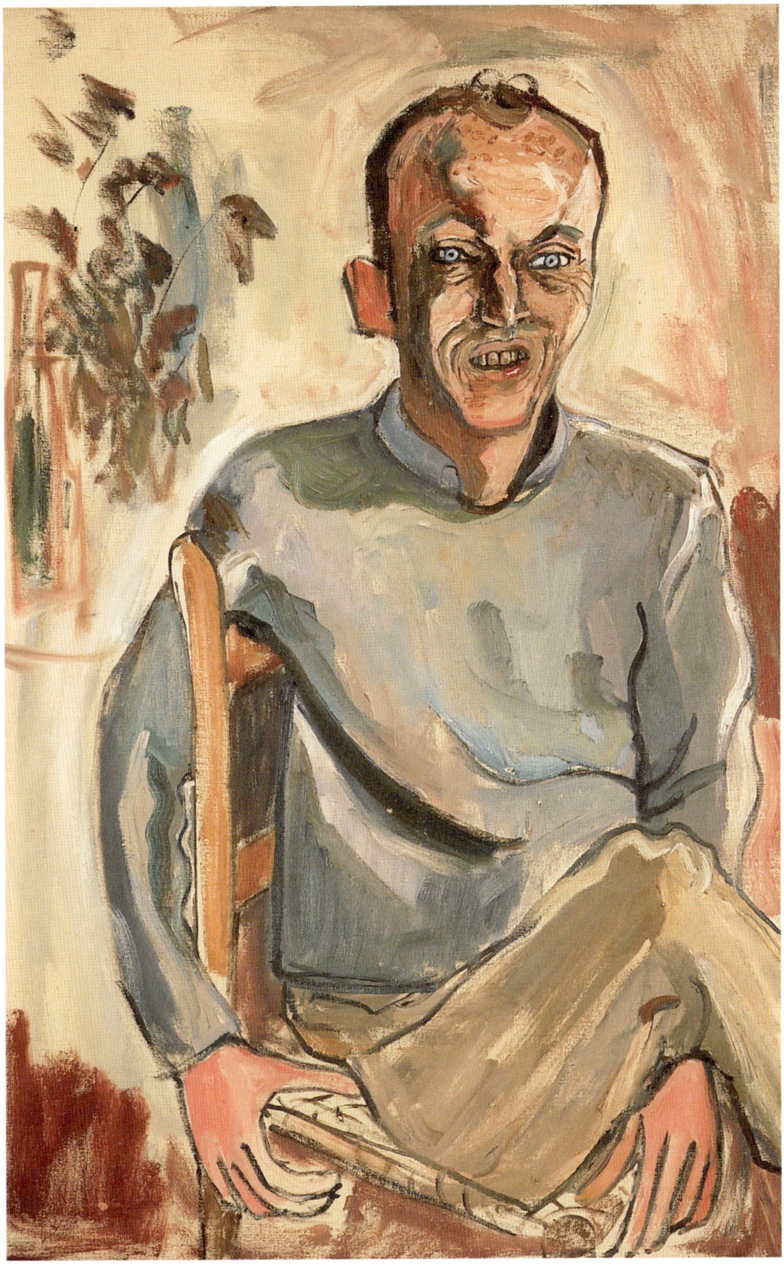

Alice Neel

Frank O'Hara No. 2, 1960

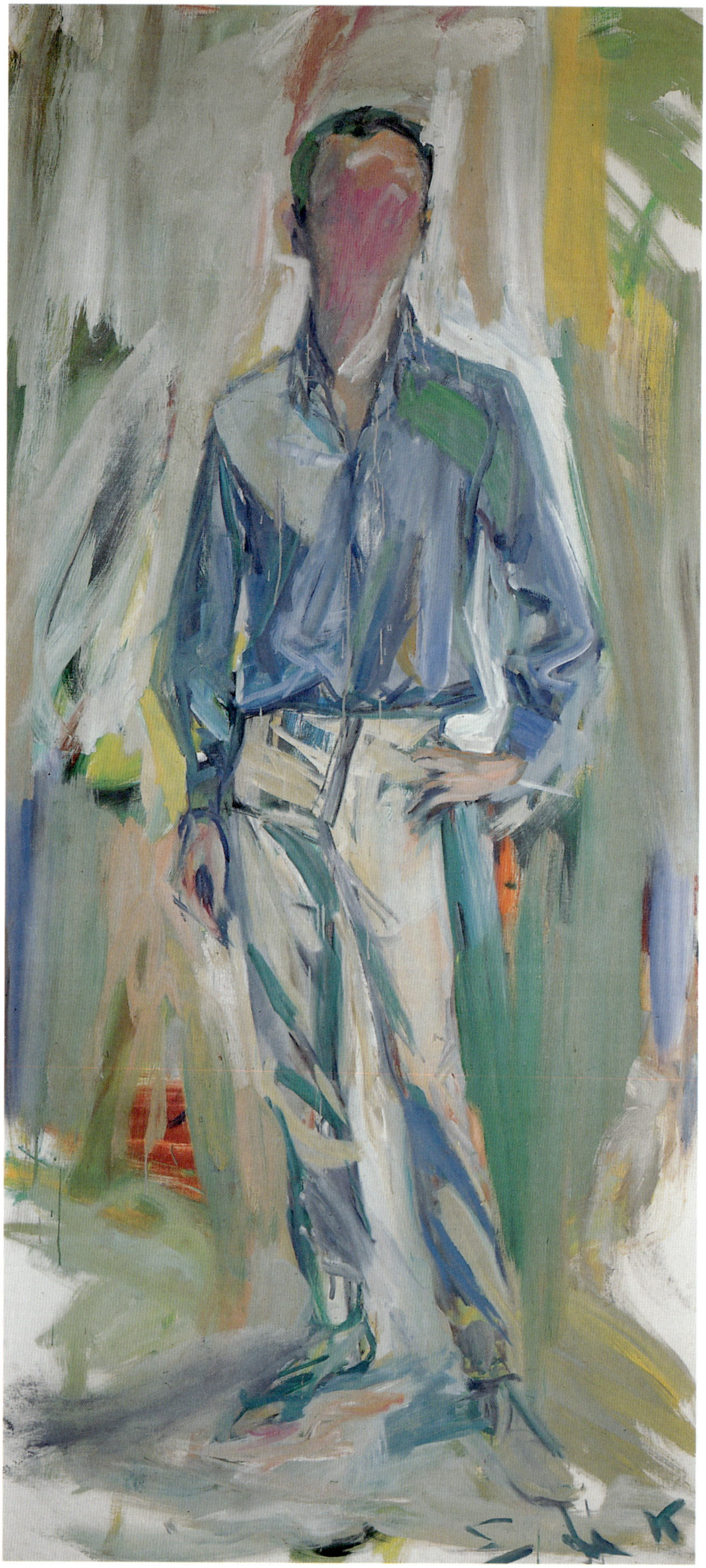

Elaine de Kooning
Frank O'Hara, 1962

Grace to be born and live as variously as possible

Elaine de Kooning painted O'Hara's portrait in 1962. He emerges full-length from a swirling cloud of Abstract Expressionist brushstrokes. "The thing about people one knows intimately is, you don't even have to look," de Kooning said. "You just paint, let's say, Frank O'Hara, in pale blue or some kind of color, and he *occurs* within the painting." O'Hara certainly occurs in the painting, but he is strikingly without a face, which is replaced by a few completely abstract brushstrokes. "Frank was standing there. First I painted the whole structure of his face; then I wiped out the face, and when the face was gone, it was more Frank than when the face was there."[75]

It is quite true that the slight figure of O'Hara is clearly recognizable, standing *contrapposto* with his hand on his hip. But de Kooning was hinting at a deeper issue in O'Hara's personality, an issue that separates him irrevocably from the first-generation New York School artists whose institutional champion he remained. I argued earlier that O'Hara's distaste for the confessional mode did not preclude a commitment to the authentic. But for O'Hara, the truly authentic was always likely to be multiple, filtered through his intense relationships with friends and lovers. It is at this point that O'Hara's view of the world begins to part company with the single-minded search for an *essential* and uniquely individual authenticity that characterized much of Abstract Expressionism.[76] As Pollock put it in a typical remark, "Painting is self-discovery. Every good artist paints what he is."[77] The comment makes clear the artist's belief in a unitary self that must be excavated through an inner-directed process, and could not be more different from O'Hara's:

> **My eyes, like millions of**
> **glassy squares, merely reflect.**[78]

William Carlos Williams, a poet that O'Hara admired, was widely quoted as advocating "no ideas but in things." O'Hara, it could be said, had developed his own variation, lying somewhere between Pollock and Williams, which might perhaps be expressed as "no ideas but in other people." In pursuit of that belief, he could take on many guises.

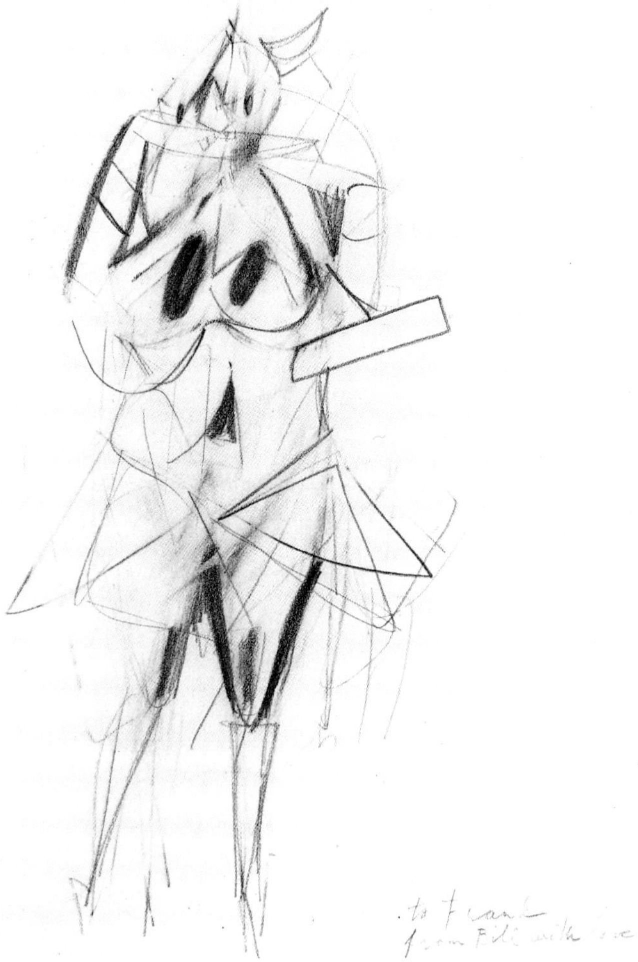

Elaine de Kooning painted him without a face, and felt that "it was more Frank." In 1954, Grace Hartigan painted him as *The Masker,* an ambiguous figure ready to take on any character. Larry Rivers too painted a number of portraits of O'Hara that suggest this sense of masking and doubling of identity, most notably his version of Courbet's *Studio,* in which O'Hara hovers to the side in a double incarnation. This embrace of multiplicity could hardly be further from the driven rhetoric of a single-minded authenticity characteristic of Abstract Expressionism. In this light O'Hara seems much more a precursor to the kind of surface-oriented attitude characteristic of Andy Warhol, the Warhol who could say that "I never fall apart because I never fall together."[79]

O'Hara embraces an explicitly multiple identity. "My quietness has a number of naked selves," he writes in "In Memory of My Feelings."

Willem de Kooning
Untitled, c. 1950

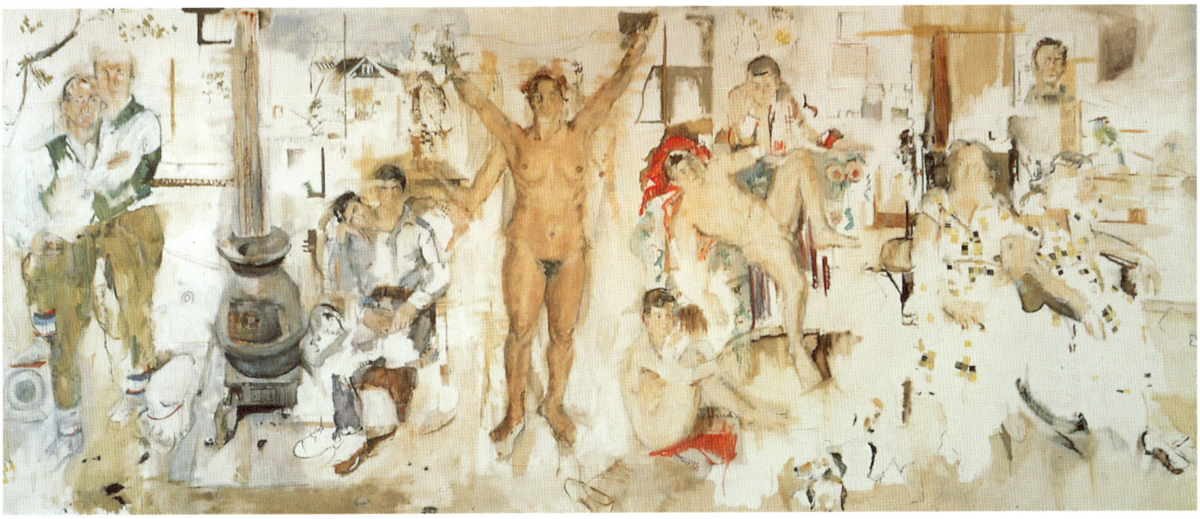

Grace

to be born and live as variously as possible. The conception
of the masque barely suggests the sordid identifications.
I am a Hittite in love with a horse. I don't know what blood's
in me I feel like an African prince I am a girl walking downstairs
in a red pleated dress with heels I am a champion taking a fall
I am a jockey with a sprained ass-hole I am the light mist
in which a face appears
and it is another face of blonde I am a baboon eating a banana
I am a dictator looking at his wife I am a doctor eating a child
and the child's mother smiling I am a Chinaman climbing a mountain
I am a child smelling his father's underwear I am an Indian
sleeping on a scalp
and my pony is stamping in the birches,
and I've just caught sight of the *Niña*, the *Pinta* and the *Santa Maria*.
What land is this, so free?[80]

In this kaleidoscopic vision O'Hara takes on race after race; he is ancient and modern; he is young and old; and he is man and woman. He is even an animal, a baboon. He is the weather, the light mist, and when the mist clears he is an archetype of an America waiting to be born. Twisting the rhetoric of the McCarthy era in which this poem was written, he claims this land so free as a playground of shifting identities. If it is free, it is free because we have the freedom to play many roles, not just one.

Larry Rivers
The Studio, 1956
Oil on canvas
82½ x 193½ inches
The Minneapolis Institute of Arts

The old camp grounds

O'Hara died in 1966, three years before the riot at the Stonewall Inn in Greenwich Village that is usually taken to mark the beginning of the end of the closeted era. For most of the gay men in O'Hara's bohemian milieu, however, it is clear that the metaphor of the closet is of limited value, since these men had succeeded in creating a world for themselves in which they were sustained by a wide circle of gay friends, and in which their homosexuality was at least tacitly accepted by many straight friends (Willem de Kooning always greeted O'Hara with a kiss on the mouth; Robert Motherwell wrote to him that, "Whenever I hear talk about homosexuals, I remember that Proust's book is the greatest epic poem of the century"[81]). George Chauncey has documented the existence of extensive gay subcultures in New York going back long before O'Hara's time, and he has pointed out some of the dangers of an ahistorical approach to the pre-Stonewall era:

Given the ubiquity of the term today and how central the metaphor of the closet is to the way we think about gay history before the 1960s, it is bracing—and instructive—to note that it was never used by gay people themselves before then. Nowhere does it appear before the 1960s in the records of the gay movement or in the novels, diaries, or letters of gay men and lesbians. The fact that gay people in the past did not speak of or conceive of themselves as living in a closet does not preclude us from using the term retrospectively as an analytic category, but it does suggest that we need to use it more cautiously and precisely, and to pay attention to the very different terms people used to describe themselves and their social worlds. Many gay men, for instance, described negotiating their presence in an often hostile world as living a double life, or wearing a mask and taking it off.[82]

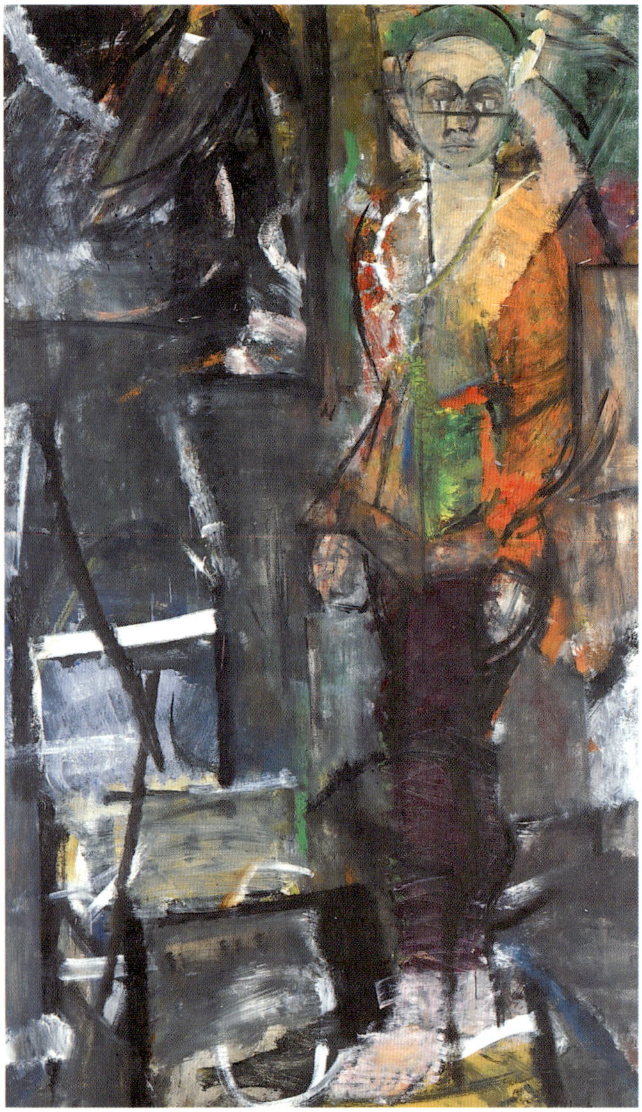

Grace Hartigan
The Masker, 1954

The sense of having to hide a central part of one's identity, to wear one mask and then another, was to some extent shared by almost all gay men in the fifties and early sixties. O'Hara seems, as I have indicated, in some part to have positively relished this constantly shifting series of masquerades. In a number of his poems he explicitly focuses on the exhilarating pleasure of letting the mask suddenly drop:

> **all day you act like**
> **someone else and then, at dusk,**
> **you go down on someone for the first**
> **time, down, down, as only a boy**
> **like a French horn goes down**
> **on a man.**[83]

O'Hara wrote a number of poems dealing directly with gay issues, many of which are extraordinarily explicit for a period in which even veiled allusions were considered daring. In a poem of 1954, "Homosexuality," in part inspired by a James Ensor self-portrait with masks, O'Hara begins sardonically: "So we are taking off our masks are we, and keeping / our mouths shut?" only to shift abruptly into a paean to New York's public bathrooms, where anonymity and veiled identity offered a kind of extraordinary freedom from the official world, his voice clearly one of experience and pleasure:

> **It's wonderful to admire oneself**
> **with complete candor, tallying up the merits of each**
>
> **of the latrines. 14th Street is drunken and credulous,**
> **53rd tries to tremble but is too at rest. The good**
>
> **love a park and the inept a railway station**

"At The Old Place" (1955) evokes the ambience of a pre-Stonewall gay dance bar in Greenwich Village. O'Hara's companions this night are John Ashbery, Joe LeSueur, John Button, and the pianist Alvin Novak:

> **Down the dark stairs drifts the steaming cha-**
> **cha-cha. Through the urine and smoke we charge**
> **to the floor. Wrapped in Ashes' arms I glide.**
> **(It's heaven!) Button lindys with me. (It's**
> **heaven!) Joe's two-steps, too, are incredible,**
> **and then a fast rhumba with Alvin, like skipping**
> **on toothpicks. And the interminable intermissions,**
>
> **we have them. Jack, Earl, and Someone drift**
> **guiltily in. "I knew they were gay**
> **the minute I laid eyes on them!" screams John.**
> **How ashamed they are of us!   we hope.**[84]

Button, asked much later what O'Hara would have thought of gay liberation, replied with true camp, "Oh, he would have thought it was silly, but he would have *loved* the dances!"[85] Camp is a contested term today, but it can still serve to indicate the kind of coded, half-secret pleasure that could serve as an entrée and as a bond in an era when codes and secrecy were virtually inescapable for gay people. There is no doubt that O'Hara could be very camp: "We scream / chatter prance and / wash our hair!"[86] After seeing Judy Garland at the Palace Theater, he told Button that "she's *better* than Picasso."[87] In his poetry, too, O'Hara made consistent use of the exclamation points and quotation marks that are integral to camp: "I jacked 'off'"; "a hot 'dog'"; "after 'hitting' the beach at Endzoay we drank up the liebfraumilch."[88] One has the prevailing sense of someone always ready to take a little ironic step back from the events of the day, anxious not to be seen taking anything too seriously, always pretending to be pretending. This is what Susan Sontag defined as "Being-as-Playing-a Role."[89] But where Sontag saw camp as a way of avoiding real depth of feeling, O'Hara's stance by no means precludes powerfully felt emotion. In a poem

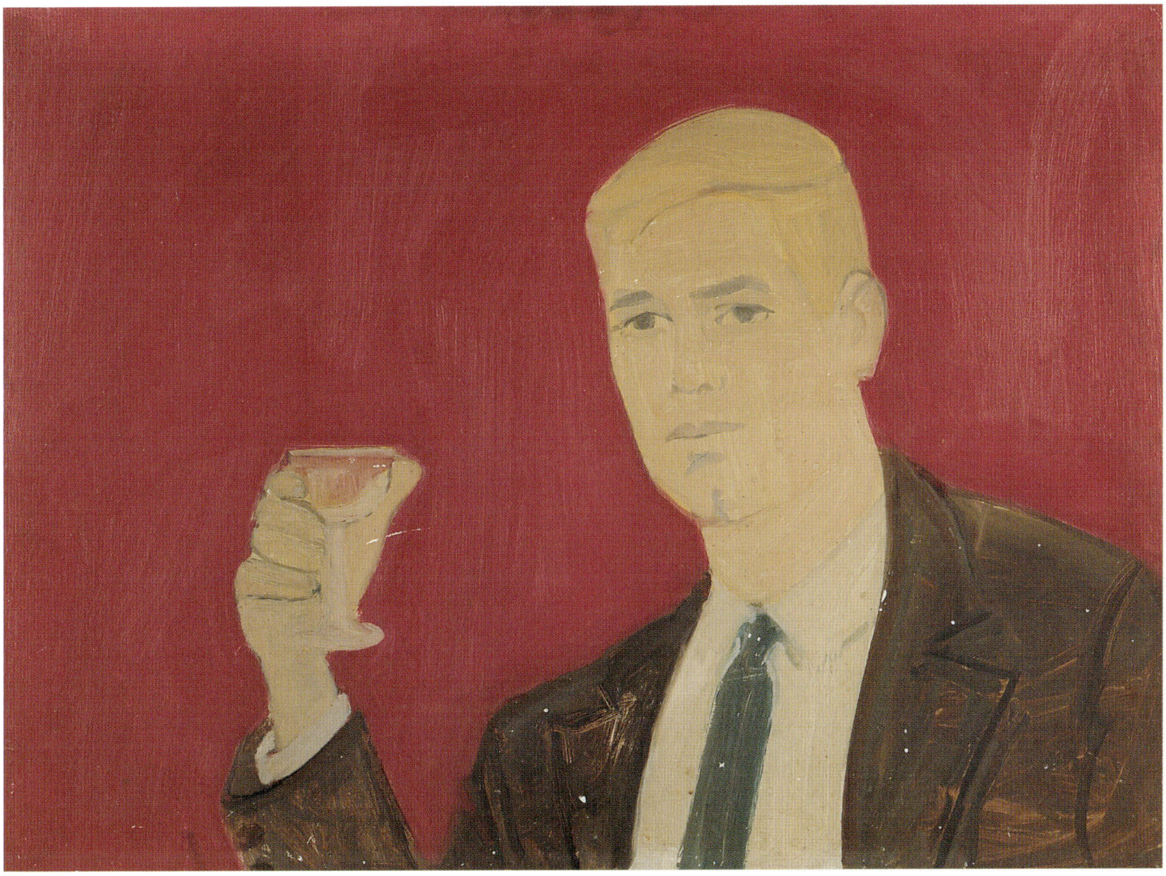

addressed to Button on his birthday in 1957, he celebrated their nights together in a tone that is at the same time camp and movingly elegiac:

> **And the lift of our experiences**
> **together, which seem to me legendary. The long subways**
> **to our old neighborhood the near East 49th and 53rd,**
> **and before them the laughing in bars till we cried,**
> **and the crying in movies till we laughed, the tenting**
> **tonight on the old camp grounds!**[90]

Alex Katz
Here's To You, 1962

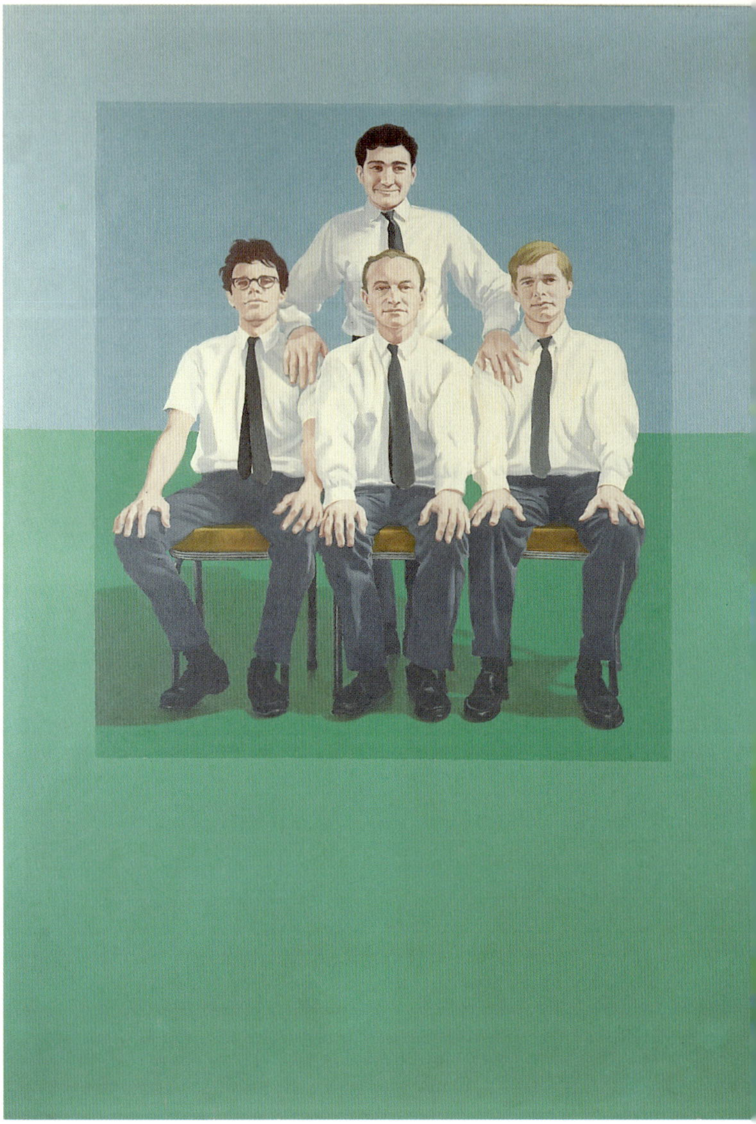

Wynn Chamberlain's audacious double portrait of 1964 first shows O'Hara, LeSueur, the artist Joe Brainard, and the poet Frank Lima dressed in bourgeois office attire. They stare somberly at the viewer. In the second version they are completely naked, and all four sport cheery grins. Chamberlain overtly invokes the playful quality that some gay men of the period could bring to the masking and unmasking that was an unavoidable part of their lives.

While O'Hara certainly had to endure his share of slights based on his sexual orientation, most bitterly his rejection by Grace Hartigan in 1960, whose psychiatrist persuaded her that she could not have a fulfilling marriage and also have close relation-

Wynn Chamberlain
Poets (Joe Brainard, Frank O'Hara, Joe LeSueur, Frank Lima) (Clothed), 1964

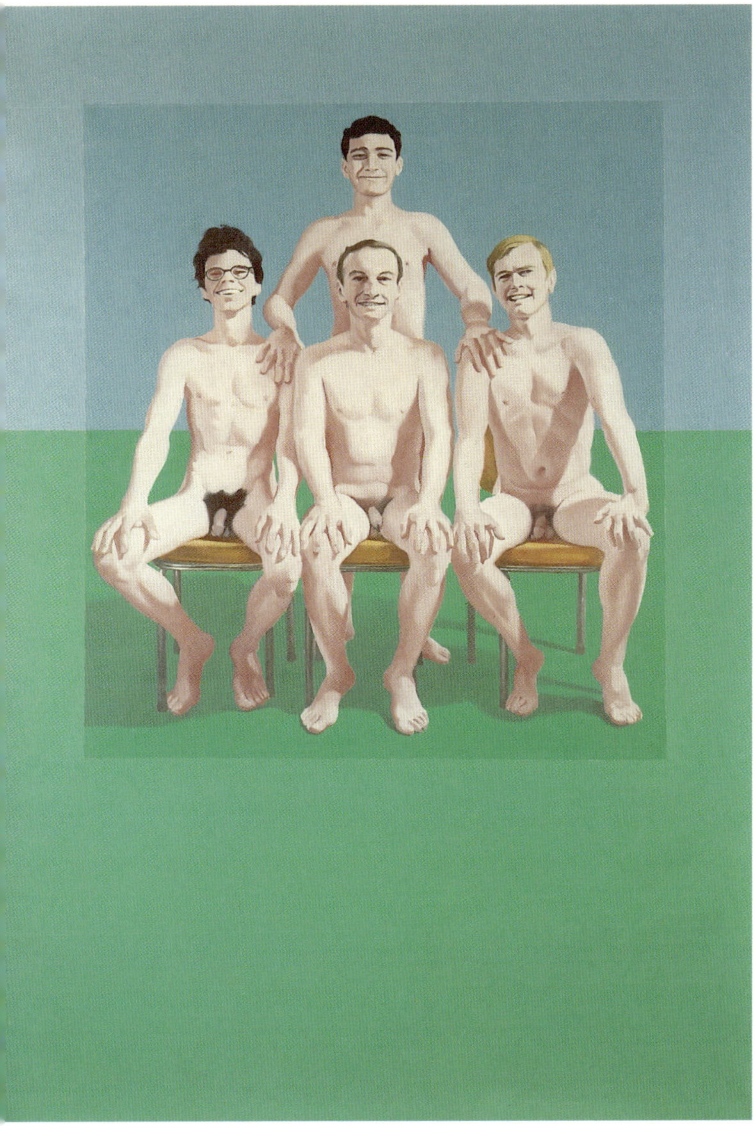

ships with homosexuals,[91] his attitude is perhaps best summed up by this passage from "Biotherm (for Bill Berkson)" (1962):

> **the other day I was walking through a train**
> **with my suitcase and I overheard someone say "speaking**
> **of faggots"**
> **now isn't life difficult enough without that**
> **and why am I always carrying something**
> **well it was a shitty looking person anyway**
> **better a faggot than a farthead**[92]

Wynn Chamberlain
Poets (Joe Brainard, Frank O'Hara, Joe LeSueur, Frank Lima)
(Naked), 1964

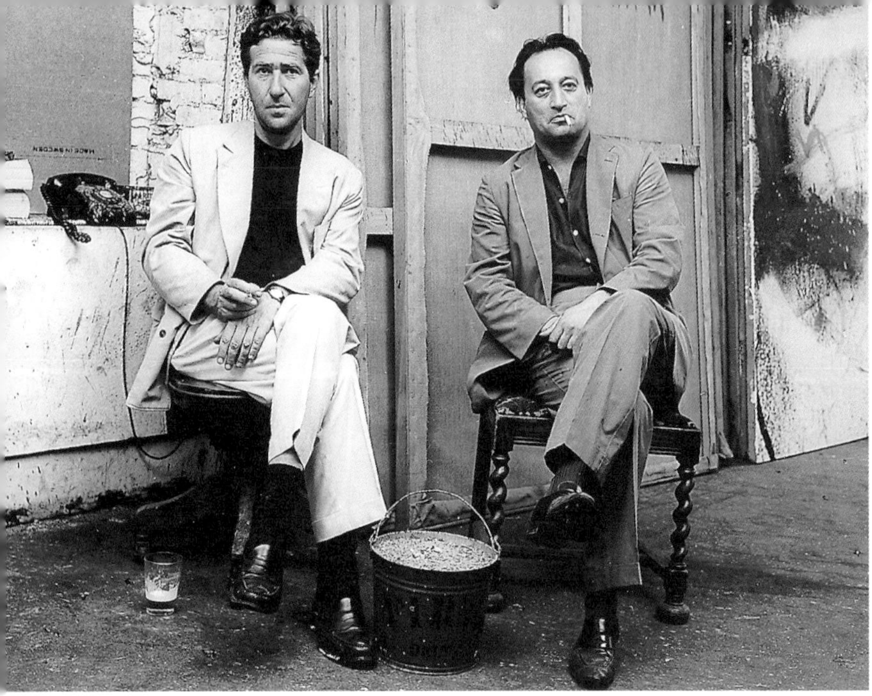

Joe LeSueur found something a little odd in O'Hara's close friendships with Goldberg and Bluhm: "a curious trio, I always thought: Mike and Norman, earthbound and burly, resolute in their heterosexuality, and Frank, with his birdlike frame, nasal tenor voice, slightly effeminate way of walking on the balls of his feet, another story altogether." But LeSueur, who himself was portrayed as a handsome *bon vivant* in Alex Katz's *Here's to You* (1962), also acknowledges that, despite the macho tone of the Cedar Bar, O'Hara was accepted there. "So far as I know, only Jackson Pollock, the least secure, the most conflicted, was known to have expressed hostility towards gays."[93] "The Cedar Bar *was* a macho place," Goldberg agrees. "A lot of us had been in the service. Even the few women in there were tough cookies." But, he adds, "Even the people who didn't read respected poets."[94] Perhaps the respect universally accorded poets seems more remote to us now than the macho antics. O'Hara himself wrote in a letter from Madrid that, "It is just like New York in that one has the same kind of relationships here. (Unlike Paris or Rome.) That is, the queens always hate me and the heterosexual painters seem to like me. So naturally I prefer them socially."[95]

To Goldberg, "Frank was macho himself. He wasn't effeminate."[96] O'Hara had, after all, been in the wartime Navy. Katz's great double portrait of 1961, *Marine and Sailor,* shows O'Hara and Berkson in uniform, and O'Hara's distinctive broken nose certainly makes him look tough as well as distinguished. In a poem inspired by a Guston painting, O'Hara remembered not only the breaking of his nose, but also his vigorous response:

Michael Goldberg and Norman Bluhm, ca. 1958

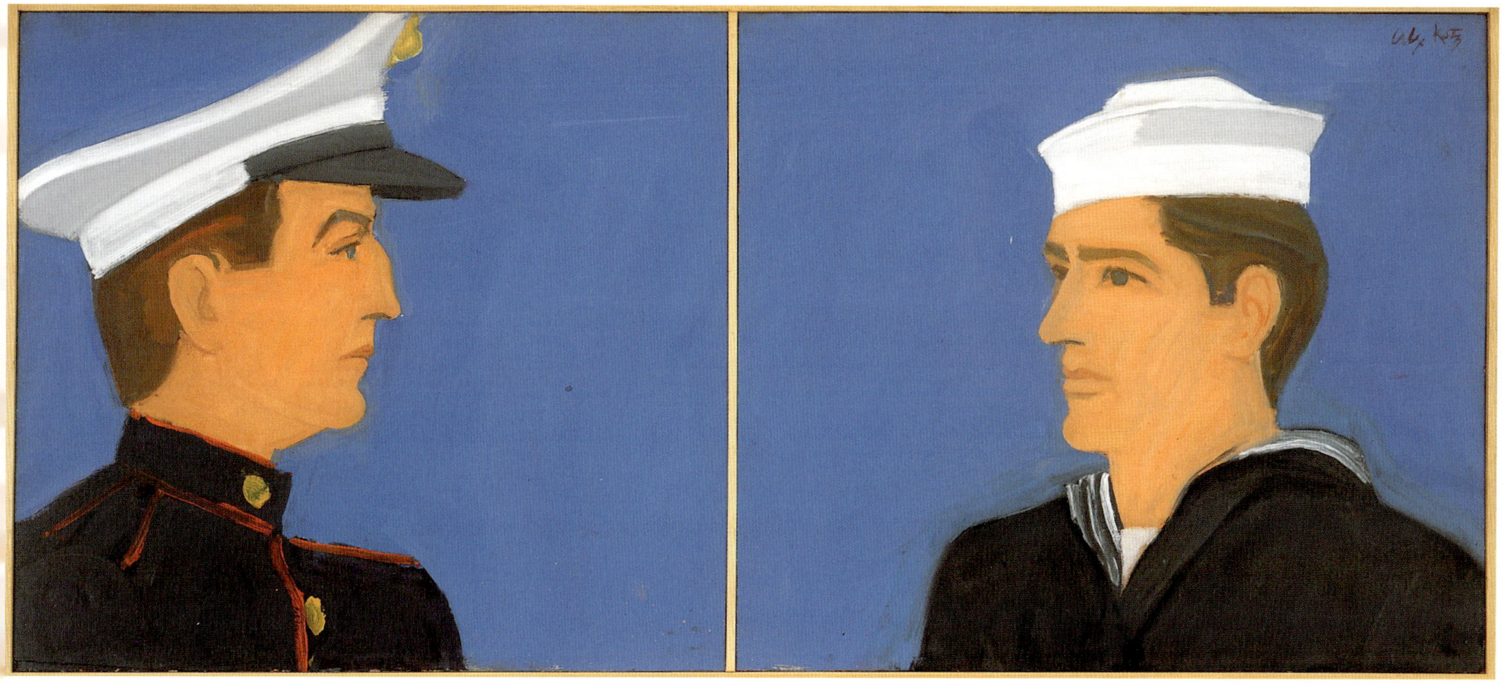

To be always in vigilance away

from the bully who first broke my nose

and so I had to break his wristwatch

I hit him

it fell off

I stepped on it

and he

will never again know

the time

A surprising violence in the sky

inspired me to my first public act[97]

Occasional outbursts of drunken violence did not intimidate O'Hara. "If Jackson Pollock tore the door off the men's room in the Cedar it was something he just did and was interesting, not an annoyance. You couldn't see into it anyway, and besides there was then a sense of genius."[98] The last sentence combines a deflating pragmatism with a fan's embrace of the glamour still associated with the out-of-control artist.

Alex Katz

Marine and Sailor, 1961

Life-giving vulgarity

As the sixties progressed, a new generation of artists began to emerge, artists who were less and less in thrall to the heroic generation of the New York School. They were simply not interested in its macho rhetoric. As Andy Warhol put it, "I tried to imagine myself in a bar striding over to, say, Roy Lichtenstein and asking him to 'step outside' because I'd heard he'd insulted my soup cans. I mean, how corny."[99] These Pop artists were less engaged by Jung and the quest for elemental truths than they were by the fabric of contemporary life in America. Rejecting the rigid distinction between High Art and kitsch, they embraced movies, comics, and all kinds of consumer goods.

O'Hara himself was ambivalent about the distinction. He remained deeply committed to both poetry and painting as vehicles through which the most profound issues could be addressed. From the beginning, however, his writing embraced not only a passionate moral seriousness but also a fascination with every detail of modern culture, including its most popular manifestations. "And after all, only Whitman and Crane and Williams, of the American poets, are better than the movies."[100] One of the earliest reviews of his poetry, by Kenneth Rexroth, had presciently suggested that there was a problem with attempting to read his poems as a correlative to New York School painting. "Frank O'Hara is a friend and interpreter of many of the leading Abstract Expressionist painters. I believe he fancies himself as doing much the same sort of thing in poetry. If so, he is mistaken. This is the poetry of flat, dead-pan colloquialism."[101] This insight makes it easy to understand the enthusiasm with which O'Hara would respond to Claes Oldenburg's *Store* when it opened in his neighborhood in 1961, calling it "the best thing since L. L. BEAN." In it, "you find cakes your mother never baked, letters you never received, jackets you never stole when you broke into that apartment."[102] Oldenburg's writing of the period celebrating the detritus of the city bears traces of O'Hara's influence. An O'Hara poem such as "Spring's First Day" (1956), with its virtually collaged

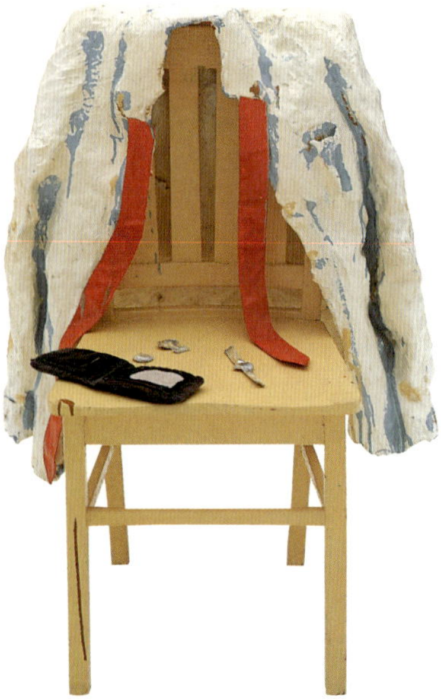

BEANS — **regularly 2 cans 35¢**

TUNAFISH — **regularly 2 cans 35¢**

Claes Oldenburg
White Shirt on a Chair, from **The Store,** 1962

The Store, 107 East 2nd Street, New York, December, 1961

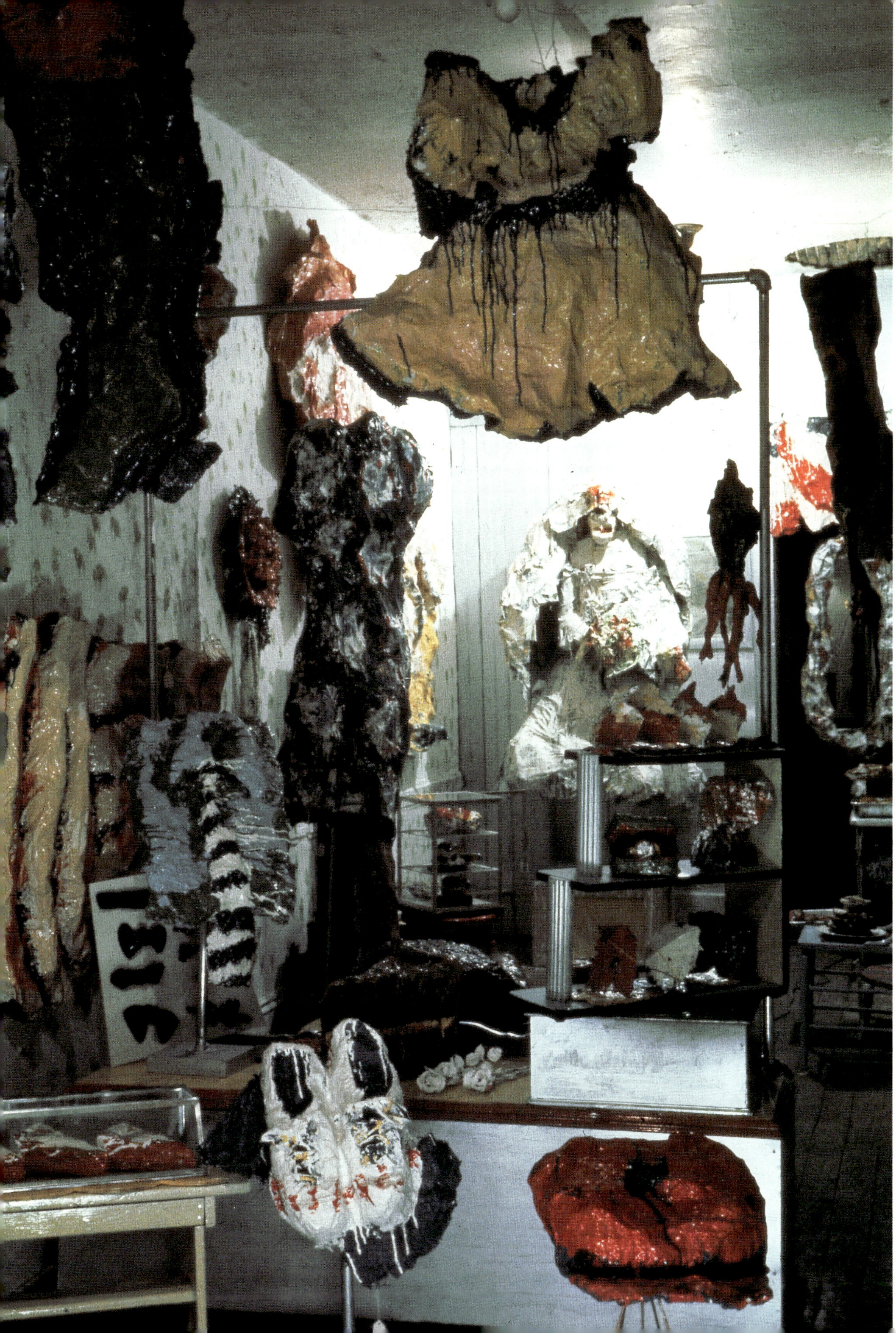

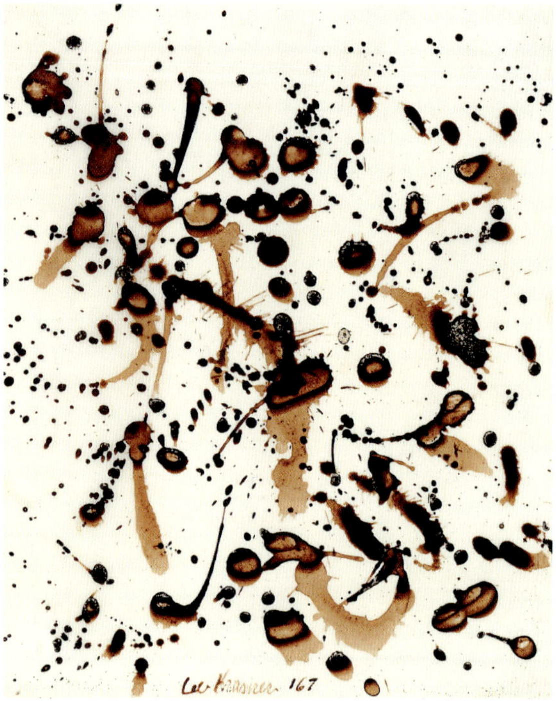

or its "All this merchandise has been and will go on FIRE SALE at this EVENT" or "'53 Chev., '51 Ford, '53 Willys, '55 Chev., '50 Chrysler" seems a direct precursor of Oldenburg's torn-up retail aesthetic: "I am for an art that embroils itself with the everyday crap & still comes out on top."[103] Oldenburg's love for the gritty details of the city was completely in tune with O'Hara's sensibility, and the poet was also quick to recognize that this "direction in itself must be taken quite apart from the work of Jasper Johns or Jean Follett or Robert Rauschenberg," characteristically throwing in the name of a woman artist alongside the two better-known men. O'Hara was by far the most important critical and institutional supporter of women artists of his time, most notably of Nell Blaine, Freilicher, Hartigan, Lee Krasner, Joan Mitchell, and Jane Wilson. There is no evidence that he took this role in any kind of deliberate or programmatic way: it simply reflects a consistent openness to new work from any source, an openness that was notably lacking in many other critics.

Other supporters of Abstract Expressionism were quick to denounce Pop. Max Kozloff, for example, condemned this "pin-headed and contemptible style of gum-chewers, bobby soxers, and, worse, delinquents."[104] Despite the fact that O'Hara's own poetry could be (and occasionally still is) criticized in virtually the same terms ("huge trash-heaps... of campy gossip, silly jokes, travel notes, subway rides, newspaper headlines, movie stars"[105]), O'Hara too remained largely unimpressed by early Pop, telling Joan Mitchell that most of the work in the groundbreaking Sidney Janis Gallery "New Realists" exhibition of October 1962 (which included works by Oldenburg, Lichtenstein, Rosenquist, and Warhol, among others) was (Oldenburg excepted) "boring and crappy."[106] But O'Hara's instincts were too generous and inclusive for him to take up a rigidly anti-Pop position. He regretted the partisanship that had led Philip Guston, Robert Motherwell, and Mark Rothko to leave the Janis Gallery in protest. "Around here, the Abstract-Expressionism New-Realism situation is pretty 'Thou art either for me or agin me'" he regretfully wrote to John Ashbery, who had written the catalogue essay for the "New Realists" exhibition.[107]

Lee Krasner
Untitled (Study for Frank O'Hara Illustration), 1967

Beginning in 1964, O'Hara began a series of collaborations with Joe Brainard that took him closer than ever to the Pop aesthetic. Brainard was a unique artist who remains impossible to classify, but he loved comics and commercial culture, and he completely lacked the high seriousness of the Abstract Expressionists. "Could we make a place for Joe Brainard as a Pop artist?" Robert Rosenblum has asked. "Turning away, but only when he felt like it, from the self-taught art-school techniques of modeled, realist drawing and painting to the brash flatness of Nancy or Pluto, might he not be put in a lineage with Lichtenstein and Warhol? But on the other hand, where's the irony and rebellion?"[108] The collages he and O'Hara made together have a modesty of scale and a lightness of touch that brings to mind the work of Joseph Cornell, but they also often have a biting sarcasm that precludes any danger of their becoming too precious. Their comics have the same edgy wit, deflating pretension without losing the sweet, playful feeling that pervades almost all of Brainard's work. They also display a sharp consciousness of an emerging sexual politics. For O'Hara, these collaborations were an opportunity to explore Pop themes and give his camp spirit free rein. They are resolutely unassuming and piercingly funny.

Brainard's eccentric spirit and his almost complete lack of ambition (he would later give up art to devote himself entirely to reading Victorian novels) positioned him to a certain extent away from the more serious challenge to Abstract Expressionism that, say, Andy Warhol was making. Warhol made a concerted effort to win O'Hara over. There was a clear overlap of interest in movies, popular culture, and the minutiae of everyday life in the city. And Warhol had been for many years a regular at downtown poetry readings, including O'Hara's.[109] In 1963, for a special issue of *C* magazine devoted to the poetry of O'Hara's close friend Edwin Denby, Warhol made a portrait of Denby kissing Gerard Malanga, staking a claim for his own group among the gay elite of an earlier generation. Joe Brainard had done the cover of the previous issue, and O'Hara himself was a contributor to the Denby issue. Warhol filmed O'Hara reading, offered him the coyly erotic drawings he often gave to friends, and in general tried to win his approval, which was not immediately forthcoming.

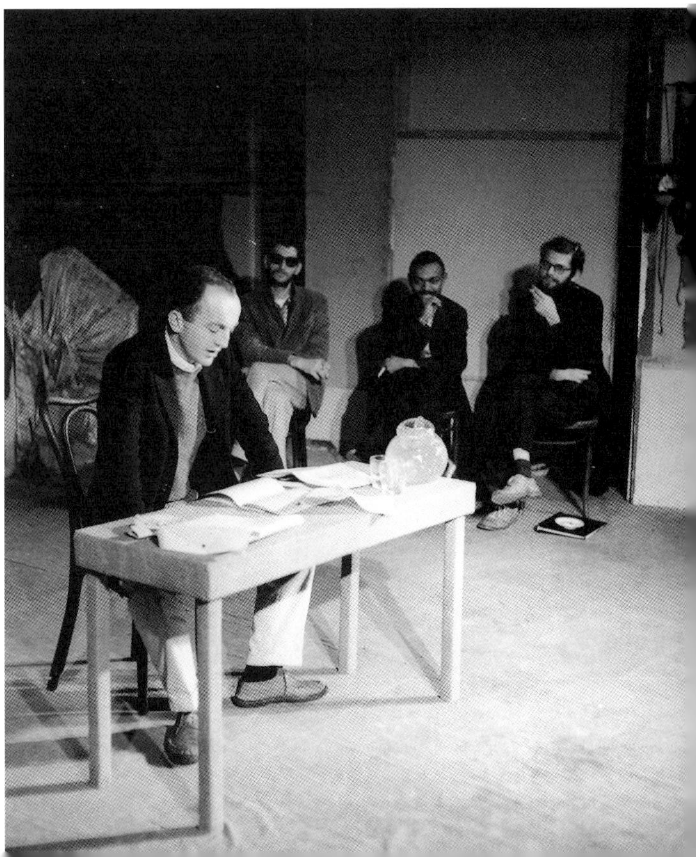

Fred W. McDarrah
Frank O'Hara reading at a benefit for Yugen Press at the Living Theater, 530 Sixth Avenue, New York, November 2, 1959.
Left to right: O'Hara, Ray Bremser, LeRoi Jones, and Allen Ginsberg

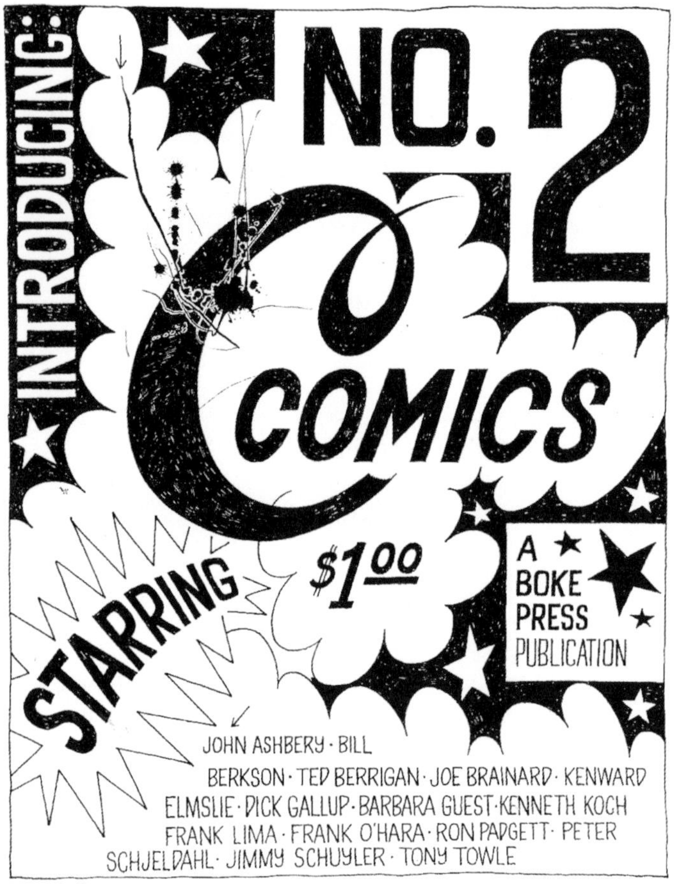

Joe Brainard

cover, **C Comics No. 2**, c. 1966

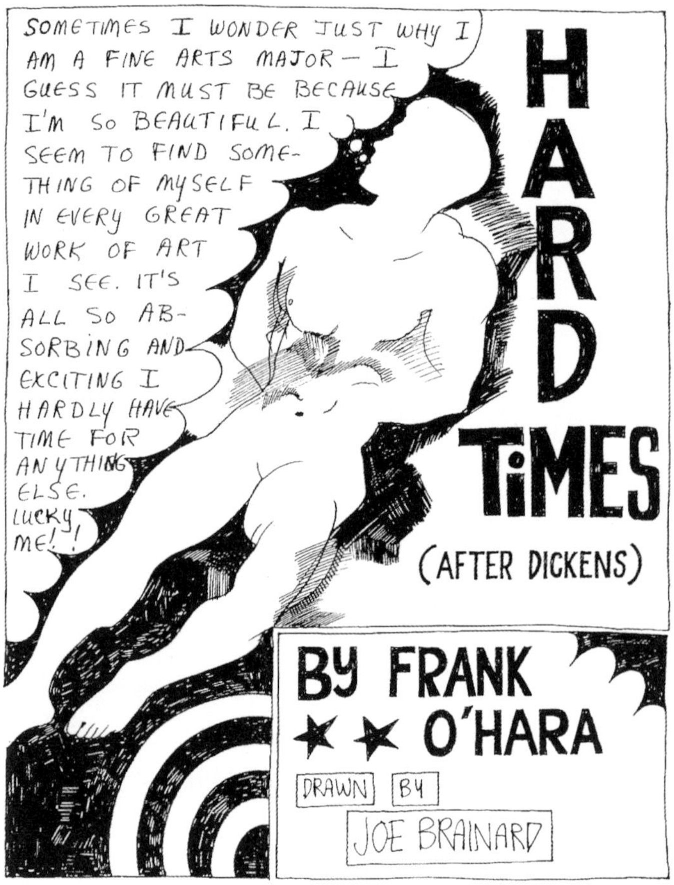

page from **C Comics No. 2**, c. 1966

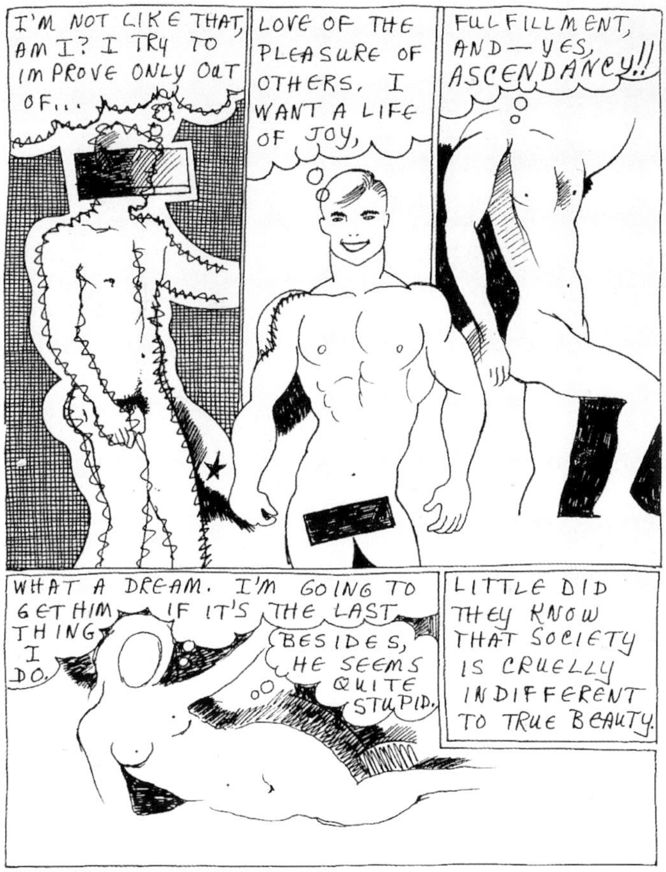

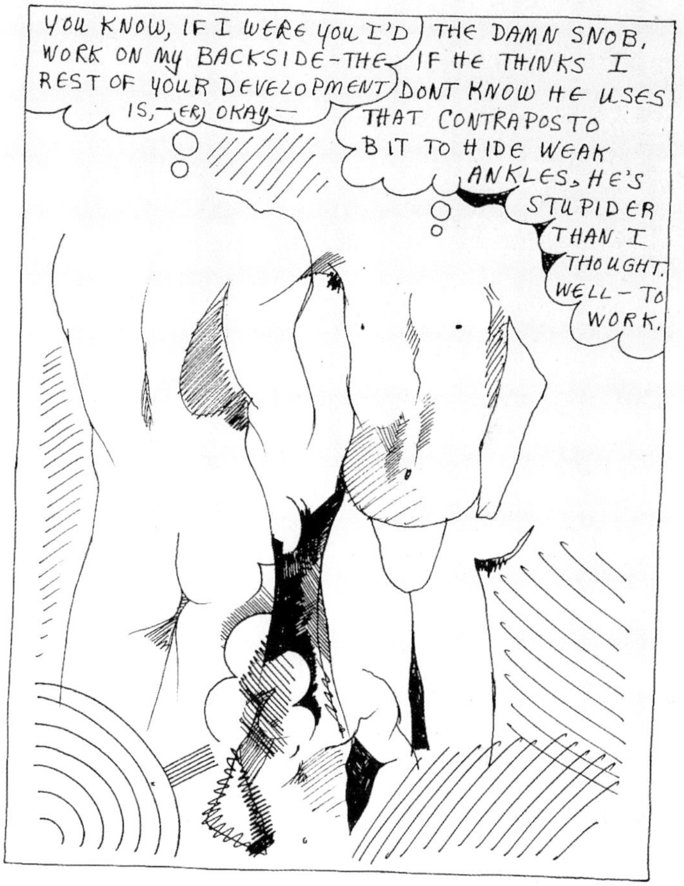

pages from **C Comics No. 2**, c. 1966

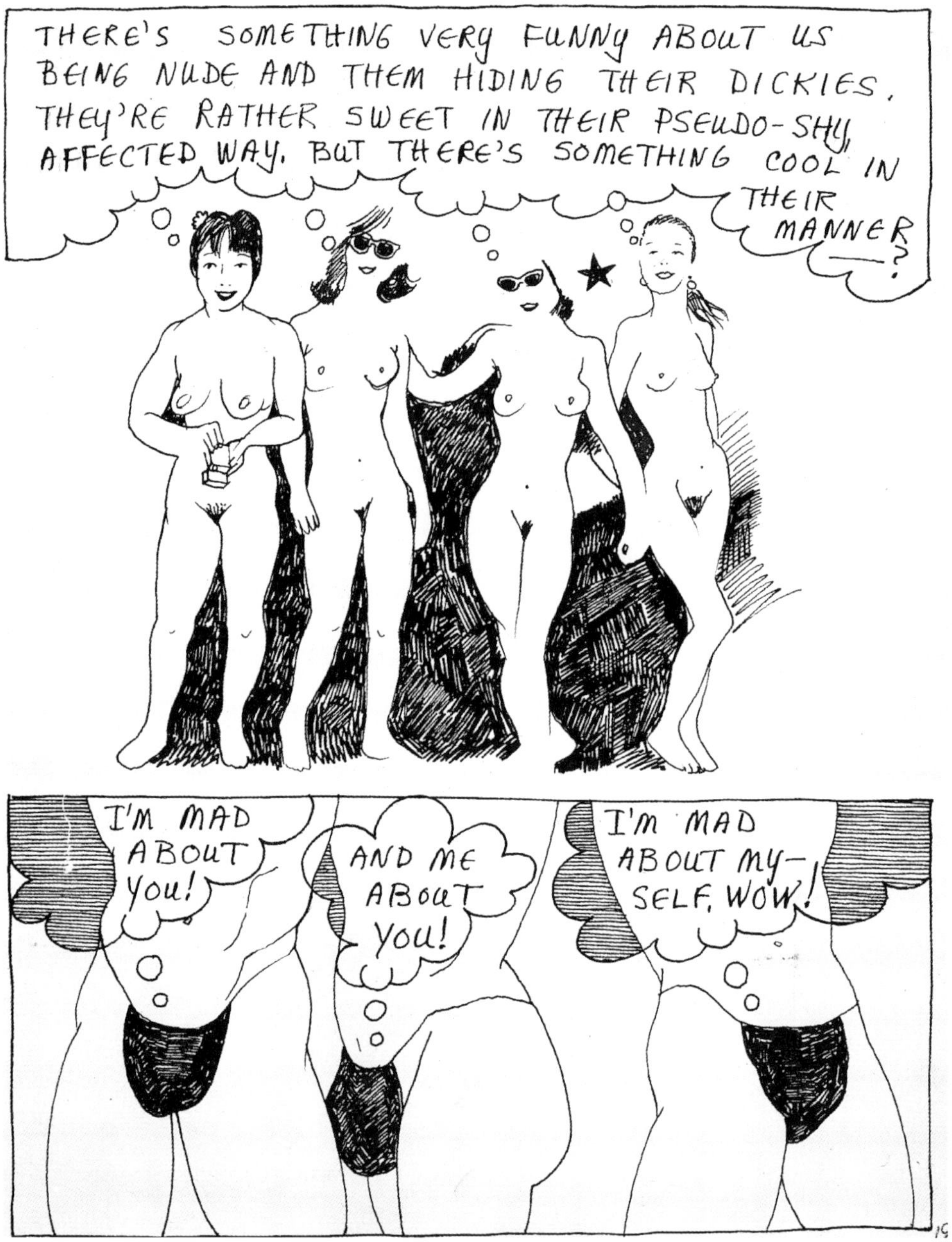

Joe Brainard and Frank O'Hara

"There's Something Very Funny About Us. . .", 1964

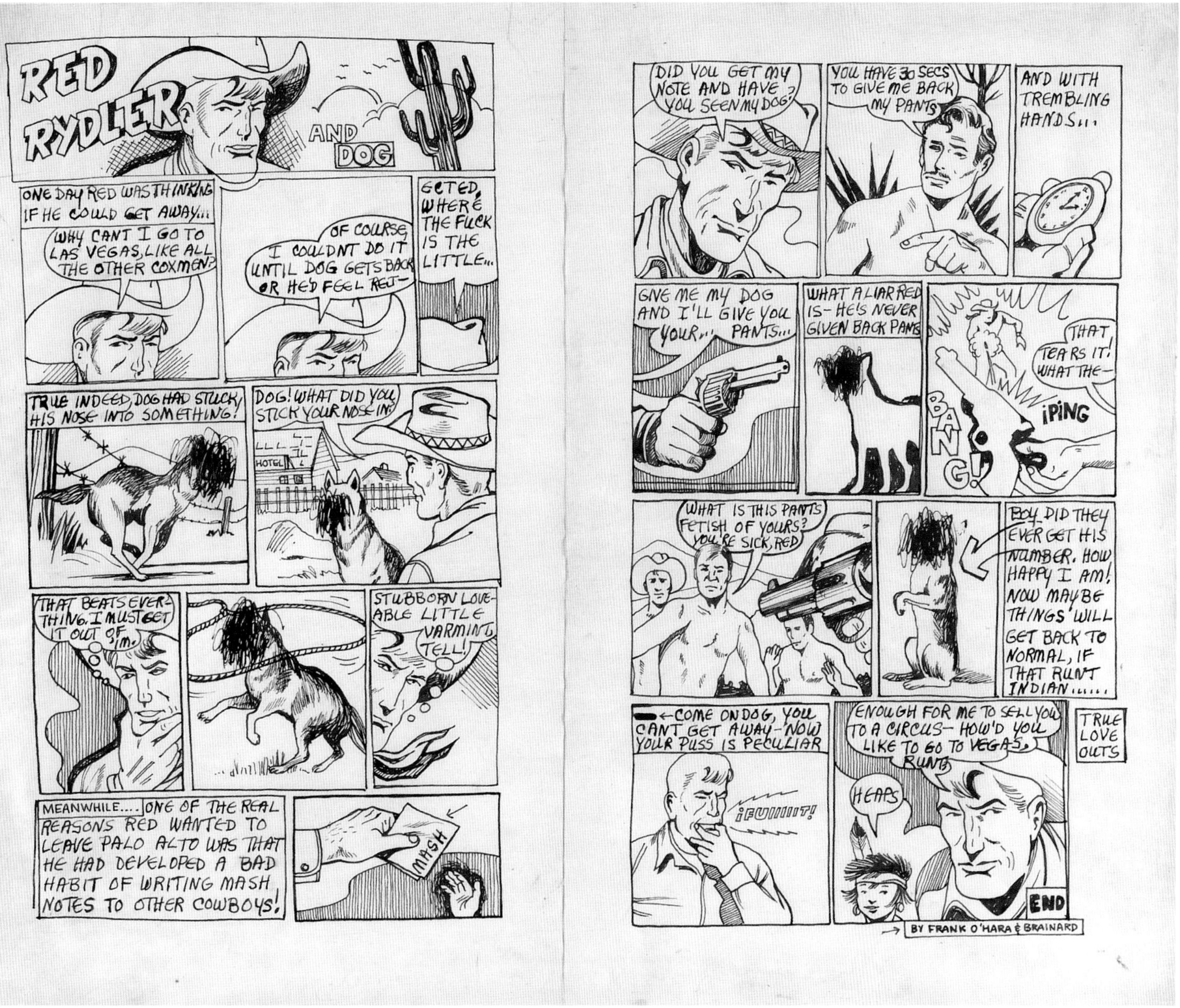

Red Rydler and Dog, c. 1964

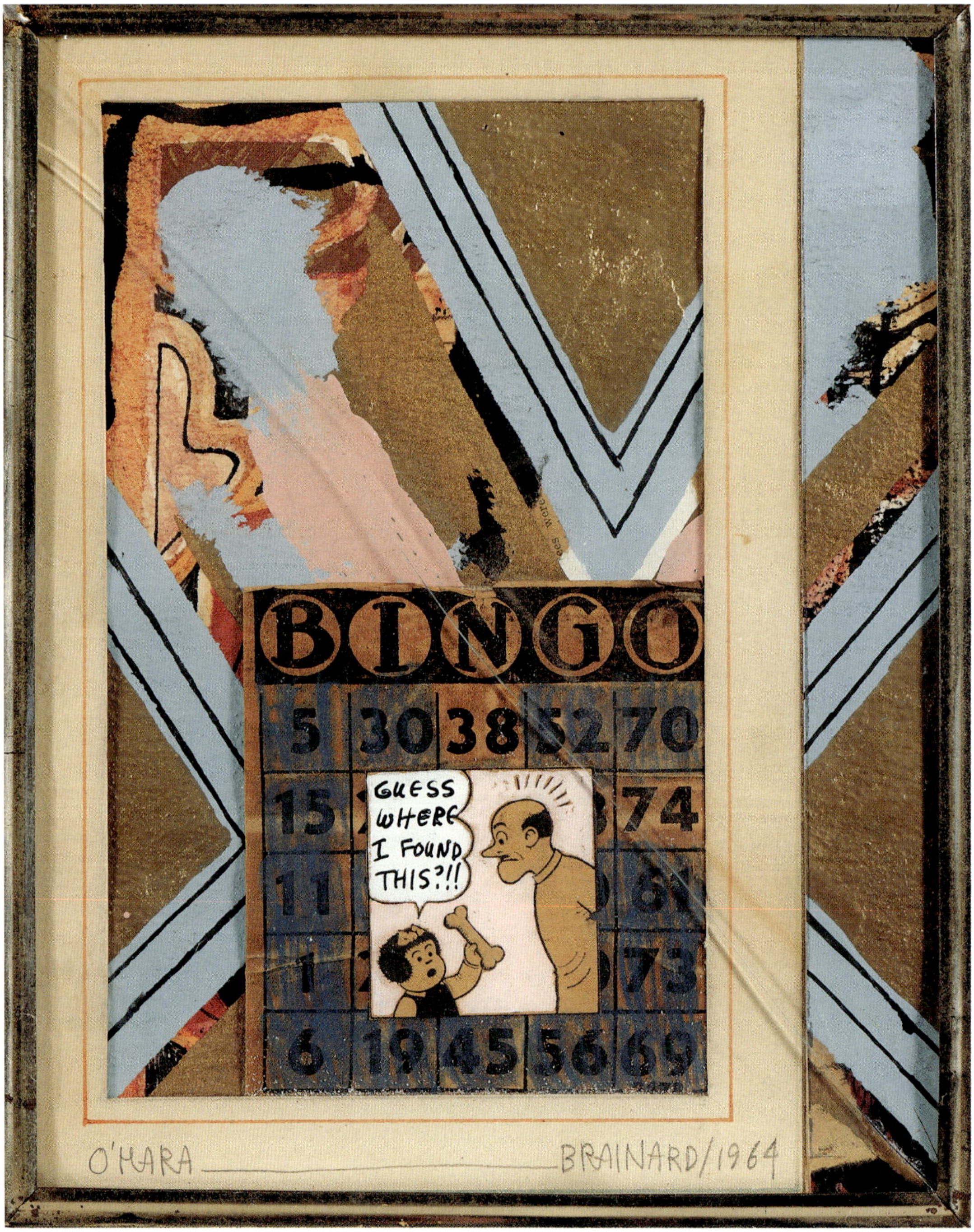

Joe Brainard and Frank O'Hara

"Guess Where I Found This?!!", 1964

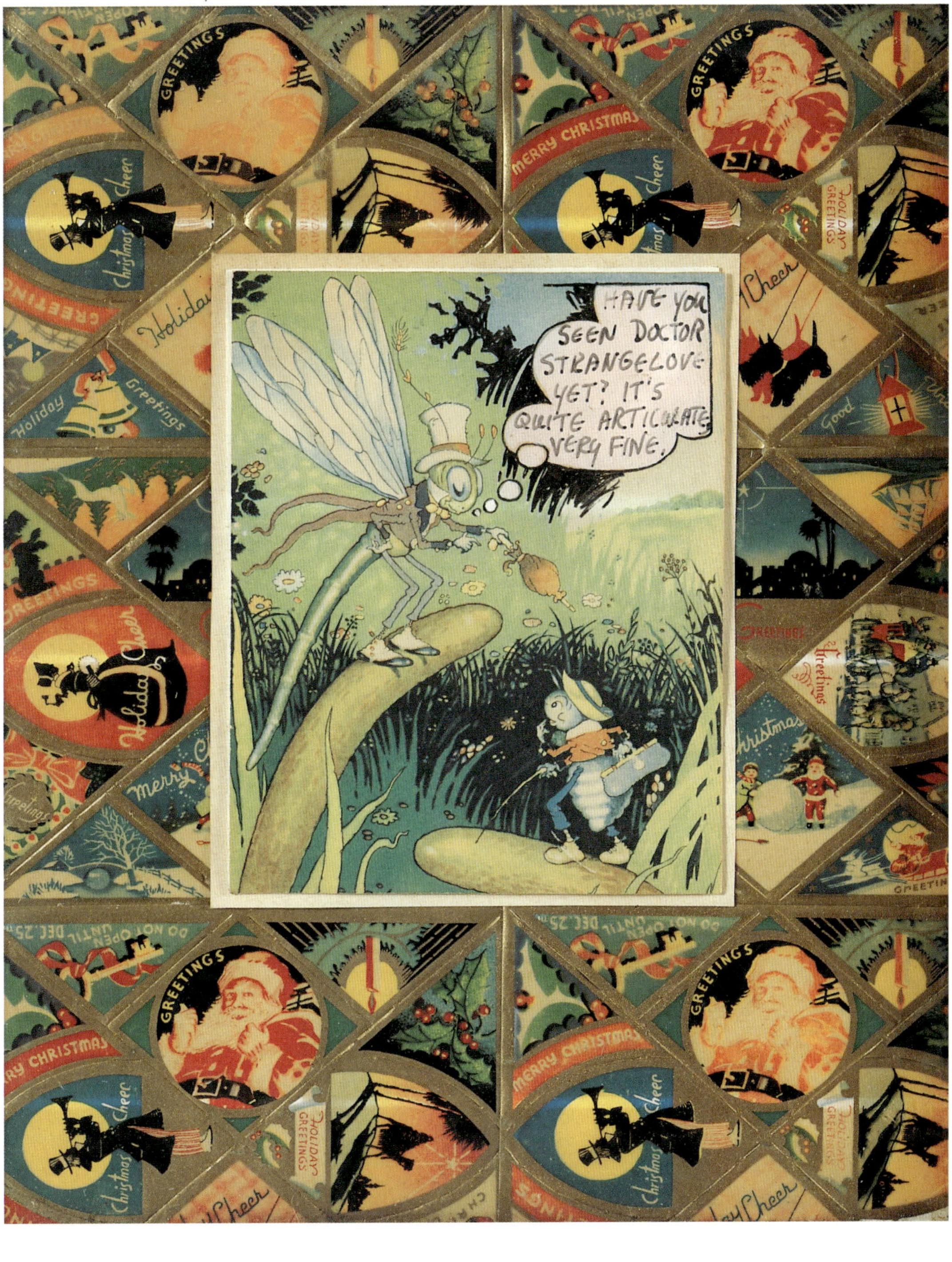

"Have You Seen Dr. Strangelove Yet? It's Quite Articulate, Very Fine", 1964

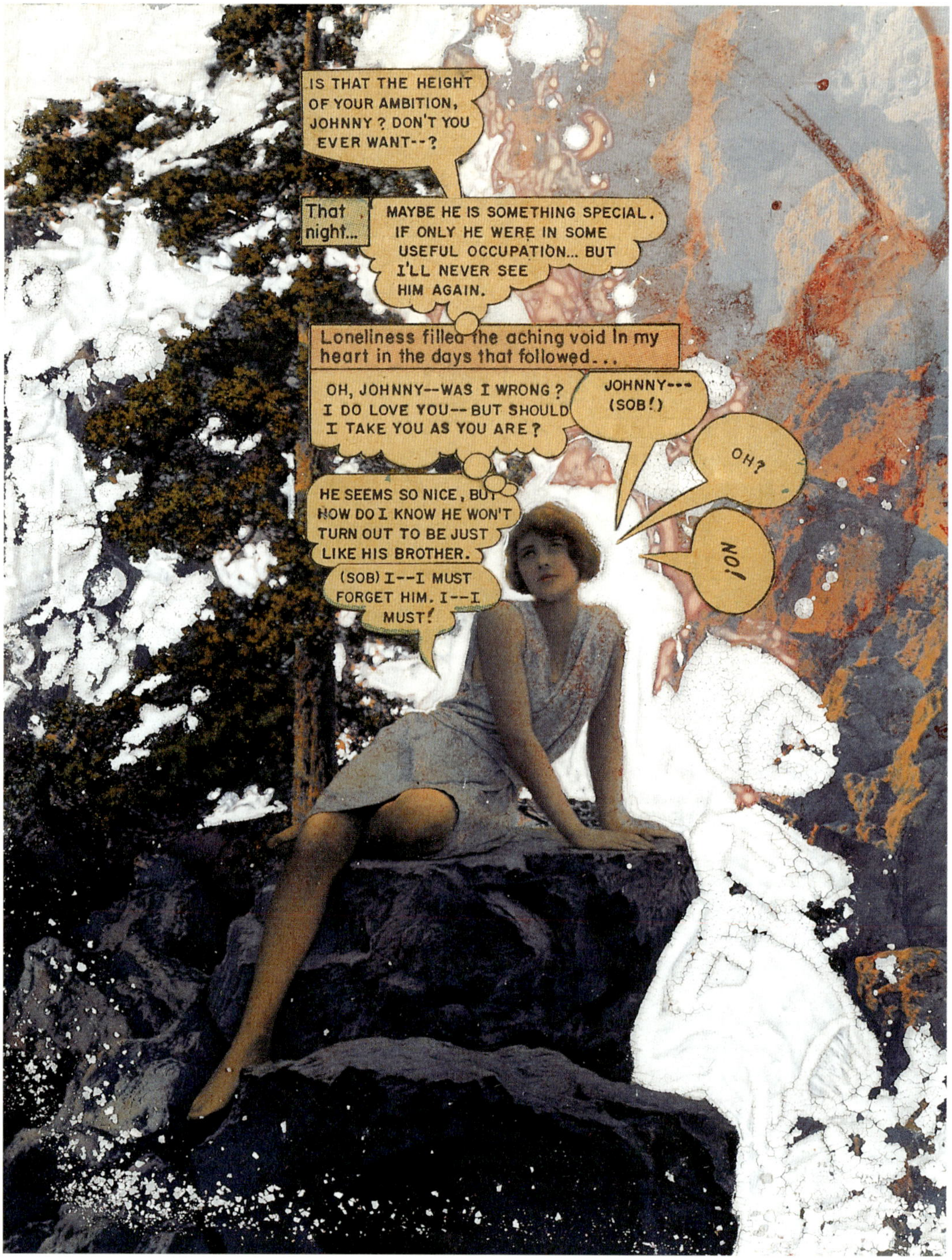

Joe Brainard and Frank O'Hara

"Is That the Height of Your Ambition Johnny?", 1964

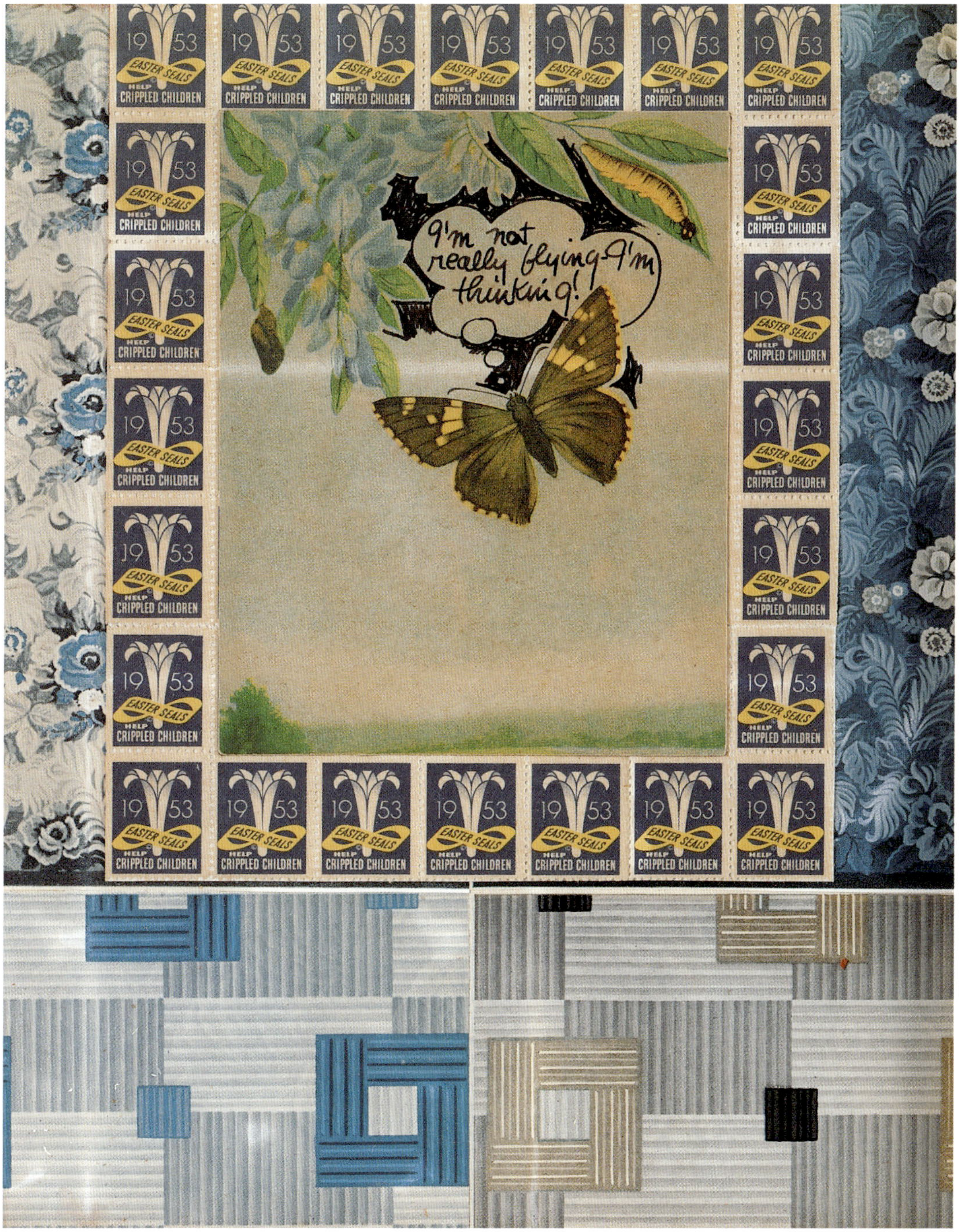

"I'm Not Really Flying I'm Thinking", 1964

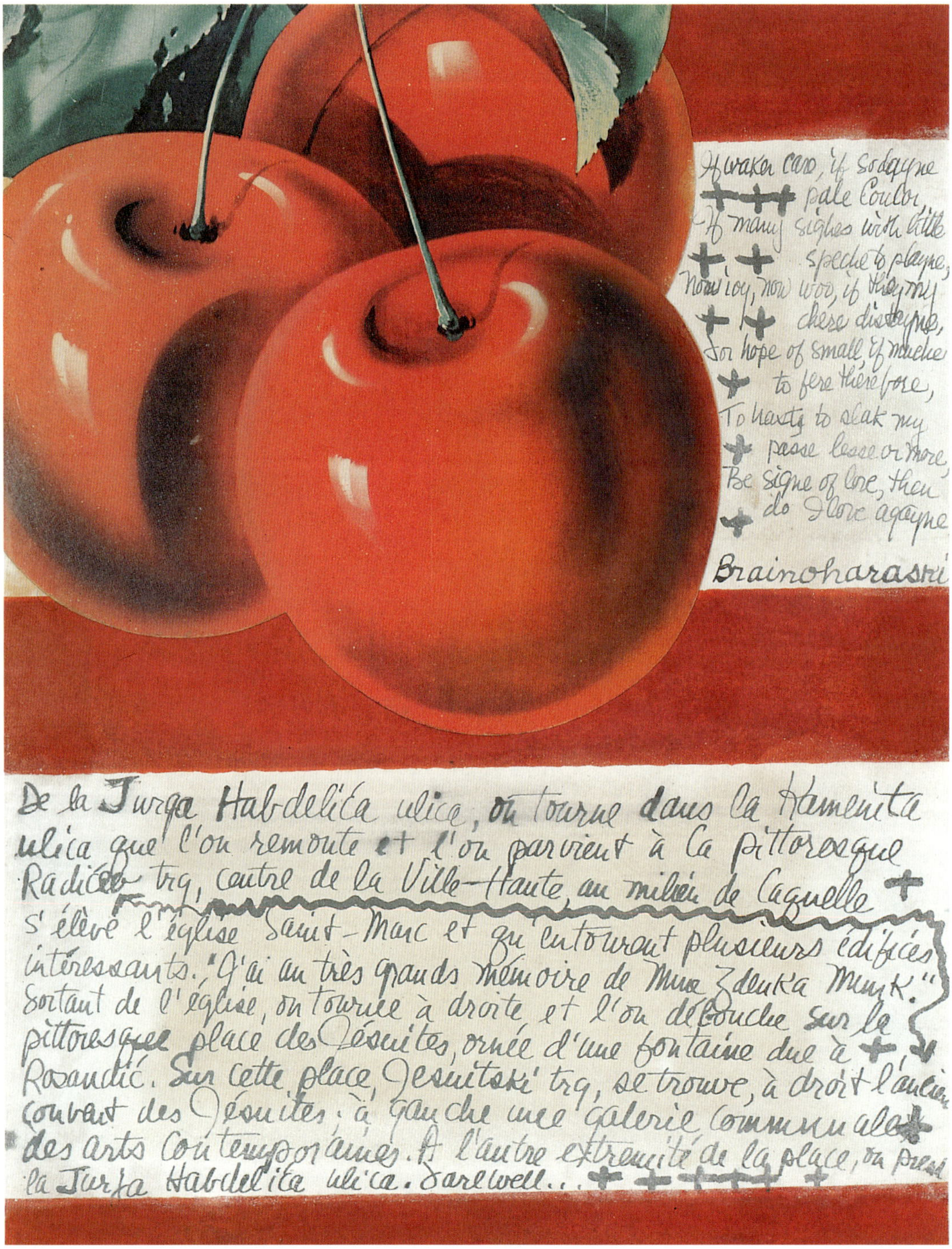

Joe Brainard and Frank O'Hara

Untitled (Cherries), 1964

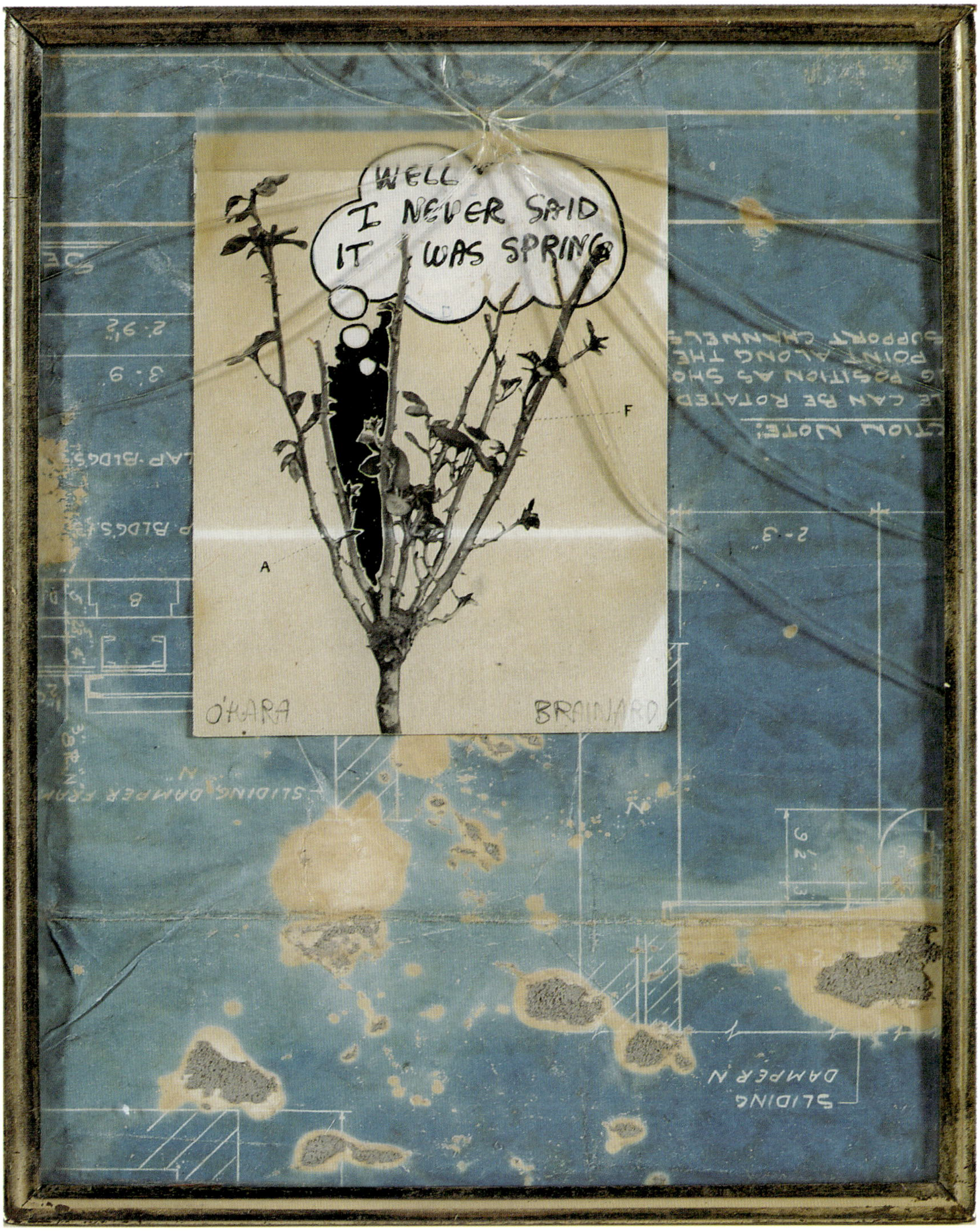

"Well, I Never Said It Was Spring", 1964

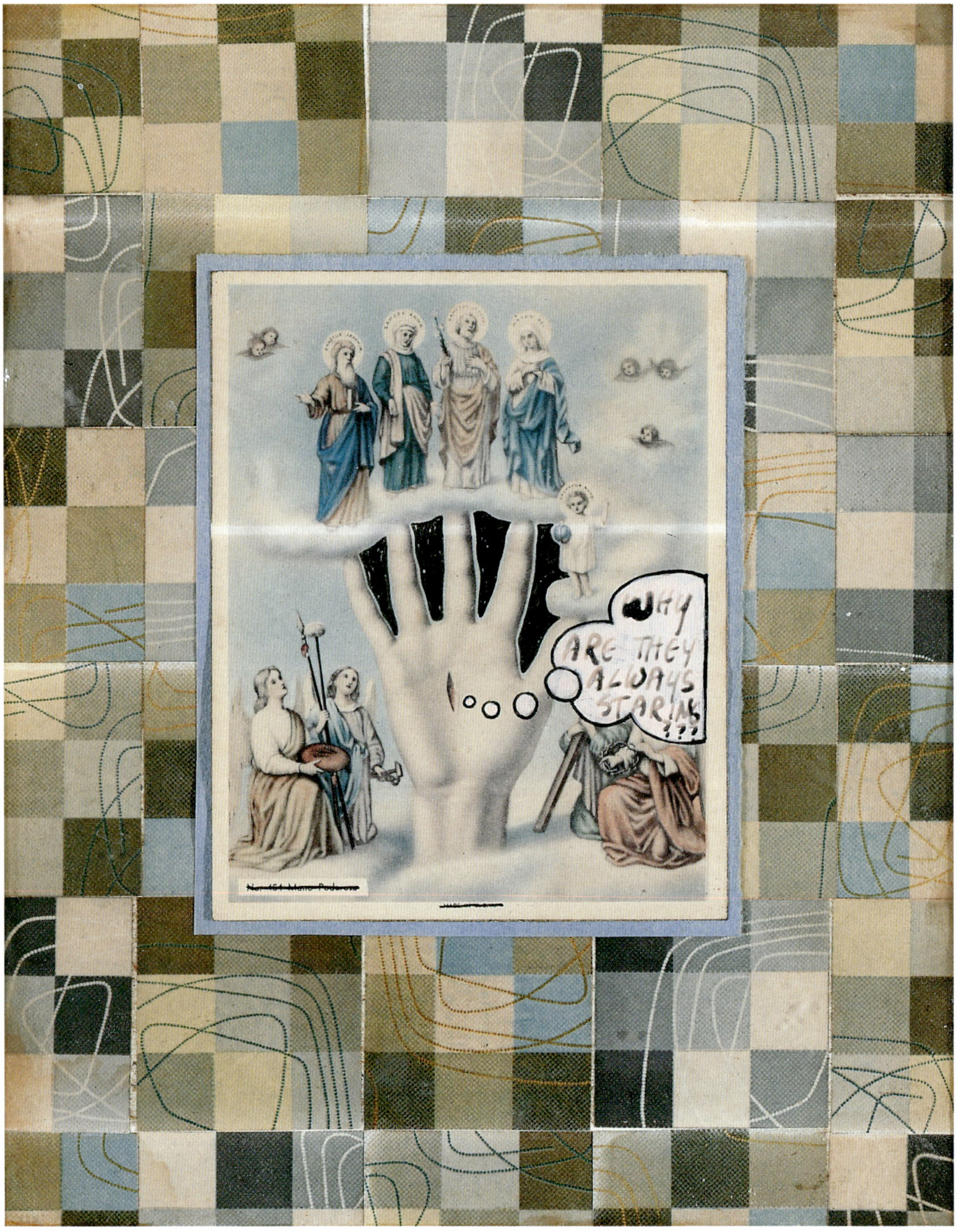

Joe Brainard and Frank O'Hara

"Why Are They Always Staring???", 1964

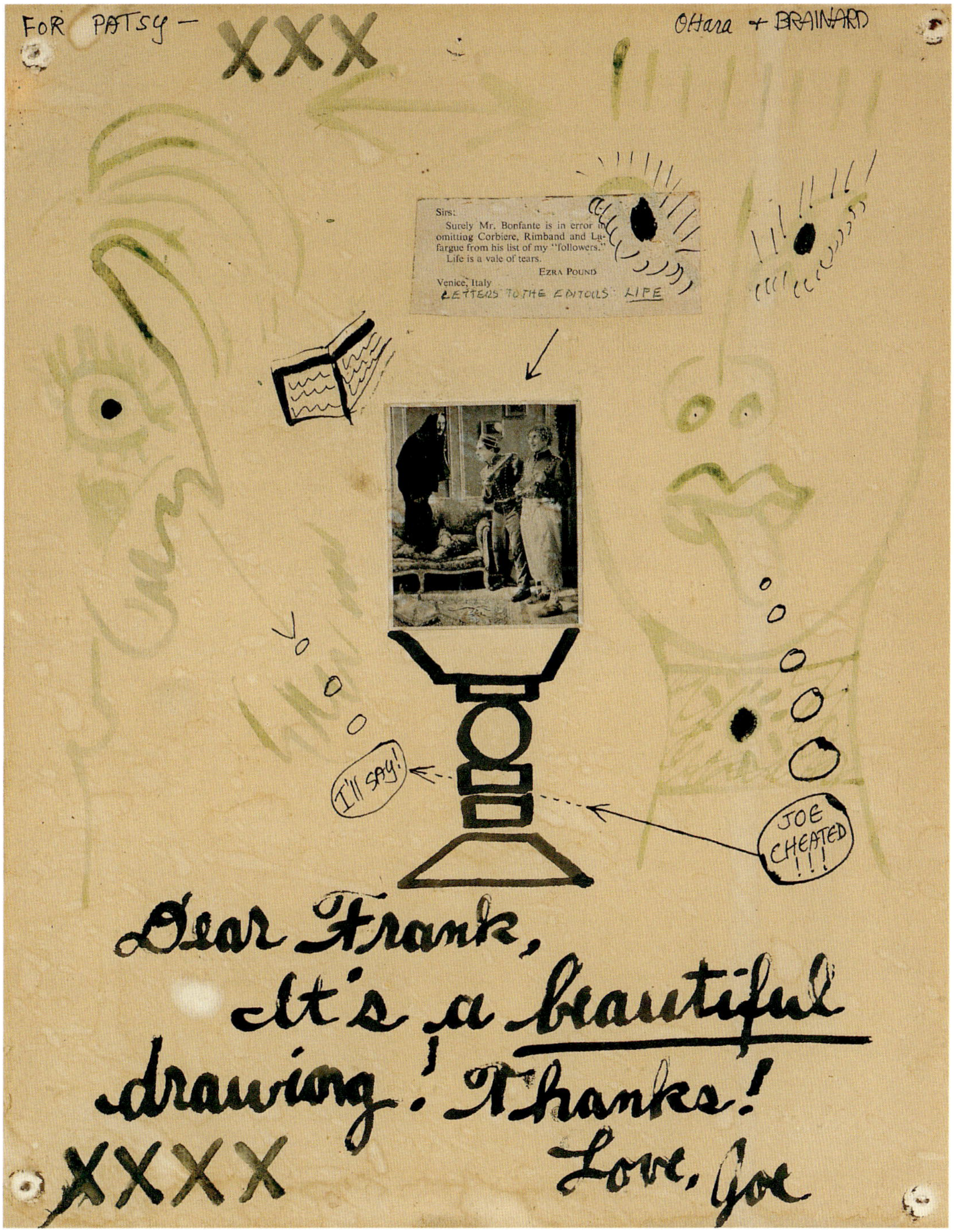

For Patsy, c. 1964

Despite all their manifest similarities, their sensibilities were perhaps too different to find much common ground. Where Warhol was devoted to the permanent fixing of iconic images, including images of people, O'Hara remained fundamentally committed to a shifting aesthetic that was constantly changing through passionate human relationships. "How many repetitious forms of your least favorite actress, or even most favorite, do you want to contemplate?"[110] he asked. His poem "Having a Coke with You" (1960) would seem in its title to prefigure a quintessential Warhol image, but its position is in fact quite different. O'Hara stresses the *failure* of static art—whether statues or painted portraits—to rival the nuances of a real love affair.

> **it is hard to believe when I'm with you that there can be anything as still**
> **as solemn as unpleasantly definitive as statuary when right in front of it**
> **in the warm New York 4 o'clock light we are drifting back and forth**
> **between each other like a tree breathing through its spectacles**
>
> **and the portrait show seems to have no faces in it at all, just paint**
> **you suddenly wonder why in the world anyone ever did them**[111]

O'Hara could never have said "I want to be a machine," as Warhol did. His own ironic manifesto was called "Personism," which he described as "evoking overtones of love without destroying love's life-giving vulgarity.... It was founded by me after lunch with LeRoi Jones on August 27, 1959, a day in which I was in love with someone (not Roi, by the way, a blond)."[112]

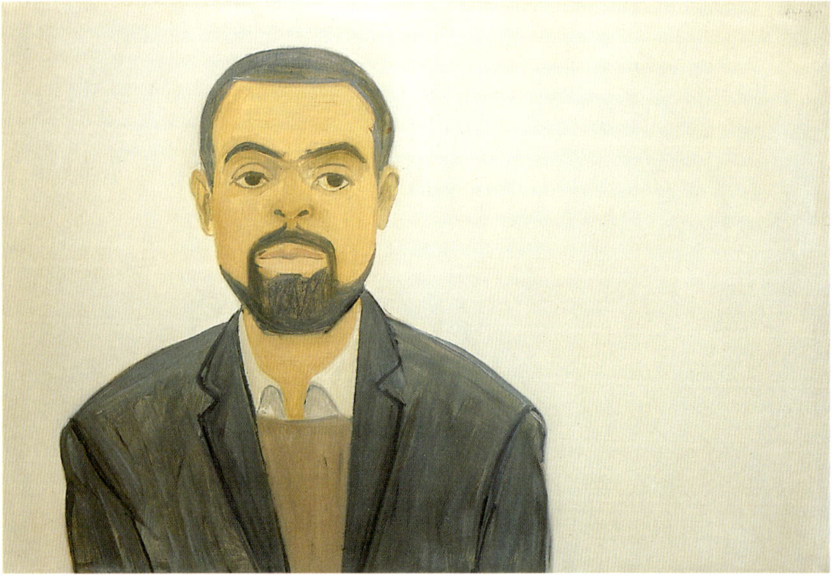

Alex Katz
LeRoi Jones, 1963
Oil on canvas
48½ x 71½ inches
Private Collection

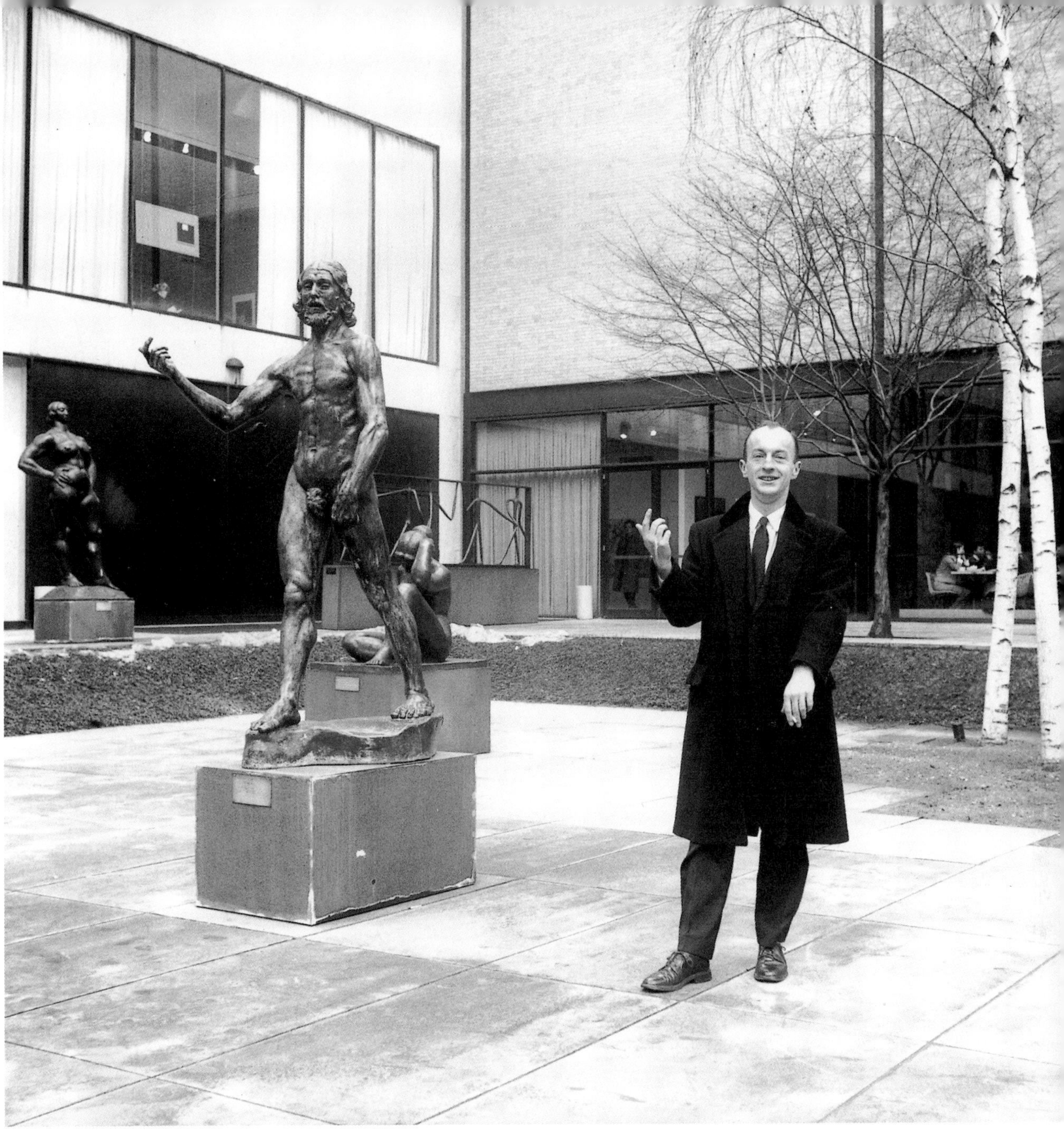

Fred W. McDarrah

Frank O'Hara in The Museum of Modern Art's Sculpture Garden, January 20, 1960, with Auguste Rodin's **St. John the Baptist Preaching**

The heavenly glass doors

As Warhol's eagerness to win his approval indicates, O'Hara was by the early sixties an increasingly influential figure at The Museum of Modern Art, and thus a significant power in the art world. He had rejoined the museum in 1955 to work in the International Program, where he assisted with the organization of "The New American Painting" (1958), the first major exhibition of Abstract Expressionism to travel to Europe. He also participated in the selection of works for the São Paulo Bienals of 1957 and 1961, the Venice Biennale of 1958, and Documenta II, in 1959. In 1960 he was made an Assistant Curator in the Department of Painting and Sculpture in the museum proper, and was promoted to Associate Curator in 1965.

Alex Katz's cutout portrait of O'Hara shows him as the suave man about town that he was. Katz's work is cool, the self-contained quality of the figure emphasized by its literal separation from any background. O'Hara had written a prescient review for *Art News* of Katz's first exhibition in 1954, and the two became friends. "He was a huge influence on me," says Katz. "He was one of the style people, like John Cage and Clement Greenberg. He gave you an aesthetic."[113] As O'Hara does in his poetry, Katz takes the everyday elements of his milieu and presents them purposely flat, just as they are. In both cases the cumulative effect is surprisingly grand. O'Hara described Katz's figures as "neither deprived nor dismayed.... They knew they were there."[114] O'Hara is of course included among these cutouts, and this is indeed how he appears: self-confident as well as literally self-contained, ready to play the required role wherever he might find himself.

O'Hara's increasing responsibilities at the museum required him to do some juggling with his continuing activities as a poet and as a friend to countless artists. He would arrive at the museum late in the morning, and his working day was interspersed with constant phone calls and visits from friends. Within the museum, according to his colleague Waldo Rasmussen, "His very closeness to the artists was questioned as a danger to critical objectivity.... Essentially he was the artist's spokesman, and that was considered in some quarters a questionable role for a museum professional and compromising to the institution."[115] At lunch he would go out, often writing poetry on the sample typewriters at the nearby Olivetti showroom (his collection *Lunch Poems* was published in 1964). While

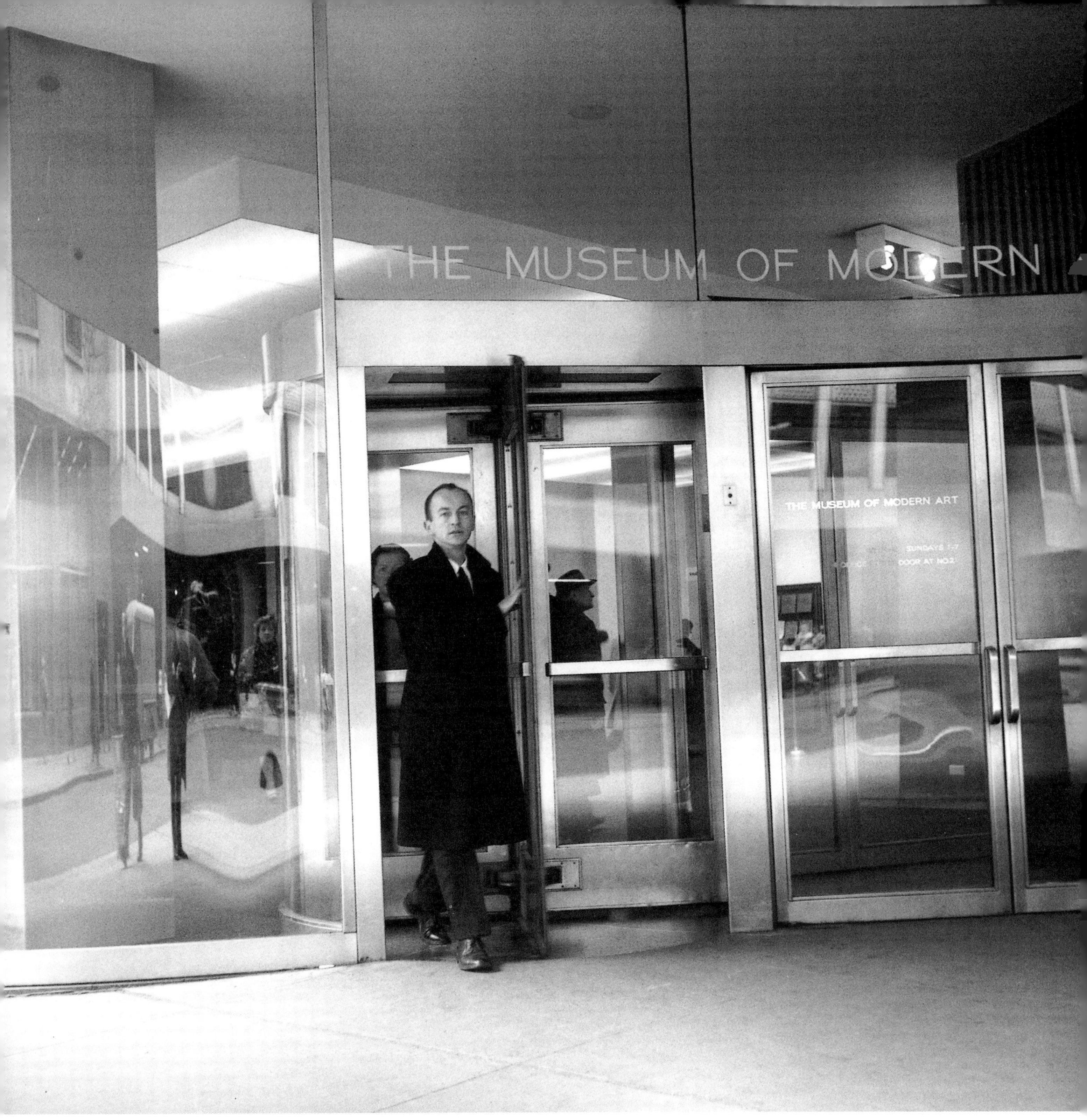

Fred W. McDarrah
Frank O'Hara at The Museum of Modern Art, New York,
January 20, 1960

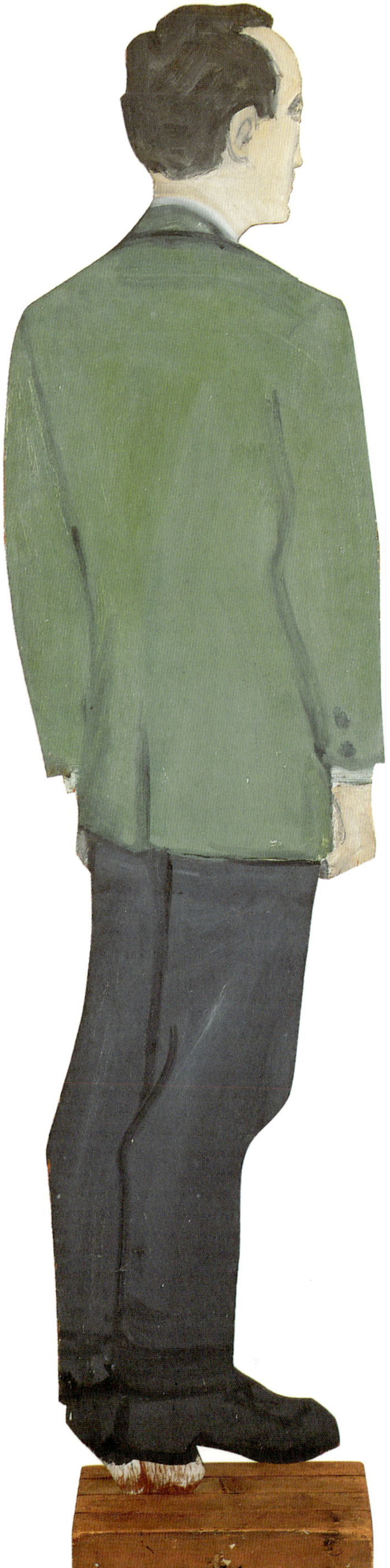

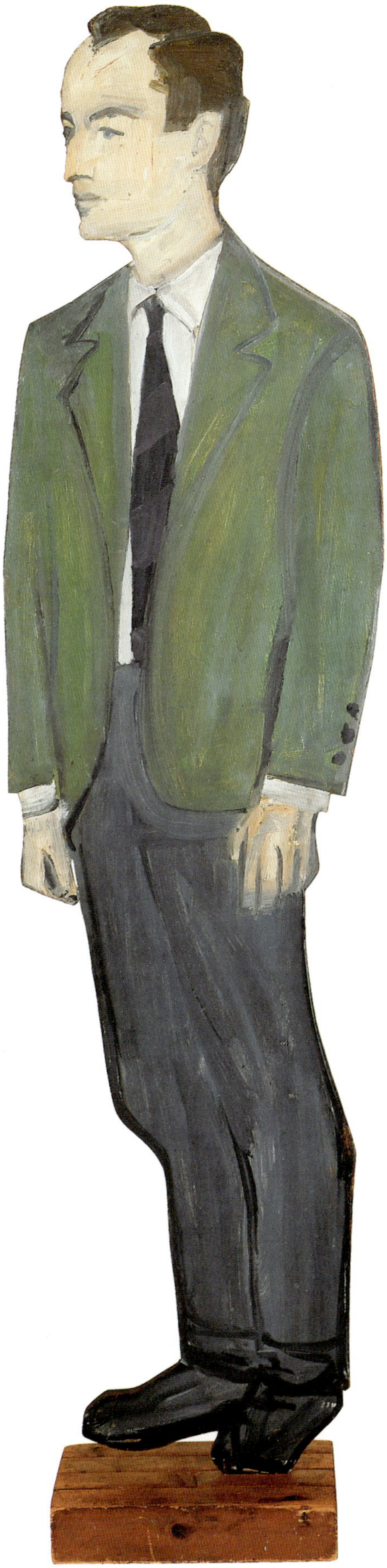

Alex Katz

Frank O'Hara, 1959-60

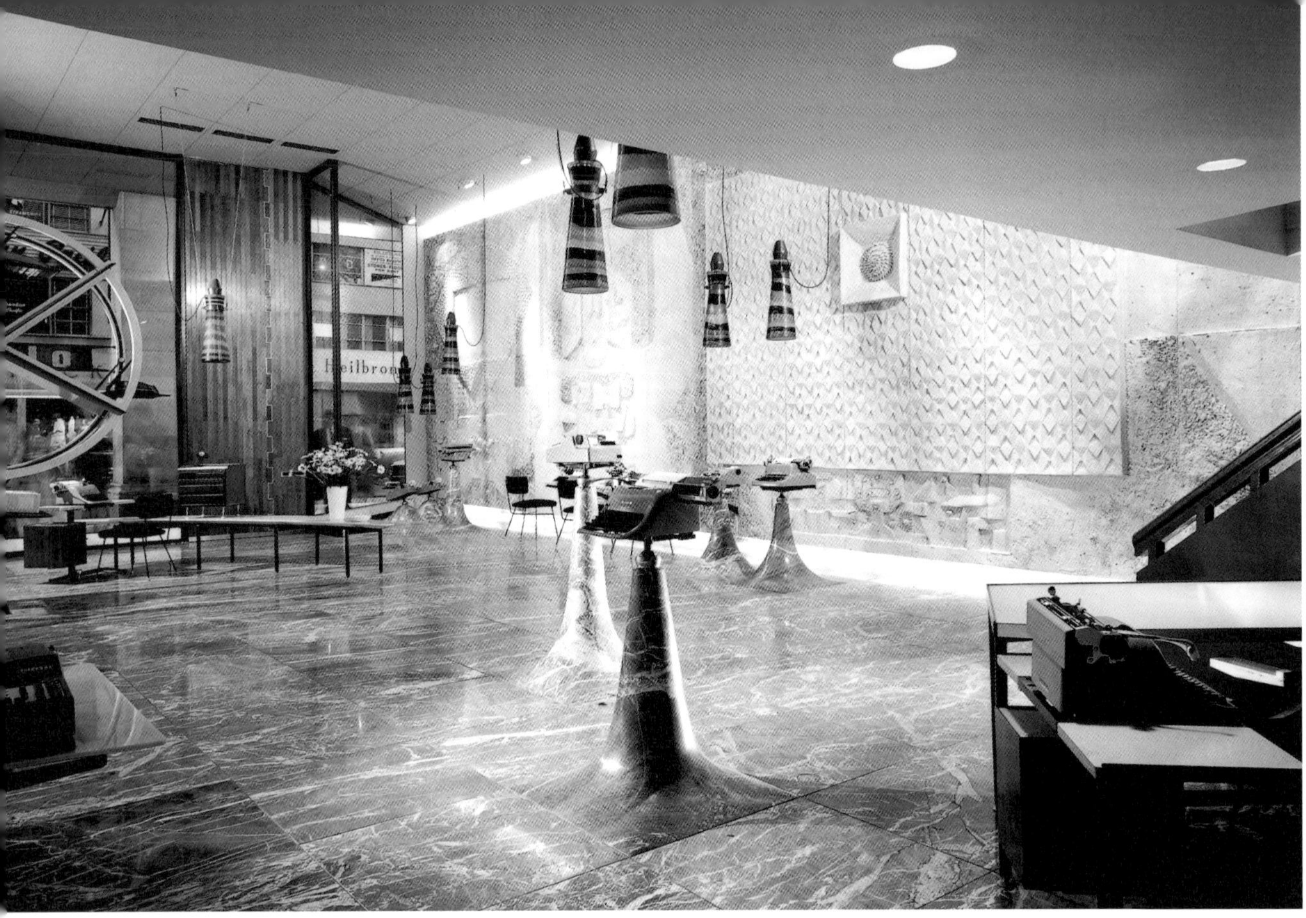

O'Hara loved the museum and his work there, he also sometimes felt trapped behind "the heavenly glass doors" of the institution, away from the New York streets that inspired him:

> **I just saw a nun in blue walking along with a valise**
> **in one hand and a package in the other wrapped**
> **with brown paper and tied with white string**
> **it was astounding**
> **she was completely defenseless she couldn't even have**
> **scratched herself if bitten by a bug**
> **unless of course she dropped the package or the valise**
> **after which epiphany the heavenly glass doors opened**
> **(I opened them)**
> **and I was back at work**
> **now I will have to wait till four o'clock for something**
> **interesting to happen**
> **this isn't Manhattan this is hell**[116]

Olivetti Showroom, New York City, 1954

Bill Berkson says that O'Hara dealt with his museum position by "approaching it as an imaginative composite of salons at the court of Louis XVI and the 1930s Warners' lot."[117] John Ashbery remembers him in black tie at the opening of the Reuben Nakian exhibition he organized, "moving from group to group with the purposeful but effortless grace of a Balanchine dancer."[118]

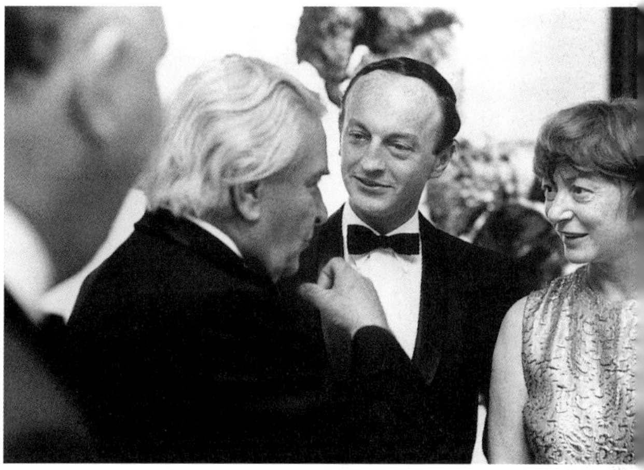

In 1965 O'Hara's exhibition of Robert Motherwell's work opened. Motherwell was not only a painter but had also edited the hugely influential anthology, *The Dada Painters and Poets* (1951), in the series he oversaw, Documents of Modern Art. O'Hara called this series "The Gospels for myself and many other poets."[119] Motherwell's *Automatism* series (one of which he dedicated to O'Hara) was a clear acknowledgment of his debt to Surrealism, an equally important influence on O'Hara's early writing. Unlike many of the artists with whom O'Hara was associated, however, Motherwell was not a regular at the Cedar Bar in the Village. That O'Hara was working with this "uptown" artist caused some jealousy among artists downtown, who felt that he might be leaving them behind, or bowing to institutional pressure. There is no doubt, however, that O'Hara had the greatest respect for Motherwell's work. For him its greatest strength was its claim to moral seriousness, the artist's "passionate affirmation of experience against despair."[120] O'Hara's last poem, the "Little Elegy for Antonio Machado" (1966), written for the catalogue of a benefit exhibition to aid refugees from Franco, makes a direct connection with Motherwell's *Elegies for the Spanish Republic,* which O'Hara deeply admired. He made the connection clear by sending Motherwell a copy of the poem.[121]

"When it isn't ignored in the work of the New York poets, politics is neutralized and transformed," David Lehman has written.[122] It is certainly true that for O'Hara politics, like everything else, was always experienced as it was filtered through his own hyper-acute sensibility, where it would take its place next to whatever else passed into his consciousness

Frank O'Hara with Elaine de Kooning and Reuben Nakian at the Nakian opening, The Museum of Modern Art, New York, 1966

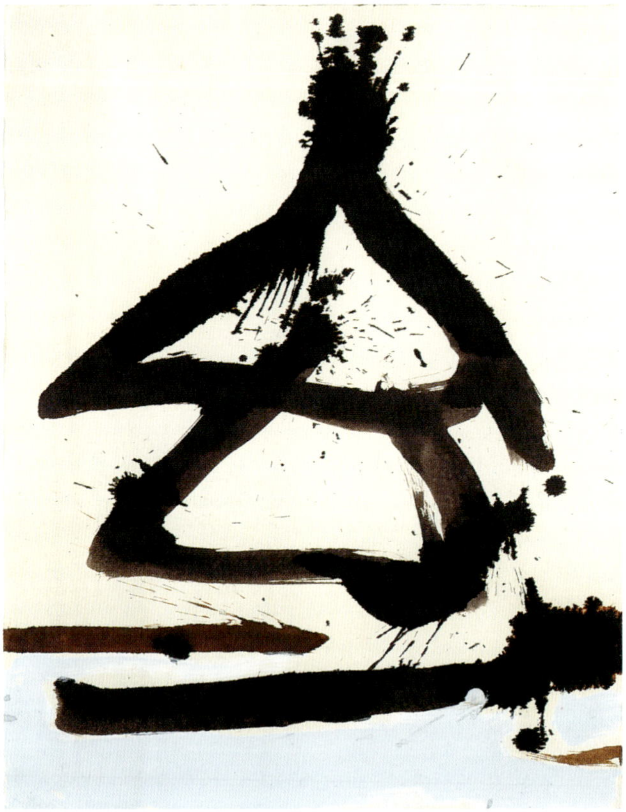

at the same time. "Khrushchev is coming on the right day!" he proclaimed, but the significance of the Soviet leader's visit to New York is subsumed into his own enjoyment of the fall weather.

> **New York seems blinding and my tie is blowing up the street**
> **I wish it would blow off**
> **though it is cold and somewhat warms my neck**
> **as the train bears Khrushchev on to Pennsylvania Station**
> **and the light seems to be eternal**
> **and joy seems to be inexorable**[123]

Robert Motherwell
Automatism #2A (For Frank O'Hara), 1965

Robert Motherwell

Untitled (Elegy), 1950

In his essay for the Motherwell catalogue, however, O'Hara makes it explicit that he is by no means disengaged. "The measure of the success of the abstract expressionist artists may be gauged by our response to the movement's ethical stand," he writes. He praises Motherwell in particular for his internationalism, which he paradoxically identifies as part of a profoundly *American* movement towards a modernity "both political and aesthetic." Specifically, O'Hara singles out for praise Motherwell's commitment to the left in the Spanish Civil War, "that perfect mirror of all that was confused, venal and wrong in national and international politics and has remained so." O'Hara's discussion here gives a clear insight into the way in which he saw political engagement as inextricably linked with individual sensibility. Speaking of the origins of the New York school, he writes that,

> While the other protesting artistic voices of the time were bound by figuration and overt symbolism, the abstract expressionists chose the open road of personal responsibility, naked nerve-ends and possible hubris, and this separated them from the surrealists, the Mexican school, and the American social realists. Belief in their personal and ethical responses saved them from aestheticism on the one hand and programmatic contortion on the other.[124]

In his politics O'Hara was a man of the fifties rather than the sixties. He had an unshakable belief in the United States as a bastion of freedom. He refused, for example, to join other intellectuals in protesting the war in Vietnam. Yet he was also committed to a sense of "personal responsibility" that often cut against the dominant tenor of the times. Opposition, however, was always expressed in the most personal terms. His poetry "does not attack the establishment," Ashbery wrote. "It merely ignores its right to exist, and is thus a source of annoyance to partisans of every stripe."[125] His intense commitment to the particular set of individuals that made up his world was one of his most attractive features, but it also made it very difficult for him to imagine a broader frame of reference. For O'Hara everything had to be experienced in relation to his own individual sensibility. For him the political was personal because everything was personal. The idea of collective action was almost inconceivable. His manifesto was "Personism."

The scene of my selves

O'Hara rarely employed metaphor in his poetry. Instead he tended to string things together, one after the other, until they coalesced into something greater than the sum of the parts, like a web in which each element seems to connect outward in apparently infinite succession. The critic Richard Howard has expressed the somewhat disorienting and flattening sense produced by that approach.

> Each time I read "Second Avenue" I bear off a handful of glittering lines, gold flakes that have quite literally panned out of the sand, but they are never the same lines and never suggest anything converging, opposing, or even subordinating in the kind of tension that makes for a unity.[126]

No artist has been more in tune with this aspect of O'Hara's work than Jasper Johns. As Kirk Varnedoe has written, Johns's "ambition was to present reality not as more integrally complete, but as more fragmented and discontinuous."[127] His patient accumulations of everyday signs and objects can be compared to O'Hara's "I do this, I do that" aesthetic, although Johns's attention is given more to objects than to personalities:

> Take an object
> Do something to it
> Do something else to it[128]

In his scrutiny of what is normally taken for granted, however, Johns echoes O'Hara's conviction that clarity of vision is an essential quality of all art. "Mentally my preference would be the mood of keeping your eyes open and looking."[129] And, like O'Hara, Johns sees things in terms of juxtapositions and relationships that pass through his own sensibility. "I tend to focus upon a relationship between oneself and a thing that is flexible, that can be one thing at one time and something else at another time. I find it interesting, although it may not be very reassuring."[130]

Johns and O'Hara first met in 1957. Johns's memory of O'Hara's conversation is familiar from the accounts of others: "There was this weird thing of Frank's interest in and understanding of other artists that seemed to put no obligation on his own work, neither threatened, nor helped, but was in a sense disassociated from his work.... I had no sense that he needed anything from me about his work but that his interest in me was about my work."[131]

One of O'Hara's greatest poems, "In Memory of My Feelings" (1956), was to provide the starting point for one of Johns's greatest paintings, *In Memory of My Feelings—Frank O'Hara* (1961). As I have already noted, the poem is a study in fragmentation. In its appropriation of the quintessential American myth of discovery, its conversion of that myth into a highly personal hymn to shifting identity, and in its dreamlike changes of scene, this poem could not but have resonated with the artist who had painted his own American flag two years before, after seeing it in a dream. The opening lines of the poem call up more images that Johns was in the process of making his own:

> **My quietness has a man in it, he is transparent**
> **and he carries me quietly, like a gondola, through the streets.**
> **He has several likenesses, like stars and years, like numerals.**
> **My quietness has a number of naked selves**[132]

While Johns had already been painting numerals for several years when the poem was written, it is also worth noting that when he made a major series of paintings in 1985 and 1986, *The Seasons,* which look backward through his life and are packed with allusions both art historical and personal, the dominant element is a mysterious, silhouetted figure who is often transparent.

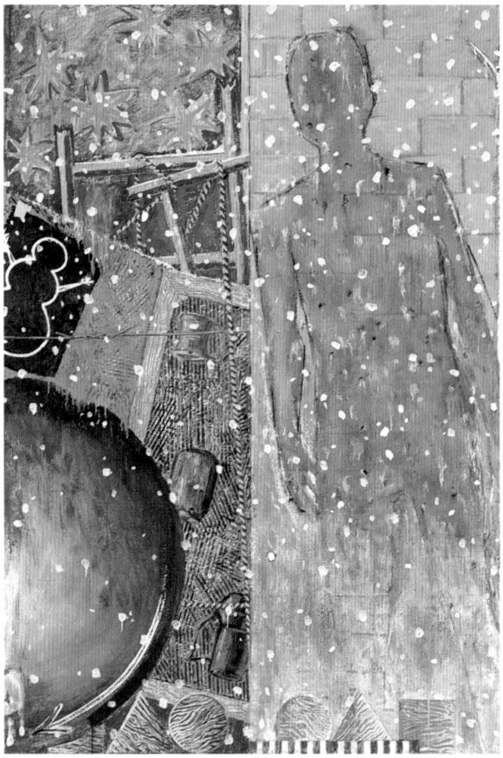

Jasper Johns
Winter, 1986
Encaustic on canvas
75 x 50 inches
Private Collection

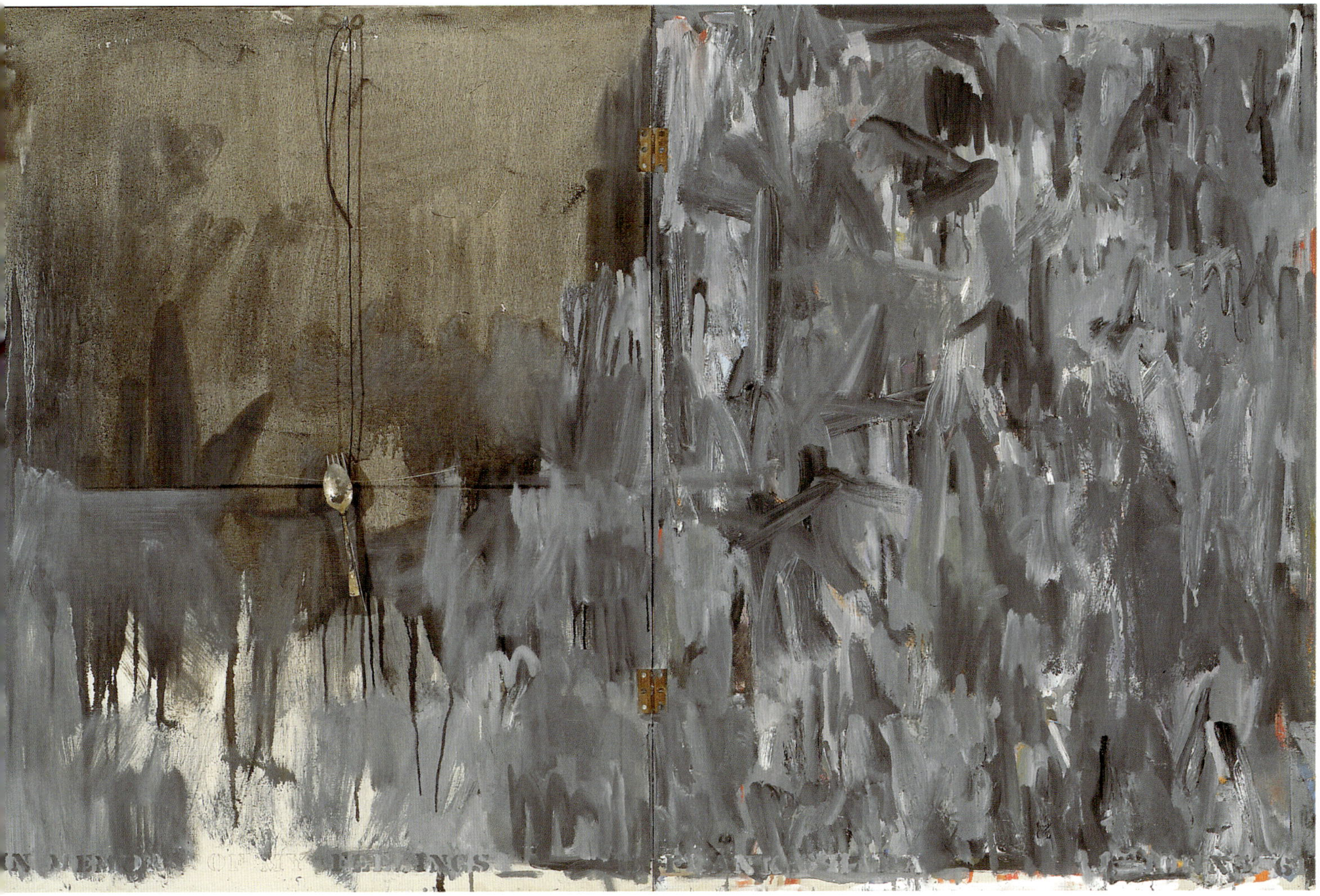

Jasper Johns

In Memory of My Feelings—Frank O'Hara, 1961

Grace Hartigan, to whom the poem is dedicated, has suggested that its subject is "how to be *open* but not violated, how *not to panic.*"[133] It is possible to draw just this sense from the paintings that Johns was making in the fifties: basic information, repeated obsessively—flags, numbers, letters, body parts. It is easy to read these paintings as products of compulsive behavior, as the work of someone trying *not to panic.* Moira Roth has seen them as a barely veiled response to McCarthyism and the Cold War threat of imminent nuclear annihilation. She tells the story of Johns going to see Leonardo da Vinci's "Deluge" drawings, because, in his words, "here was a man depicting the end of the world and his hand was not trembling."[134] In this reading, Johns is searching for a way out of a desperate situation. In both the poem and the painting, however, the desperation seems profoundly personal. The poem concludes with images of desolation and despair:

> **I have forgotten my loves, and chiefly that one, the cancerous**
> **statue which my body could no longer contain,**
> **against my will**
> **against my love**
> **become art,**
> **I could not change it into history**
> **and so remember it,**
> **and I have lost what is always and everywhere**
> **present, the scene of my selves, the occasion of these ruses,**
> **which I myself and singly must now kill**
> **and save the serpent in their midst.**

The loss of love, which has passed from the immediacy of experience to "become art," seems to precipitate a psychological crisis. Rather than such a crisis resulting in a fragmentation of personality, however, in this case it is the "scene of my selves," unequivocally plural, that has been lost, leaving only "the serpent." For O'Hara the normal, even desired, state is the one in which his multiple selves can move freely in and out of the scene.

Johns's painting is made up of two panels, hinged together, with a fork and spoon attached. This additive technique is in a way a visual correlative to O'Hara's own method of composition, simply adding one thing to another without trying to force an overarching unity. Fred Orton has suggested that the stencilled title that runs along the painting's lower edge—*In Memory of My Feelings—Frank O'Hara*—also acts "as a kind of hinge between the painting and O'Hara's poem, designating difference and articulation, marking a correspondence and co-operation between the meanings that proliferate for the painting and the poem, the painter and the poet, their practices and lives."[135] It is this hinge, Orton argues, that gave Johns the distance he needed to make a painting that dealt with his own emotions. Kenneth Silver has written that "in the name of vacating the place of his own feelings, Johns performs a kind of ventriloquism."[136] The painter lets the poet speak for him, but the painter also speaks through the poet.

The hinged construction suggests the possibility of the two elements breaking apart completely, yet it simultaneously holds out the opposite option: that of coming together completely. The second option is not so clear-cut, however. The folding together of the panels would indeed bring them together, but only at the price of concealing whatever feelings are depicted. Unification would be achieved, but only through a shutdown that would imply a kind of death. The vaguely indicated but nevertheless inescapable motif of the American flag that defines much of the composition is here reduced to a washed-out palette of brown and grey, reinforcing the sense of an identity only just holding on, capable at any moment of folding up on itself (as flags are folded for burials). Like one of O'Hara's selves watching the arrival of Columbus's ships, the identity in question is definitely American.

The fork and spoon, basic tools for feeding oneself, are bound tightly together and hang all but uselessly from a wire. Almost hidden under the covering brushstrokes, the phrase "DEAD MAN" is stencilled twice along the bottom edge. While the painting is not in any conventional sense an illustration of the poem, it does conjure up the same feeling of a breakdown so complete that it threatens to obliterate the sense of self. Orton has suggested that the subtext of the painting, for Johns, was the ending of his intense relationship with Robert Rauschenberg.[137]

After O'Hara's death, Johns used the fork and spoon as a vehicle to memorialize him in the drawings he made for The Museum of Modern Art's tribute publication, *Frank*

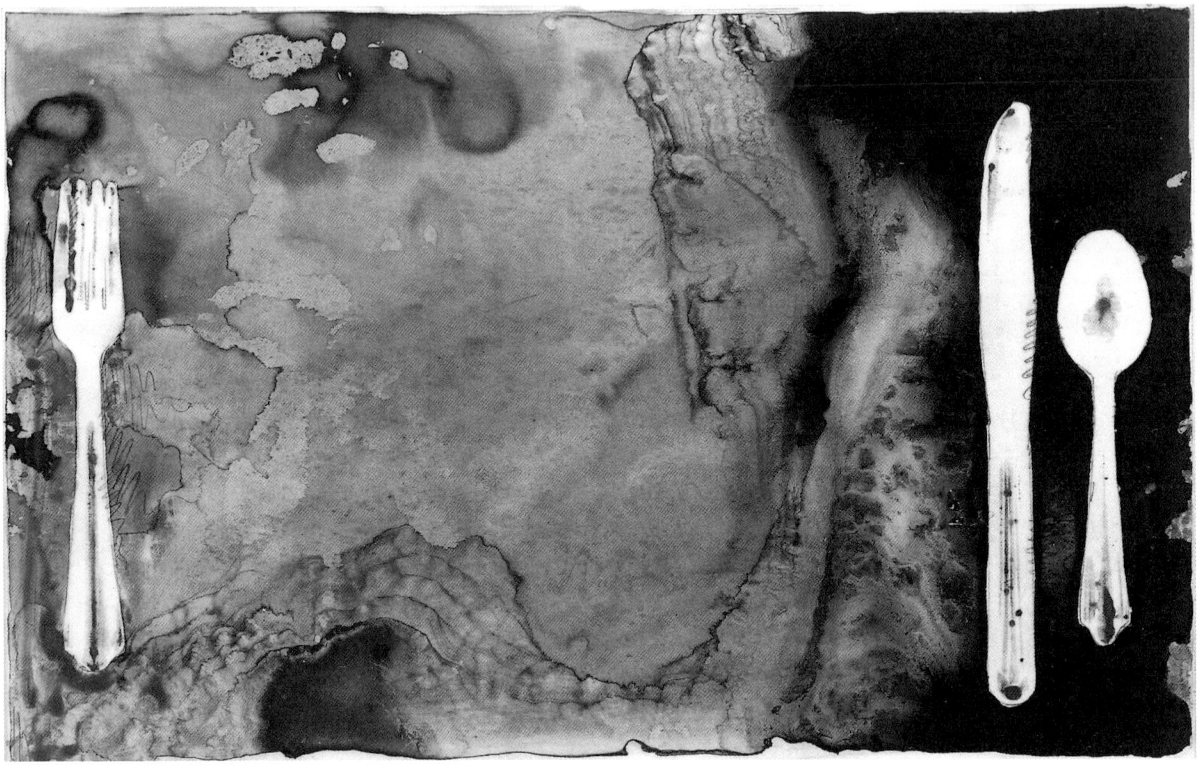

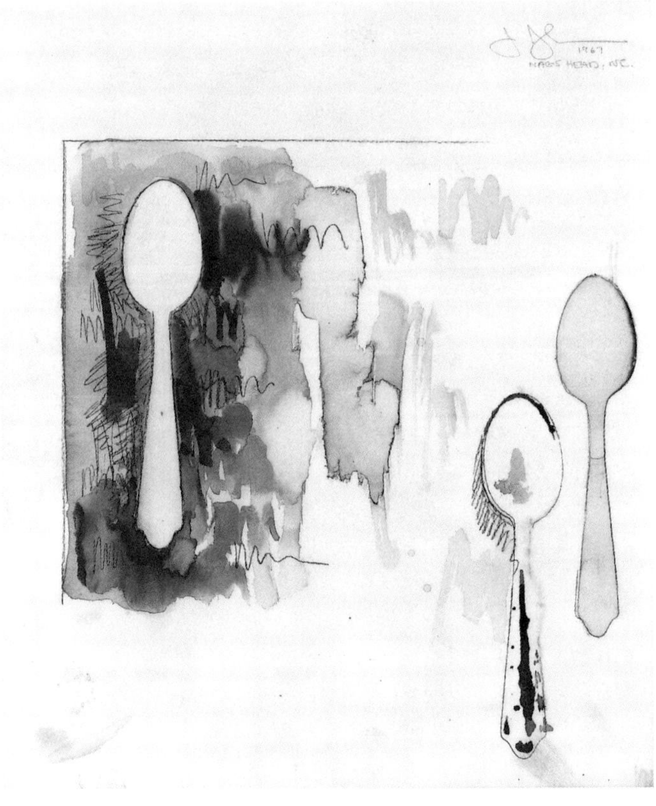

Jasper Johns

Studies for "In Memory of My Feelings", 1967

O'Hara: In Memory of My Feelings (1967). Where in the painting of 1961 the fork and spoon are hung up and bound together by a twisted wire, in the later drawings they are laid out in simple place settings, suggesting a kind of resolution to the suffering that they seem to represent in the original painting.

In 1961, the same year that Johns made the painting, O'Hara visited the artist in Edisto, South Carolina, where Johns had a house. It was at this time that Johns made a plaster cast of O'Hara's left foot. (In a poem of 1963 addressed to Johns, O'Hara wrote, "when I think of you in South Carolina I think of my foot in the sand."[138]) In 1970, four years after O'Hara's death on the beach at Fire Island, Johns completed the sculpture he had envisaged making, *Memory Piece (Frank O'Hara)*. The cast is attached to the lid of a box that contains a layer of sand. Each time the lid is closed, a fresh footprint is impressed into it. The sculpture makes an intimate kind of memorial, keeping O'Hara's physical footprint in the world in an echo of the way his poetry lives on in the minds of his readers.

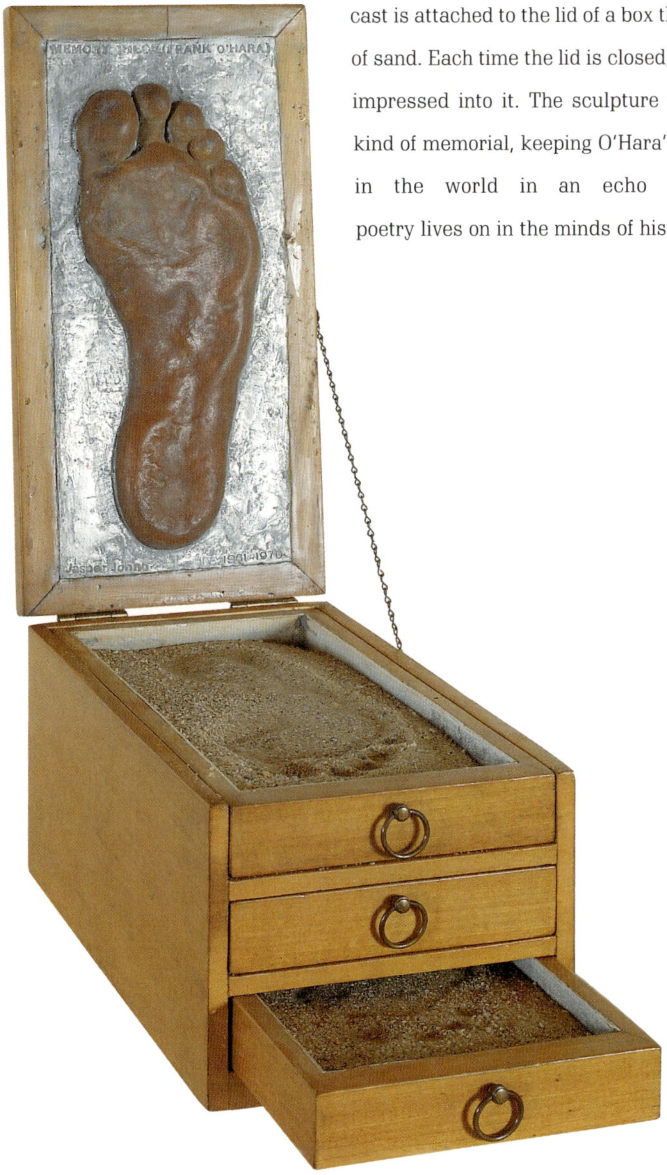

Jasper Johns
Memory Piece (Frank O'Hara), 1961-70

In Rauschenberg's illustrations for Dante's *Inferno* (1959-60) he had outlined his own foot as part of the drawing to accompany the canto dealing with the punishment of sodomites. The punishment, according to the poem, was to run forever barefoot on hot sand.[139] Johns's even more literal version of the bare foot on sand can perhaps be seen as an extension of Rauschenberg's gesture of the previous year. Such an interpretation is supported by Johns's print *Pinion* (1966), which was originally intended to incorporate a poem by O'Hara.[140] *Pinion* bears the foot and hand prints (and one knee print) of a sprinter waiting for the starter's pistol.

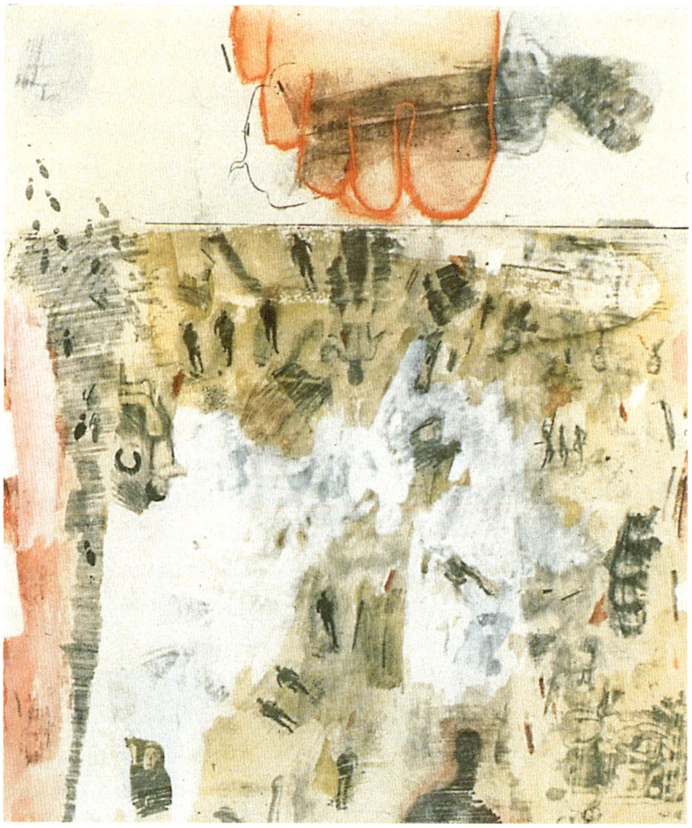

Robert Rauschenberg

(Canto XIV), from **XXXIV Drawings for Dante's *Inferno***, 1959-60

Offset lithograph

14½ x 11½ inches

The Museum of Contemporary Art, Los Angeles. Gift of Marcia Simon Weisman

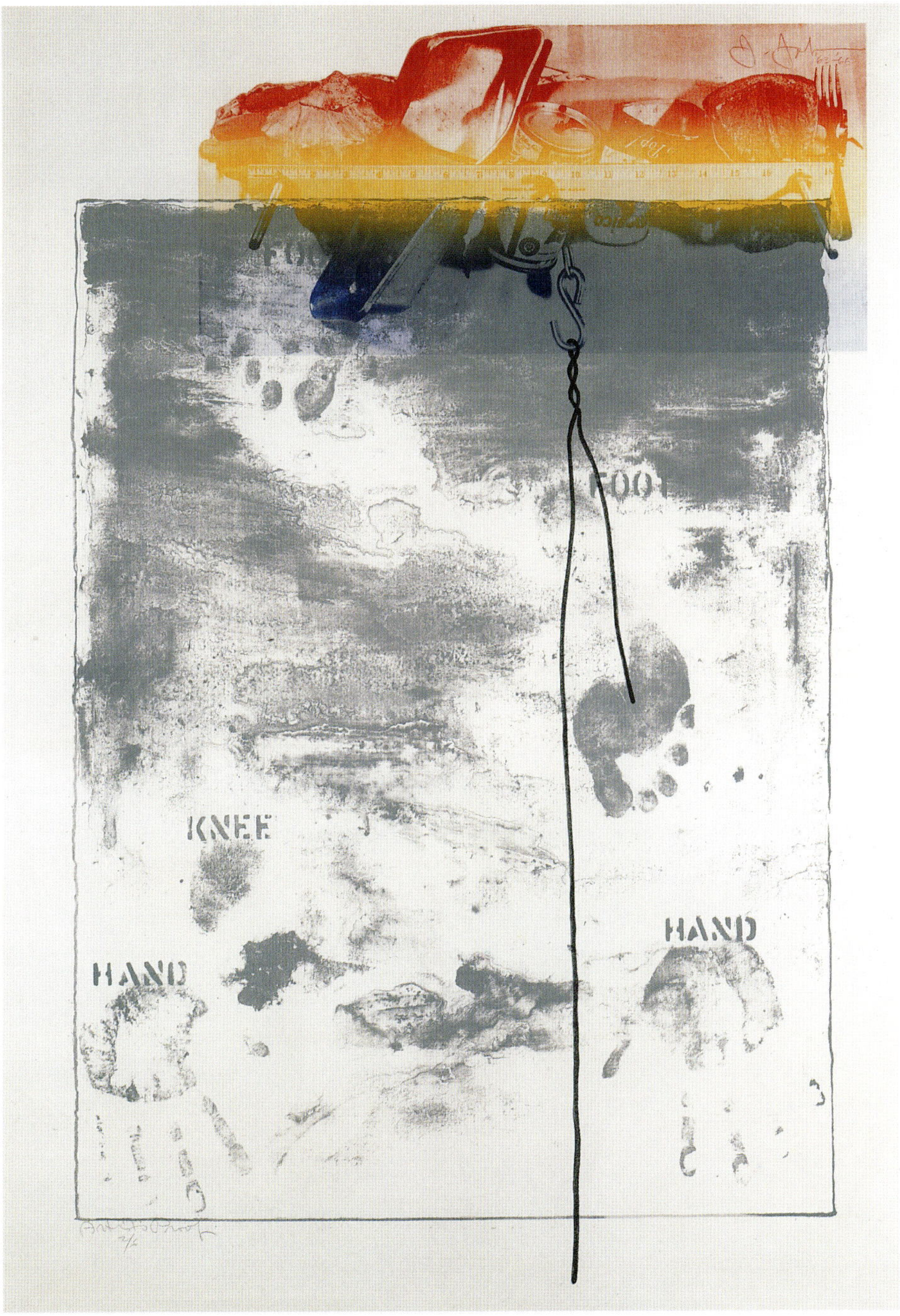

Jasper Johns

Pinion, 1966

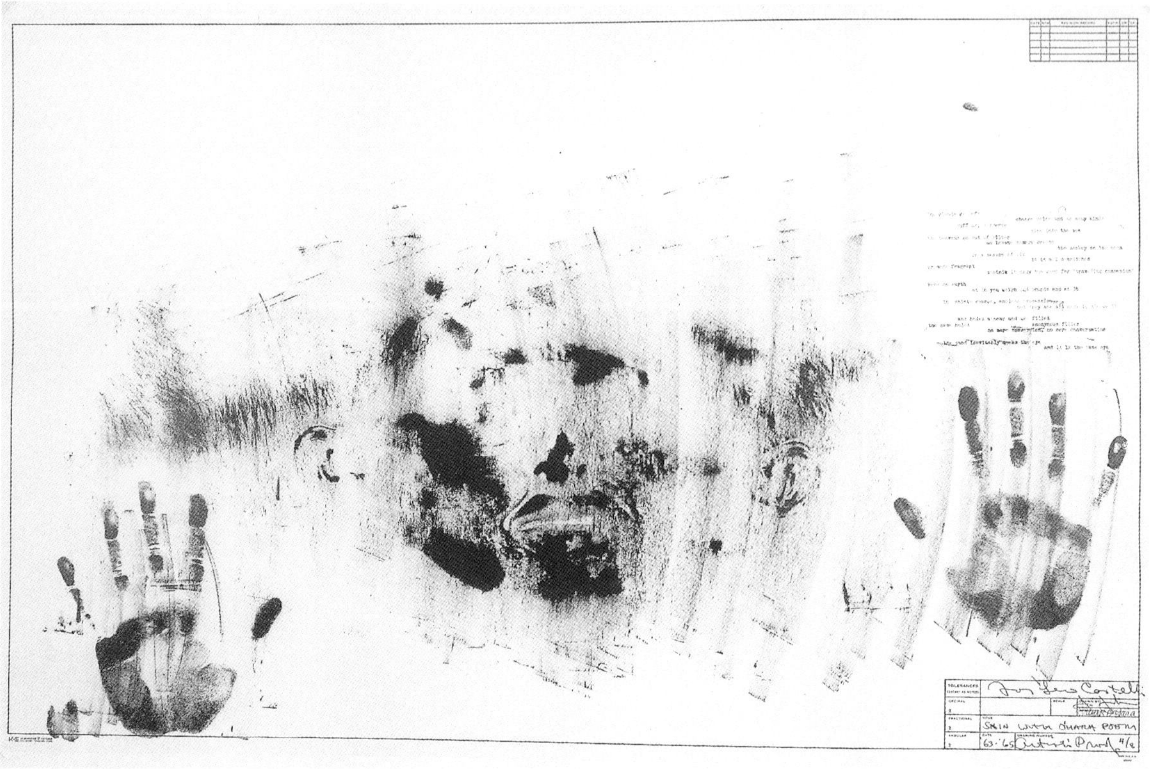

Although Johns and O'Hara had planned to collaborate on a series of prints, the only one completed before O'Hara's death was *Skin with O'Hara Poem* (1963-65). It is not a collaboration in the sense in which O'Hara had collaborated with Bluhm and Rivers, although it is signed by both men. The print was essentially made by Johns in 1963, with O'Hara's poem added two years later. The image, on engineering drafting paper, consists of smudged impressions of Johns's face and hands. It conveys a death-shadowed, shroud-like quality that is reflected in the accompanying poem, "[The clouds go soft]" (1963), where holes in the fabric of O'Hara's shirts are transformed into graves that are then filled:

the shirts change, endless procession
but they are all neck 14 sleeve 33

and holes appear and are filled
the same holes anonymous filler
no more conversion, no more conversation

Jasper Johns
Skin with O'Hara Poem, 1963-65

A step away from them

The attention to death in poems such as "[The clouds go soft]" makes it all the more tempting to read significance into O'Hara's sudden death in 1966. He died after being hit by a jeep on the beach at Fire Island, late in the evening. It is the kind of arbitrary, unsatisfying ending that makes one want to search for portents of a death foretold. Norman Bluhm, for example, told me that the week before his death, O'Hara had spent the weekend at the beach with the Bluhms, and at one point asked their young children to bury him in the sand "like I was dead."[141] Appearing in *Once upon an El* (1955), a film by Daisy Aldan, he had pretended to throw himself in front of a train. A watercolor that Motherwell dedicated to him is called *Night Beside the Sea.* More pernicious is the suggestion that there might have been something suicidal about O'Hara's actual death. Such speculation is fueled, understandably, by the desire to have his life come to some kind of coherent conclusion, even if it were one of despair. But sometimes an accident is just an accident, and lives can end without fulfilling the demands of narrative.

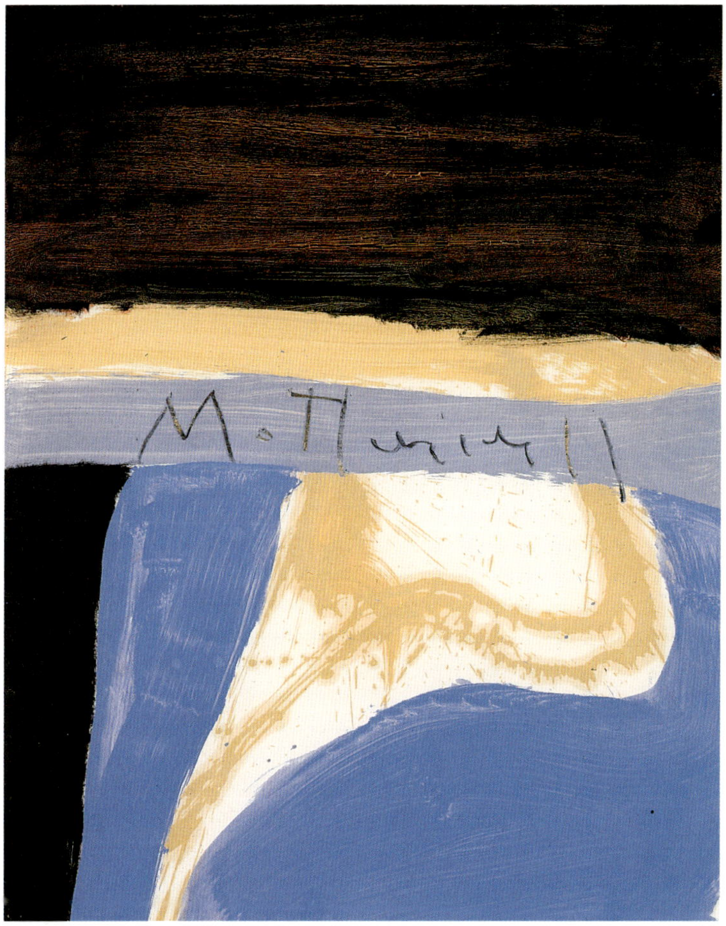

Robert Motherwell

Night Beside the Sea, 1962

Alfred Leslie, however, has succeeded in making a moving series of works out of the desire that any death, especially this sudden and unexpected one, might offer up meaning to those who remain. In a series of monumental paintings, *The Killing Cycle,* painted between 1967 and 1978, Leslie attempted to allegorize O'Hara's death as part of a bigger meditation on death in general. In a number of preparatory works for this series, Leslie made studies, many of them painted at the site of the accident, that stay closer to the specifics of O'Hara's death, and are, if anything, more emotionally loaded through that specificity. In a number of these works, Leslie has made use of the subtitles that O'Hara originally wrote for *The Last Clean Shirt,* quite consciously providing them with an eerie new context:

I have the other idea about guilt.
It's not in us, it's in the situation.

You don't say the victim is responsible
for a concentration camp or a Mack Truck.

Leslie's use of these lines in a deliberately anachronistic way transforms the natural tendency to seek significance from death into paintings that go beyond such speculation to constitute new and independent works of art.

It is true that the theme of death was becoming increasingly important in O'Hara's poetry. "I historically / belong to the enormous bliss of American death"[142] he wrote. A notebook he had with him on his fatal trip to Fire Island contains only three lines, under the rubric, "Oedipus Rex":

He falls, but even in falling
he is higher than those who
fly into the ordinary sun.

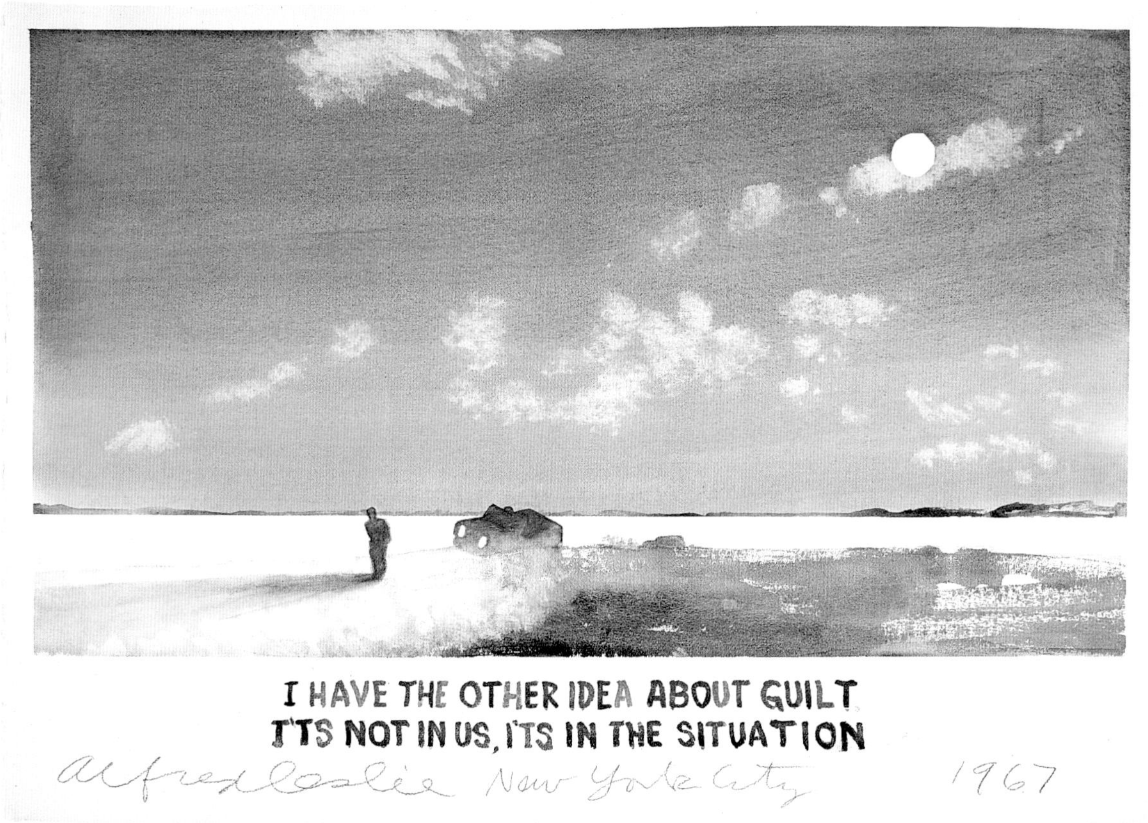

Alfred Leslie

Study for *The Killing Cycle*

(I have the other idea about guilt), 1967

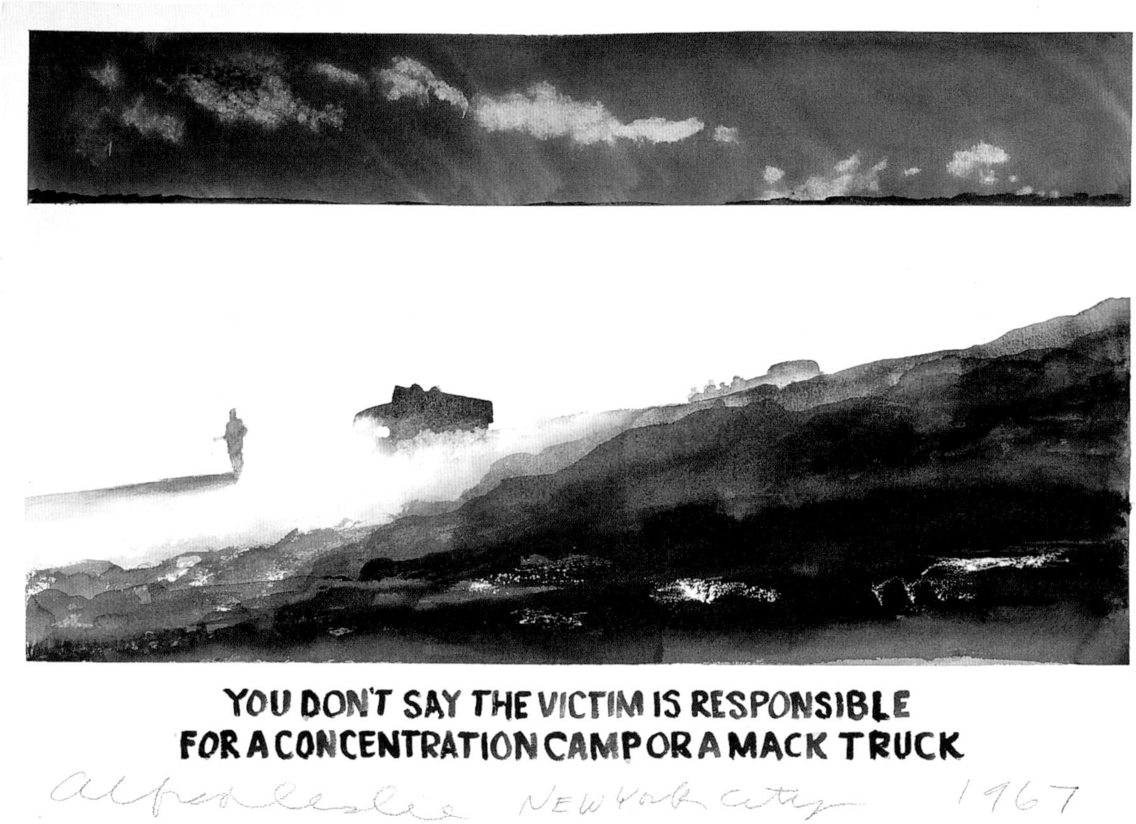

Alfred Leslie

Study for *The Killing Cycle*

(You don't say the victim is responsible), 1967

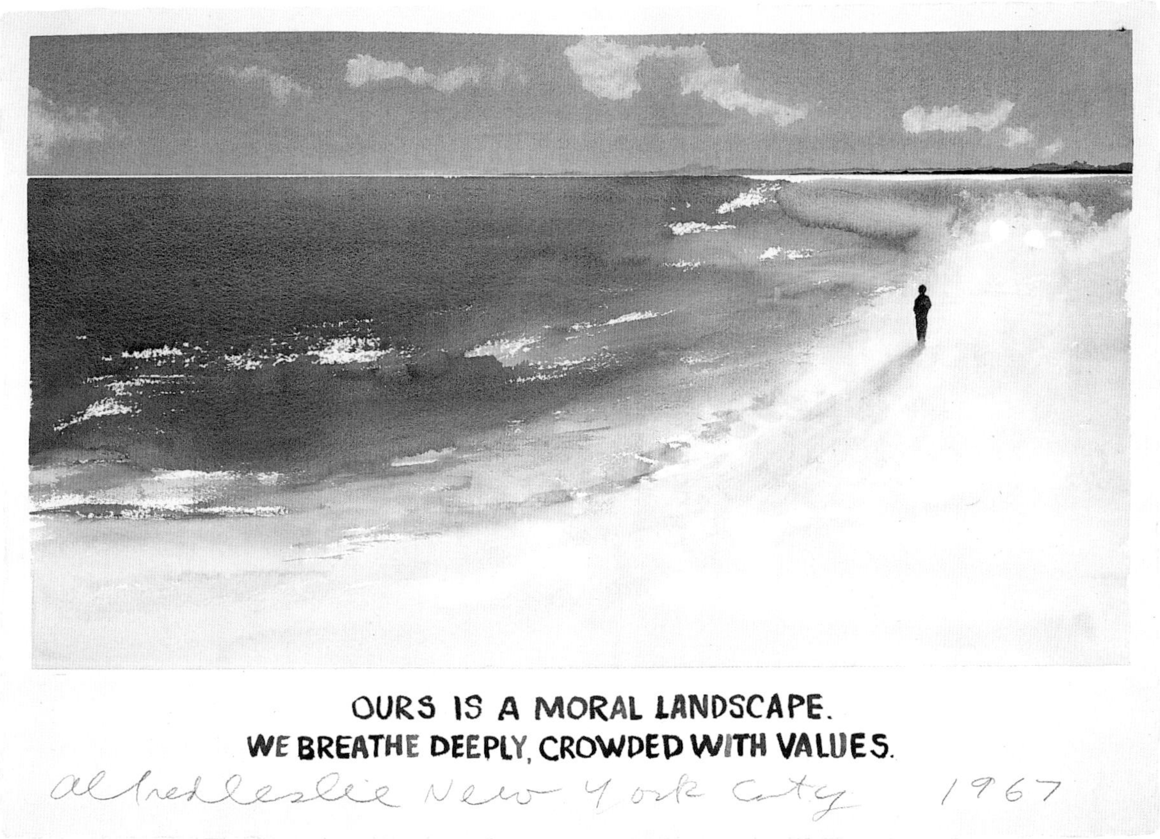

Alfred Leslie

Study for *The Killing Cycle*

(Ours is a moral landscape), 1967

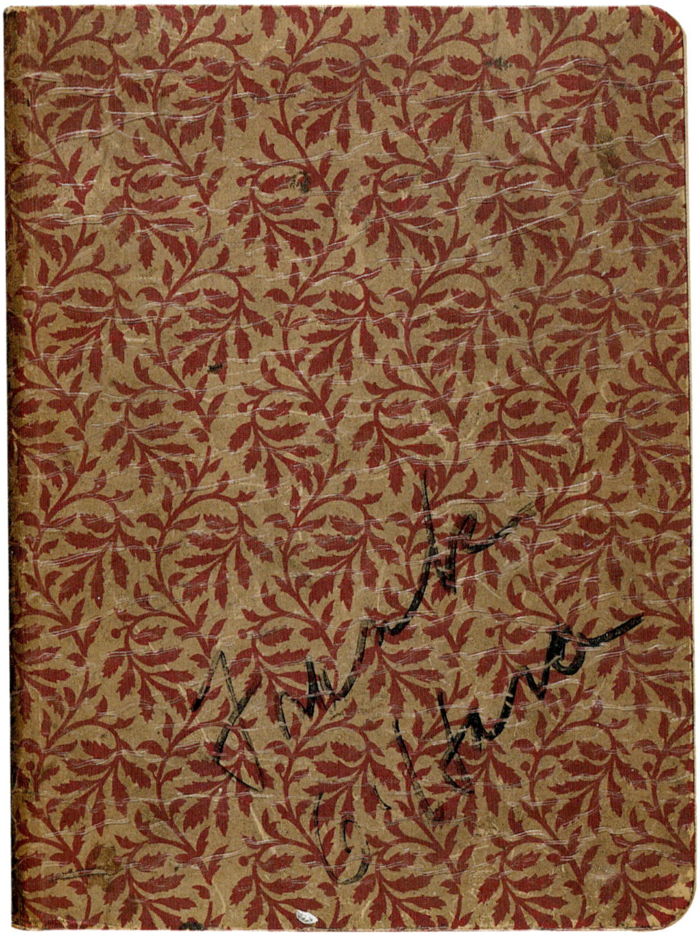

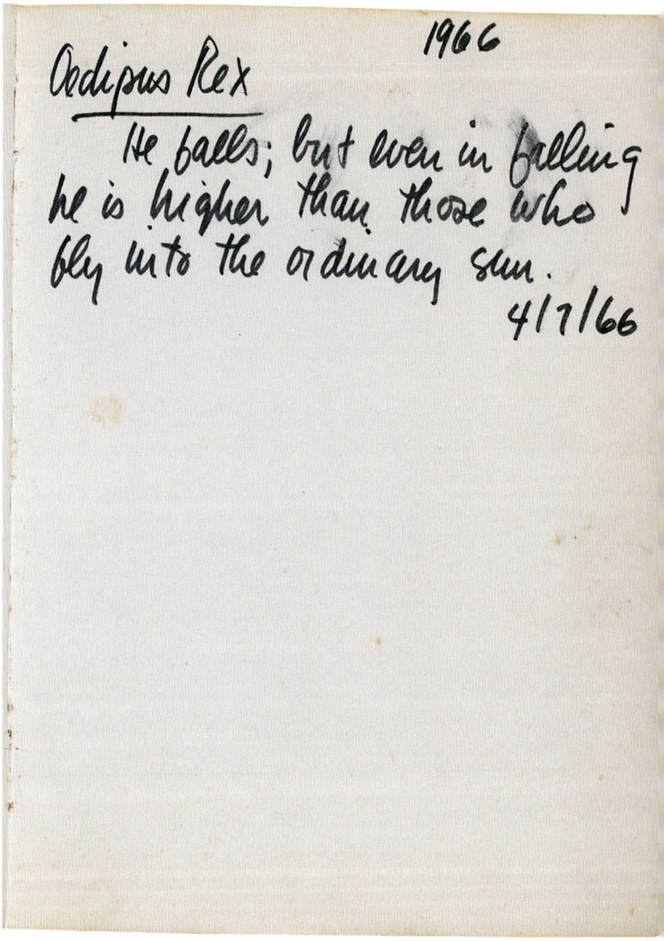

Frank O'Hara

front cover of journal, 1966

first page of journal, 1966

O'Hara counted on love and friendship to sustain him against "despair's sharp snake"[143] and to keep the presence of death at bay. In one of his few poems that are not devoted entirely to the experience of the present, the one he wrote to celebrate John Button's birthday, he tried to glimpse the future:

And in 1984 I trust we'll still
be high together. I'll say "Let's go to a bar"
and you'll say "Let's go to a movie" and we'll go to both;[144]

Even more essential than love, although he insisted love was the highest value, was poetry. "I am mainly preoccupied with the world as I experience it," he wrote, "and at times when I would rather be dead the thought that I could never write another poem has so far stopped me. I think this is an ignoble attitude. I would rather die for love, but I haven't."[145]

In "A Step Away From Them" O'Hara's pleasurable wanderings in the city are abruptly interrupted. He has just finished a cheeseburger and a chocolate malted, when he is suddenly jolted by memories:

First
Bunny died, then John Latouche,
then Jackson Pollock. But is the
earth as full as life was full, of them?

His only answer is to keep on walking.

And one has eaten and one walks,
past the magazines with nudes
and the posters for BULLFIGHT and
the Manhattan Storage Warehouse,
which they'll soon tear down. I
used to think they had the Armory
Show there.

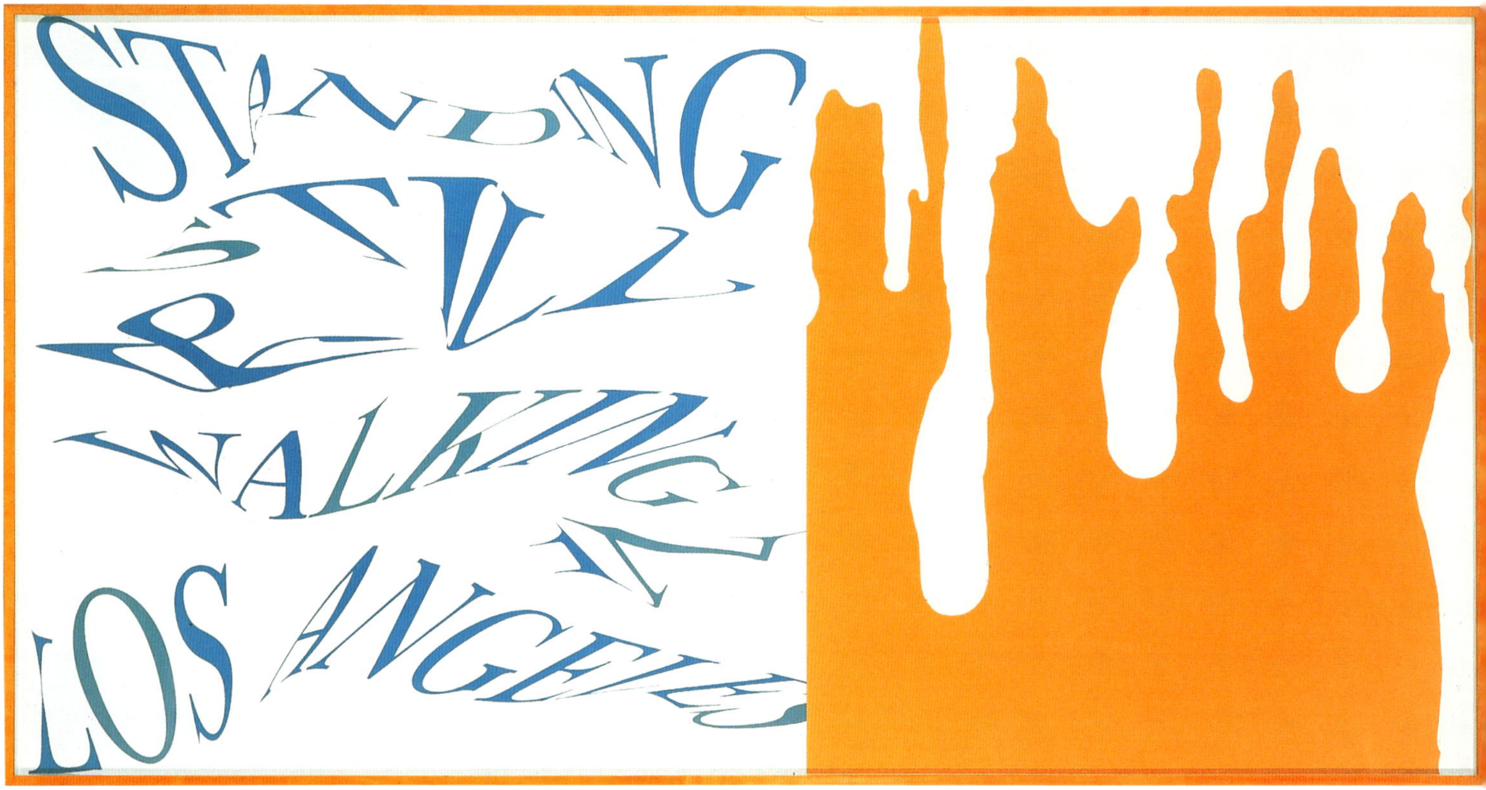

The earth itself has become a vast warehouse for the buried dead, and buried memories. And, as the poem's title reminds us, we are just "A Step Away From Them." More than forty years later, we might also be reminded of O'Hara's foot in Johns's *Memory Piece,* still stepping down on its bed of sand.

For O'Hara, just as love and sudden revelation are everywhere in the city streets, so is death, and its sudden appearance can also be a kind of ecstasy. In the great elegy he wrote for Billie Holliday, "The Day Lady Died" (1959), a poem of twenty-nine lines, Holliday does not appear until the twenty-fifth. Until then O'Hara has given us a precise account of his strolling around midtown Manhattan shopping for gifts to take on a visit to Mike Goldberg and Patsy Southgate, until he suddenly sees a copy of the *New York Post* with Holliday's photograph and the news of her death. The poem ends in a rush as O'Hara is swept backward in time to a memory of her singing:

Larry Johnson
Untitled (Standing Still and Walking in Los Angeles), 1994

and I am sweating a lot by now and thinking of
leaning on the john door in the 5 SPOT
while she whispered a song along the keyboard
to Mal Waldron and everyone and I stopped breathing[146]

We feel the suddenness of the end. It is not only Holliday who has stopped breathing but also O'Hara and everyone else in the club. The ecstatic, breathtaking quality of great singing, great art, is linked inextricably with the literal stopping of the breath.

O'Hara himself has been gone for more than thirty years now. His poetry, of course, has lasted, and is more widely read today than ever before. He remains an inspiring figure to young poets, and to artists. Larry Johnson's *Untitled (Standing Still and Walking in Los Angeles)* (1994), is an example of recent work that invokes his legacy, transforming the line from the "Ode on Causality": "standing still and walking in New York," into a transcontinental homage to the man who never referred to Los Angeles, only to "Hollywood," always in search of the mythic element in everyday life.

O'Hara loved the process of one thing becoming another. Countless poems salute the occasions that mark change and new beginnings. When his friends and family had to find an epigraph for him, they recognized this quality in his work and in his life. They chose for his gravestone his own words, "grace to be born and live as variously as possible." But perhaps O'Hara had already written his own testament, on life as well as on death, as early as 1956:

When I die, don't come, I wouldn't want a leaf
to turn away from the sun—it loves it there.
There's nothing so spiritual about being happy
but you can't miss a day of it, because it doesn't last.[147]

Notes

1
For O'Hara's poetry, see *The Collected Poems of Frank O'Hara*, ed. Donald Allen (Berkeley: University of California Press, 1995), Marjorie Perloff's *Frank O'Hara: Poet Among Painters* (Chicago: The University of Chicago Press, 1977), and the anthology edited by Jim Elledge, *Frank O'Hara: To Be True to a City* (Ann Arbor: The University of Michigan Press, 1990). For O'Hara's life, see Brad Gooch, *City Poet: The Life and Times of Frank O'Hara* (New York: Knopf, 1993). Bill Berkson and Joe LeSueur, eds., *Homage to Frank O'Hara* (Berkeley: Creative Arts, 1980) is invaluable. See also Alexander Smith's *Frank O'Hara: A Comprehensive Bibliography* (New York: Garland, 1979), as well as the bibliography included in this catalogue.

2
Greenberg, 1952, quoted in Kirk Varnedoe, *Jackson Pollock* (New York: The Museum of Modern Art, 1998), 43.

3
Feldman, "Lost Times and Future Hopes," in *Homage to Frank O'Hara*, 12.

4
Button, "Frank's Grace," in *Homage to Frank O'Hara*, 42.

5
O'Hara, in the television film *David Smith: Sculpting Master of Bolton Landing*, WNDT-TV, New York, 18 November 1964.

Reprinted in Frank O'Hara, *What's With Modern Art?*, ed. Bill Berkson (Austin, Tex.: Mike & Dale's Press, 1999), 27.

6
O'Hara, letter to Fairfield Porter, 7 July 1955.

7
Feldman, in *Homage to Frank O'Hara*, 12.

8
Katz, "Memoir," in *Homage to Frank O'Hara*, 99.

9
Interview with the author, 4 September 1998.

10
Schuyler, "Frank O'Hara: Poet Among Painters," in *Homage to Frank O'Hara*, 82.

11
Guston, in *Homage to Frank O'Hara*, 101.

12
Rivers, in *Homage to Frank O'Hara*, 138.

13
Gruen, *The Party's Over Now: Reminiscences of the Fifties* (New York: Viking, 1972), 143.

14
See David Lehman's *The Last Avant-Garde: The Making of the New York School of Poets* (New York: Doubleday, 1998) for a comprehensive study of the group.

15
Perloff, *Radical Artifice* (Chicago: The University of Chicago Press, 1991), 174.

16
Rexroth, from "Two Voices Against the Chorus," in Elledge, *Frank O'Hara: To Be True to a City*, 3.

17
O'Hara, in "Sorrows of the Youngman: John Rechy's *City of Night*" (1963), in Frank O'Hara, *Standing Still and Walking in New York*, ed. Donald Allen (Bolinas, Calif.: Grey Fox Press, 1975), 162.

18
Ashbery, "Frank O'Hara's Question," *Book Week* 25 (September 1966): 6.

19
"Radio" (1955), in *Collected Poems*, 234.

20
See Perloff, *Frank O'Hara: Poet Among Painters*, 25.

21
O'Hara, *Jackson Pollock* (New York: Braziller, 1959), 12.

22
Ashbery, quoted in Lehman, 305.

23
Ashbery, "Frank O'Hara's Question," 6. See also Daniel Belgrad, *The Culture of Spontaneity* (Chicago: The University of Chicago Press, 1998).

24
Kenneth Koch, interview with the author, 22 February 1999.

25
David Shapiro, "Conversations with Michael Goldberg," in Shapiro, Jeremy Gilbert-Rolfe, and Elisabetta Longari, *Michael Goldberg* (Viterbo: Primaprint, 1997), 21.

26
Lucie-Smith, "An Interview with Frank O'Hara," in *Standing Still and Walking in New York*, 21.

27
Koch, "All the Imagination Can Hold," in Elledge, *Frank O'Hara: To Be True to a City*, 33.

28
Berkson, "Frank O'Hara and His Poems," in *Homage to Frank O'Hara*, 162.

29
O'Hara, interview with Lucie-Smith, 13.

30
"Who Is William Walton?" (1961), in *Collected Poems*, 395.

31
O'Hara, "Meditations in an Emergency" (1954), in *Collected Poems*, 197.

32
O'Hara, "Song" (1959), in *Collected Poems*, 327. O'Hara wrote on the manuscript: "If I called this *Vilanelle* it would seem like Empson but I call it Hangover."

33
"Corresponding Foreignly," in Frank O'Hara, *Poems Retrieved*, ed. Donald Allen (San Francisco: Grey Fox Press, 1996), 161.

34
O'Hara, "Nature and New Painting," in *Standing Still and Walking in New York*, 42.

35
Quoted in Gooch, *City Poet*, 218. O'Hara was in tune with his times. There was virtually no preservation movement in New York until after the destruction of the old Pennsylvania Station in 1963. The Landmarks Preservation Commission was formed in 1965.

36
O'Hara, "A Step Away from Them" (1956), in *Collected Poems*, 257.

37
Collected Poems, 265.

38
Berkson, in "Frank O'Hara and his Poems," in *Homage to Frank O'Hara*, 161.

39
Guest, in *Homage to Frank O'Hara*, 77.

40
Perloff, *Frank O'Hara: Poet Among Painters*, 21.

41
"The Day Lady Died," in *Collected Poems*, 325.

42
O'Hara, "A Step Away from Them," in *Collected Poems*, 257.

43
O'Hara, "[There's nothing more beautiful]" (1958), in *Poems Retrieved*, 190.

44
O'Hara, interview with Lucie-Smith, 3.

45
Interview with the author, 6 March 1998.

46
Homage to Frank O'Hara, 218.

47
Interview with the author, 6 March 1998.

48
Ashton, *The New York School: A Cultural Reckoning* (New York: Penguin, 1972), 196.

49
See Irving Sandler, "Avant-Garde Artists of Greenwich Village," in Rick Beard and Leslie Cohen Berlowitz, eds., *Greenwich Village: Culture and Counterculture* (New Brunswick: Rutgers University Press, 1993), 325.

50
O'Hara, "Larry Rivers: A Memoir," in *Standing Still and Walking* in New York, 169.

51
O'Hara, quoted in Robert Saltonstall Mattison, *Grace Hartigan: A Painter's World* (New York: Hudson Hills Press, 1990), 28.

52
O'Hara, interview with Lucie-Smith, 21.

53
O'Hara, "Larry Rivers: A Memoir," in *Standing Still and Walking in New York*, 169.

54
O'Hara,"Larry Rivers: A Memoir", 170.

55
"How to Proceed in the Arts," in O'Hara, *Art Chronicles 1954-1966* (New York: Braziller, 1975), 98.

56
Grosman, quoted by Calvin Tompkins, in *The Scene: Reports on Post-Modern Art* (New York: Viking, 1976), 62.

57
O'Hara, interview with Lucie-Smith, 4.

58
Rivers's own description in "Life Among the Stones," *Location* (Spring 1963): 93.

59
LeSueur, unpublished typescript.

60
Bluhm, "26 things at once," *Lingo* 7 (1997): 11.

61
"To Richard Miller" (1958), in *Collected Poems*, 301.

62
Du Plessix, "Painters and Poets," in *Art in America* 53, no. 5 (October-November 1965): 24.

63
Alfred Leslie, interview with the author, 1998.

64
Freilicher, in *Homage to Frank O'Hara*, 23.

65
Freilicher, interview with the author, 30 November 1998.

66
O'Hara, *Art Chronicles*, 4.

67
Rivers, in *Homage to Frank O'Hara*, 57.

68
O'Hara, interview with Lucie-Smith, 22.

69
O'Hara's own take on such rhetoric is expressed in an obviously occasional poem:

> Have you ever wanted
> to get in the ring
> with Tolstoy?
>
> no, but I want
> to get into bed
> with you
>
> how's that?

"[Have you ever wanted]," *Poems Retrieved*, 191.

70
O'Hara, interview with Lucie-Smith, 9.

71
O'Hara, review in *Art News* (April 1954), reprinted in *What's With Modern Art?*, 14.

72
Neel, in Patricia Hills, *Alice Neel* (New York: Harry N. Abrams, 1983), 103.

73
Allara, *Pictures of People: Alice Neel's American Portrait Gallery* (Hanover, N.H.: Brandeis University Press, 1998), 167.

74
Neel, in Hills, 103. In the 1950s Beckmann taught at the Brooklyn Museum School.

75
Elaine de Kooning, in *Homage to Frank O'Hara*, 97.

76
Michael Leja has explored this topic in depth in his *Reframing Abstract Expressionism: Subjectivity and Painting in the 1940s* (New Haven: Yale University Press, 1993).

77
O'Hara, quoted in Selden Rodman, *Conversations with Artists* (New York: Devin-Adair, 1957), 82.

78
O'Hara, "Nocturne" (1955), in *Collected Poems*, 225.

79
Warhol, *The Philosophy of Andy Warhol (From A to B and Back Again)* (New York: Harcourt Brace Jovanovich, 1975), 81.

80
Collected Poems, 256.

81
Motherwell, in O'Hara, *Robert Motherwell* (New York: The Museum of Modern Art, 1965), 59.

82
Chauncey, *Gay New York: Gender, Urban Culture, and the Makings of the Gay Male World, 1890-1940* (New York: Basic Books, 1994), 6.

83
O'Hara, "[There's nothing more beautiful]" (1958), in *Poems Retrieved*, 190.

84
Collected Poems, 223-24. Novak remembers that they would go quite regularly to The Old Place "when we were tired of the San Remo, which was home" (telephone interview with the author, 10 February 1999).

85
Button, quoted by Stuart Byron in "Frank O'Hara: Poetic 'Queertalk'", in Elledge, *Frank O'Hara: To Be True to a City*, 66.

86
O'Hara, "An Image of Leda," in *Collected Poems*, 36.

87
Button, "Frank's Grace," in *Homage to Frank O'Hara*, 42.

88
"Second Avenue" (1953), "F.M.I. 6/25/61" (1961), and "Biotherm (for Bill Berkson)" (1962), in *Collected Poems*, 144, 411, and 437.

89
Sontag, "Notes on Camp'" (1964), in *Against Interpretation* (New York: Anchor, 1966), 280.

90
"John Button Birthday," in *Collected Poems*, 268.

91
See Gooch, *City Poet*, 359-60.

92
Collected Poems, 441.

93
LeSueur, unpublished manuscript, 1998.

94
Goldberg, interview with the author, 6 March 1998.

95
Letter to Vincent Warren, quoted in Gooch, 347.

96
Goldberg, interview with the author, 6 March 1998.

97
"[Now it seems far away and gentle]" (c. 1957), in *Poems Retrieved*, 160.

98
O'Hara, "Larry Rivers: A Memoir," in *Standing Still and Walking in New York*, 169.

99
Andy Warhol and Pat Hackett, *POPism: the Warhol '60s* (New York: Harper and Row, 1980), 15.

100
O'Hara, "Personism: A Manifesto" (1959), in *Collected Poems*, 498.

101
Rexroth, 3.

102
O'Hara, "Art Chronicle," in *Art Chronicles 1954-1966*, 9.

103
Oldenburg (1961), in *Claes Oldenburg: An Anthology* (New York: Solomon R. Guggenheim Museum, 1995), 96.

104
Kozloff, "Pop Culture, Metaphysical Disgust, and the New Vulgarians" (1962), in *Renderings: Critical Essays on a Century of Modern Art* (New York: Simon and Schuster, 1968), 221.

105
Pearl K. Bell on O'Hara's *Collected Poems*, quoted in Reva Wolf, *Andy Warhol, Poetry and Gossip in the 1960s* (Chicago: The University of Chicago Press, 1997), 17.

106
Quoted in Gooch, 394.

107
Quoted in Gooch, 394.

108
Rosenblum, "Remembering Joe Brainard," in *Joe Brainard: Retrospective* (New York: Tibor de Nagy, 1997), 7.

109
For an in-depth study of Warhol's relations with the poetry world, see Wolf, *Andy Warhol, Poetry, and Gossip in the 1960s*.

110
O'Hara, "The Grand Manner of Motherwell" (1965), in *Standing Still and Walking in New York*, 175.

111
Collected Poems, 360.

112
"Personism: A Manifesto," in *Collected Poems*, 499.

113
Katz, interview, October 1998.

114
O'Hara, "Alex Katz" (1966), in *Alex Katz: Twenty Five Years of Painting* (London: Saatchi, 1997), 159.

115
Rasmussen, "Frank O'Hara in the Museum," in *Homage to Frank O'Hara*, 86.

116
O'Hara, "F.Y.I. #371 (The Nun)," in *Poems Retrieved*, 212.

117
Berkson, "A New York Beginner," in *Modern Painters* (Autumn 1998): 51-52.

118
Ashbery, "A Reminiscence," in *Homage to Frank O'Hara*, 22.

119
"The Grand Manner of Motherwell," in *Standing Still and Walking in New York*, 176.

120
"The Grand Manner of Motherwell," 179.

121
Archives, Dedalus Foundation, New York.

122
Lehman, *The Last Avant-Garde*, 306.

123
"Poem" (1959), in *Collected Poems*, 340.

124
O'Hara, *Robert Motherwell*, 10.

125
Ashbery, "Frank OHara's Question," 6. O'Hara was certainly not disengaged, however, "watching the botching of military governments, the crippling of the U.N., the ineffectual expediency of our national policies, and the mishandling of the atomic bomb, has been a bitter experience," he wrote (Lehman, 40).

126
Howard, "Frank O'Hara: 'Since Once We Are We Always Will Be in This Life Come What May,'" in Elledge, *To Be True to a City*, 114-115.

127
Varnedoe, *Jasper Johns: A Retrospective* (New York: The Museum of Modern Art, 1996), 18.

128
Johns, "Sketchbook Notes" (c. 1963-64), in *Jasper Johns: Writings, Sketchbook Notes, Interviews* (New York: The Museum of Modern Art, 1996), 54.

129
Johns, interview with David Sylvester, 1965, in *Jasper Johns: Writings, Sketchbook Notes, Interviews*, 116.

130
Johns, interview with Christian Geelhaar (1978), in *Jasper Johns: Writings, Sketchbook Notes, Interviews*, 193.

131
Johns, quoted in Gooch, *City Poet*, 332.

132
Collected Poems, 252-53.

133
Hartigan, quoted in Perloff, *Poet Among Painters*, 141.

134
Roth, "The Aesthetic of Indifference," *Artforum* (November 1977): 52.

135
Orton, *Figuring Jasper Johns* (Cambridge: Harvard University Press, 1994), 62.

136
Kenneth Silver, "Modes of Disclosure: The Construction of Gay Identity and the Rise of Pop Art," in Paul Schimmel and Donna De Salvo, *Hand-Painted Pop: American Art in Transition*, 1955-62 (Los Angeles: The Museum of Contemporary Art, 1992), 183.

137
Orton, 72-73.

138
"[Dear Jap]," in *Collected Poems*, 471.

139
See Jonathan Katz, "The Art of Code: Jasper Johns and Robert Rauschenberg," in Whitney Chadwick and Isabelle de Courtivron, eds., *Significant Others: Creativity and Intimate Partnership* (London: Thames and Hudson, 1993), 202.

140
See Riva Castleman, *Jasper Johns: A Print Retrospective* (New York: The Museum of Modern Art, 1986), 19.

141
Bluhm, interview with the author, 20 August 1998.

142
"Rhapsody," in *Collected Poems*, 326.

143
"In Favor of One's Time," in *Collected Poems*, 342.

144
"John Button Birthday," in *Collected Poems*, 268.

145
O'Hara's statement for *The New American Poetry* (1959), reprinted in *Collected Poems*, 500.

146
Collected Poems, 325.

147
"Poem," in *Collected Poems*, 244.

Checklist

U.S.A. Poetry: Frank O'Hara, 1966 **(pp. 35, 157)**
Laserdisc (originally 16mm)
Produced and directed by Richard Moore
Courtesy of Thirteen/WNET New York

Norman Bluhm

Backdrop Sketch for Loves Labor, *a play by Frank O'Hara*, 1959 **(p. 49)**
Watercolor and ink on brown paper
43 x 68 in.
Courtesy of the artist's family

Norman Bluhm & Frank O'Hara

Bang, 1960 **(p. 63)**
Gouache and ink on paper
19¼ x 14 in.
Grey Art Gallery and Study Center. New York University Art Collection.
Gift of Norman Bluhm

Chicago, 1960 **(p. 62)**
Gouache and ink on paper
14 x 19¼ in.
Grey Art Gallery and Study Center.
New York University Art Collection.
Gift of Norman Bluhm

The Endless House, 1960 **(p. 67)**
Gouache and ink on paper
19¼ x 14 in.
Grey Art Gallery and Study Center.
New York University Art Collection.
Gift of Norman Bluhm

A Haiku, 1960 **(p. 59)**
Gouache and ink on paper
19¼ x 14 in.
Courtesy of the artist's family, Vermont

Hand, 1960 **(p. 61)**
Gouache and ink on paper
19¼ x 14 in.
Grey Art Gallery and Study Center.
New York University Art Collection.
Gift of Norman Bluhm

Help! I am Alive!, 1960 **(p. 65)**
Gouache and ink on paper
19¼ x 14 in.
Grey Art Gallery and Study Center.
New York University Art Collection.
Gift of Norman Bluhm

I'm So Tired, 1960 **(p. 63)**
Gouache and ink on paper
19¼ x 14 in.
Grey Art Gallery and Study Center.
New York University Art Collection.
Gift of Norman Bluhm

May!, 1960 **(p. 65)**
Gouache and ink on paper
19¼ x 14 in.
Grey Art Gallery and Study Center.
New York University Art Collection.
Gift of Norman Bluhm

Meet Me In the Park, 1960 **(p. 64)**
Gouache and ink on paper
19¼ x 14 in.
Grey Art Gallery and Study Center.
New York University Art Collection.
Gift of Norman Bluhm

Noël, 1960 **(p. 66)**
Gouache and ink on paper
19¼ x 14 in.
Grey Art Gallery and Study Center.
New York University Art Collection.
Gift of Norman Bluhm

There I Was, 1960 **(p. 66)**
Gouache and ink on paper
19¼ x 14 in.
Grey Art Gallery and Study Center.
New York University Art Collection.
Gift of Norman Bluhm

This Is The First, 1960 **(p. 67)**
Gouache and ink on paper
19¼ x 14 in.
Grey Art Gallery and Study Center.
New York University Art Collection.
Gift of Norman Bluhm

Joe Brainard

C Comics No. 2, c. 1966 **(pp. 104-105)**
11x 8½ in. (closed)
The Museum of Contemporary Art, Los Angeles

Joe Brainard & Frank O'Hara

"Guess Where I Found This?!!", 1964 **(p. 108)**
Collage and ink on paper
10⅛ x 8⅛ in.
Collection of Jack Larson, Los Angeles

"Have You Seen Dr. Strangelove Yet? It's Quite Articulate, Very Fine", 1964 **(p. 109)**
Collage and ink on paper
10 x 8 in.
Collection of Luke Matthiessen, East Northport, New York

"I Grew This Mustache. . .", 1964 **(p. 14)**
Collage and ink on paper
13 x 9¾ in.
Collection of Bill Berkson, San Francisco

"I'm Not Really Flying I'm Thinking", 1964 **(p. 111)**
Collage and ink on paper
10 x 8 in.
Collection of Bill Berkson, San Francisco

"Is That the Height of Your Ambition Johnny?", 1964 **(p. 110)**
Collage and ink on paper
10⅛ x 8⅛ in.
Collection of Jack Larson, Los Angeles

"There's Something Very Funny About Us. . .", 1964 **(p. 106)**
Ink on paper
10 x 8 in.
Collection of Joe LeSueur, East Hampton, New York

Untitled (Cherries), 1964 **(p. 112)**
Ink and collage on paper
13½ x 10¾ in.
Collection of Kenneth Koch, New York

"Well, I Never Said It Was Spring", 1964 **(p. 113)**
Collage and ink on paper
10⅛ x 8⅛ in.
Collection of Jack Larson,
Los Angeles

"Why Are They Always Staring???", 1964 **(p. 114)**
Collage and ink on paper
10 x 8 in.
Collection of Joe LeSueur,
East Hampton, New York

For Patsy, c. 1964 **(p. 115)**
Ink and collage on paper
13¾ x 10¾ in.
Collection of Luke Matthiessen,
East Northport, New York

Red Rydler and Dog, c. 1964 **(p. 107)**
Ink on paper (two sheets)
14 x 17 in.
Collection of Ron and Pat Padgett,
New York

Untitled, ("I Sure Wish George Would Hurry Up..."), c. 1964
Ink on paper
13 x 10 in.
Collection Dan Wagoner

Untitled, c. 1964
Collage and ink on paper
9½ x 7½ in.
Collection Maureen O'Hara

Untitled, ("When I Think of What We Once Meant to Each Other!..."), c. 1964
Ink on paper
13 x 10 in.
Collection Dan Wagoner

John Button

Swimmer, c. 1956 **(p. 40)**
Oil on canvas
23½ x 30 in.
Collection of John Bergman,
New York

The Dancer, 1961 **(p. 41)**
Oil on canvas
32 x 23½ in.
Collection of Joe LeSueur,
East Hampton, New York

Wynn Chamberlain

Poets (Joe Brainard, Frank O'Hara, Joe LeSueur, Frank Lima) (Clothed), 1964 **(p. 96)**
Oil on canvas
66 x 45 in.
Collection of Mr. and Mrs. Earl
McGrath, New York

Poets (Joe Brainard, Frank O'Hara, Joe LeSueur, Frank Lima) (Naked), 1964 **(p. 97)**
Oil on canvas
66 x 45 in.
Collection of Mr. and Mrs. Earl
McGrath, New York

Elaine de Kooning

Frank O'Hara, 1962 **(p. 88)**
Oil on canvas
93 x 42 in.
Collection of Ariel Follett O'Hara,
Chicago, and J. Philip O'Hara,
Providence

Willem de Kooning

Untitled, c. 1950 **(p. 90)**
Pencil on paper board
13 x 10 in.
Collection Maureen O'Hara

Two Women with Still Life, 1952 **(p. 25)**
Pastel and charcoal on paper
22¼ x 18¾ in.
The Museum of Contemporary Art,
Los Angeles
Bequest of Marcia Simon Weisman

Jane Freilicher

Frank O'Hara, 1951 **(p. 78)**
Oil on canvas
65 x 23 in.
Collection of Ariel Follett O'Hara,
Chicago, and J. Philip O'Hara,
Providence

Early New York Evening, 1953-54 **(p. 37)**
Oil on canvas
51½ x 31¾ in.
Collection of Elizabeth Hazan,
Courtesy Tibor de Nagy Gallery,
New York

Michael Goldberg

Sardines, 1955 **(p. 23)**
Oil and adhesive tape on canvas
80¼ x 66 in.
National Museum of American Art,
Smithsonian Institution, Gift of Mr.
and Mrs. David K. Anderson,
Martha Jackson Memorial Collection

Dear Diary, 1962 **(pp. 71-74)**
Oil and collage on paper (six sheets)
14 x 16 in. each
Collection of the artist, New York

Michael Goldberg & Frank O'Hara

Ode on Necrophilia, 1960 **(p. 70)**
Silkscreen
17 x 14 in.
Collection of Joe LeSueur,
East Hampton, New York

Odes, 1960 **(p. 69)**
Book with silkscreen and letterpress prints on paper
18 x 14¼ in. (closed)
State University of New York at
Buffalo, Poetry/Rare Books Collection

Philip Guston

Frank, 1955 **(p. 19)**
Pencil on paper
11 x 8½ in.
Collection of Bill Berkson,
San Francisco

Grace Hartigan

Oranges No. 1, 1952 **(p. 44)**
Oil on paper
44¼ x 33½ in.
State University of New York at
Buffalo, Poetry/Rare Books Collection,
David and Becky Anderson
Collection

Oranges No. 7, 1952 **(p. 45)**
Oil on paper
44¼ x 33½ in.
Collection Mr. and Mrs. Richard P.
Doerer, Grosse Point, Michigan

The Masker, 1954 **(p. 92)**
Oil on canvas
72 x 42 in.
The Frances Lehman Loeb Art Center, Vassar College, Poughkeepsie, New York

Jasper Johns

In Memory of My Feelings—Frank O'Hara, 1961 **(p. 129)**
Oil on canvas with objects
40¼ x 60 x 2⅞ in.
Collection of Museum of Contemporary Art, Chicago, Partial Gift of Apollo Plastics Corporation

Memory Piece (Frank O'Hara), 1961-70 **(p. 133)**
Wood, lead, brass, rubber, sand and sculp-metal
6½–18⅜ x 6¾ x 13 in.
Collection of the artist

Skin with O'Hara Poem, 1963-65 **(p. 136)**
Lithograph
22 x 34 in.
Collection of Jack Larson, Los Angeles

Pinion, 1966 **(p. 135)**
Lithograph
40 x 28 in.
Courtesy Margo Leavin Gallery, Los Angeles

Study for "In Memory of My Feelings", 1967 **(p. 132)**
Ink and pencil on plastic
14⅛ x 11 in.
Collection of the artist

Study for "In Memory of My Feelings", 1967 **(p. 132)**
Ink and pencil on plastic
12½ x 19 in.
Collection of the artist

Larry Johnson

Untitled (Standing Still and Walking in Los Angeles), 1994 **(p. 144)**
Ektacolor photograph
45⅞ x 87¼ in.
The Museum of Contemporary Art, Los Angeles
Purchased with funds provided by James Burrows and Linda Burrows

Howard Kanovitz

The New Yorkers, 1967 **(p. 38)**
Lightbox with Plexiglas, cutouts and photos
18 x 22½ x 5¼ in.
Collection of Mr. and Mrs. Earl McGrath, New York

Alex Katz

Frank O'Hara, 1959-60 **(cover, pp. 120-121)**
Oil on wood
60 x 15 in.
Courtesy of Robert Miller Gallery, New York

Marine and Sailor, 1961 **(p. 99)**
Oil on panel
19 x 44 in.
Courtesy of Robert Miller Gallery, New York

Here's To You, 1962 **(p. 95)**
Oil on canvas
24 x 32⅛ in.
Collection of Jack Larson, Los Angeles

Franz Kline & Frank O'Hara

Plate from *21 Etchings and Poems*, 1960 **(p. 75)**
Photogravure with etching
8$\frac{5}{16}$ x 14$\frac{7}{16}$ in.
Collection of Sarah Lawrence College Library, Bronxville, New York

Lee Krasner

Untitled (Study for Frank O'Hara Illustration), 1967 **(p. 102)**
Ink on paper
14 x 11 in.
Collection of Mr. and Mrs. Eugene V. Thaw, Santa Fe, New Mexico

Alfred Leslie

The Last Clean Shirt, 1964 **(p. 76)**
Black-and-white film on laserdisc
44 minutes
Courtesy of the artist and Boil & Squeal Gallery, New York

Poem "Á la recherche d' Gertrude Stein", 1967 **(p. 77)**
India ink on mylar
26½ x 33 in.
Courtesy of the artist and Boil & Squeal Gallery, New York

Study for The Killing Cycle *(I have the other idea about guilt)*, 1967 **(p. 139)**
Watercolor on paper
30 x 41 in.
Courtesy of the artist and Boil & Squeal Gallery, New York

Study for The Killing Cycle *(You don't say the victim is responsible)*, 1967 **(p. 140)**
Watercolor on paper
30 x 41 in.
Courtesy of the artist and Boil & Squeal Gallery, New York

Study for The Killing Cycle *(Ours is a moral landscape)*, 1967 **(p. 141)**
Watercolor on paper
30 x 41 in.
Courtesy of the artist and Boil & Squeal Gallery, New York

Fred W. McDarrah

Frank O'Hara in his flat, 441 East 9th Street, New York, September 26, 1959 **(p. 2)**
Black-and-white photograph
16 x 20 in.
Collection of the artist, New York

Frank O'Hara reading at a benefit for Yugen Press at the Living Theater, 530 Sixth Avenue, New York, November 2, 1959 **(p. 103)**
Black-and-white photograph
16 x 20 in.
Collection of the artist, New York

Frank O'Hara at The Museum of Modern Art, New York, January 20, 1960 **(p. 119)**
Black-and-white photograph
16 x 20 in.
Collection of the artist, New York

Frank O'Hara in The Museum of Modern Art's Sculpture Garden, January 20, 1960, with Auguste Rodin's *St. John the Baptist Preaching* **(p. 117)**
Black-and-white photograph
16 x 20 in.
Collection of the artist, New York

Robert Motherwell

Untitled (Elegy), 1950 **(p. 125)**
Oil on linen
30 x 38 in.
Collection of the Dedalus Foundation, New York

Night Beside the Sea, 1962 **(p. 137)**
Oil on paper
29 x 23 in.
Collection of the Dedalus Foundation, New York

Automatism #2A (For Frank O'Hara), 1965 **(p. 124)**
Acrylic and oil on paper
26 x 20 in.
Collection of the Dedalus Foundation, New York

Hans Namuth

Frank O'Hara and Larry Rivers at work on *Stones*, 1958 **(p. 50)**
Black-and-white photograph
16 x 20 in.
Courtesy of Hans Namuth Ltd., New York

Frank O'Hara and Larry Rivers at work on *Stones*, 1958 **(p. 51)**
Black-and-white photograph
16 x 20 in.
Courtesy of Hans Namuth Ltd., New York

Alice Neel

Frank O'Hara, 1960 **(p. 86)**
Oil on canvas
34 x 16⅛ in.
National Portrait Gallery, Smithsonian Institution, Washington, D.C., Gift of Hartley S. Neel

Frank O'Hara No. 2, 1960 **(p. 87)**
Oil on canvas
38 x 24 in.
The Estate of the artist. Courtesy of Robert Miller Gallery, New York

Frank O'Hara

Oranges, 1953 **(p. 47)**
Bound mimeographs with painted cover by Grace Hartigan
11⅓ x 9 in. (closed)
State University of New York at Buffalo, Poetry/Rare Books Collection, David and Becky Anderson Collection

Untitled, c. 1957 **(p. 48)**
Watercolor on paper
12 x 16 in.
Estate of John Button, New York

Ode on Necrophilia, 1960 **(p. 70)**
Ink on paper
18 x 14¼ in.
Collection of Michael Goldberg, New York

Untitled ("Down at the Box Office"), 1961 **(p. 48)**
Collage and ink on paper
8½ x 11 in.
Collection of Bill Berkson, San Francisco

Fabrizio del Dongo, c. 1962 **(p. 46)**
Ink and pencil on paper
4 x 3 in.
Collection of Bill Berkson, San Francisco

Journal, 1966 **(p. 142)**
Notebook
8 x 6 x 1 in.
Collection Joe LeSueur, East Hampton, New York

In Memory of My Feelings, 1967 **(pp. 29-34)**
Loose-leaf book of poems by O'Hara with illustrations by artists published as a memorial volume by The Museum of Modern Art, New York
12¾ x 9½ in. (closed)
The Museum of Contemporary Art, Los Angeles

Claes Oldenburg

Pie A La Mode, 1962
Plaster-soaked muslin
20 x 13 x 19 in.
The Museum of Contemporary Art, Los Angeles
The Panza Collection

White Shirt on a Chair, 1962 **(p. 100)**
Plaster-soaked muslin
39¾ x 30 x 25 in.
The Museum of Contemporary Art, Los Angeles
The Panza Collection

Jackson Pollock

Untitled, 1943 **(p. 26)**
Collage and ink on paper
15⅜ x 13½ in.
The Museum of Contemporary Art, Los Angeles
Bequest of Marcia Simon Weisman

Fairfield Porter

Male Nude (Frank O'Hara), 1954 **(p. 83)**
Pencil on paper
17 x 14 in.
The Estate of Fairfield Porter. Courtesy of Hirschl & Adler Modern, New York

Untitled Male Nude (in Boots), 1954 **(p. 83)**
Pencil on paper
22 x 17 in.
The Estate of Fairfield Porter. Courtesy of Hirschl & Adler Modern, New York

Portrait of Frank O'Hara, 1957 **(p. 84)**
Oil on canvas
63⅞ x 45⅞ in.
The Toledo Museum of Art;
Purchased with funds from the
Libbey Endowment,
Gift of Edward Drummond Libbey

Larry Rivers

O'Hara Nude with Boots, 1954 **(p. 81)**
Oil on canvas
97 x 53 in.
Collection of the artist, New York

Larry Rivers & Frank O'Hara

Stones: Inner Folder, 1957–60 **(p. 52)**
Linen cuttings and blue denim
19 x 23½ in.
Courtesy of Marlborough Gallery,
New York

Stones: The End of All Existences, 1957 **(p. 54)**
Hand-colored lithograph
19 x 23½ in.
Courtesy of Marlborough Gallery,
New York

Stones: US, 1957 **(p. 53)**
Hand-colored lithograph
19 x 23½ in.
Courtesy of Marlborough Gallery,
New York

Stones: Five O'Clock, 1958 **(p. 57)**
Hand-colored lithograph
19 x 23½ in.
Courtesy of Marlborough Gallery,
New York

Stones: Love, 1958 **(p. 54)**
Hand-colored lithograph
19 x 23½ in.
Courtesy of Marlborough Gallery,
New York

Stones: Melancholy Breakfast, 1958 **(p. 56)**
Hand-colored lithograph
19 x 23½ in.
Courtesy of Marlborough Gallery,
New York

Stones: Springtemps, 1958 **(p. 53)**
Hand-colored lithograph
19 x 23½ in.
Courtesy of Marlborough Gallery,
New York

Stones: Students, 1958 **(p. 55)**
Hand-colored lithograph
19 x 23½ in.
Courtesy of Marlborough Gallery,
New York

Stones: To the Entertainment of Patsy and Mike Goldberg, 1958 **(p. 56)**
Hand-colored lithograph
19 x 23½ in.
Courtesy of Marlborough Gallery,
New York

Stones: Where Are They, 1958 **(p. 58)**
Hand-colored lithograph
19 x 23½ in.
Courtesy of Marlborough Gallery,
New York

Stones: Will We Ever Get, 1958 **(p. 58)**
Hand-colored lithograph
19 x 23½ in.
Courtesy of Marlborough Gallery,
New York

Stones: Berdie, 1959 **(p. 55)**
Hand-colored lithograph
19 x 23½ in.
Courtesy of Marlborough Gallery,
New York

Stones: Energy, 1959 **(p. 57)**
Hand-colored lithograph
19 x 23½ in.
Courtesy of Marlborough Gallery,
New York

Stones: Title Page, 1959 **(p. 52)**
Hand-colored lithograph
19 x 23½ in.
Courtesy of Marlborough Gallery,
New York

Selected Bibliography

Agee, William. *Fairfield Porter: An American Painter*. Southampton, New York: The Parrish Art Museum, 1993.

Alex Katz. Valencia: IVAM Centre Julio Gonzalez, 1996.

Alex Katz from the Early 60s. New York: Robert Miller Gallery, 1987.

Allara, Pamela. *Pictures of People: Alice Neel's American Portrait Gallery*. Hanover, N.H.: Brandeis University Press, 1998.

Allen, Donald M., ed. *The New American Poetry: 1945-1960*. New York: Grove Press, 1960.

Arnason, H. H. *Robert Motherwell*. 2nd edition. New York: Harry N. Abrams, 1982.

Altieri, Charles. *Enlarging the Temple: New Directions in American Poetry During the 1960's*. Lewisburg: Bucknell University Press, 1979.

Arnason, H. H. *Robert Motherwell*. 2nd edition. New York: Harry N. Abrams, 1982.

Art With the Touch of a Poet: Frank O'Hara. Storrs, Connecticut: William Benton Museum of Art, 1983.

Ashbery, John. "Frank O'Hara's Question." *Book Week* 25 (September 1966): 6.

———. *Reported Sightings: Art Chronicles 1957-1987*. New York: Alfred Knopf, 1989.

———. Review of *In Memory of My Feelings*. *Art News* 66, no. 9 (January 1968): 50-51, 67-68.

———. *Selected Poems*. New York: Viking, 1985.

Ashton, Dore. "Migratory Passings: Some Thoughts on Poetry and Painting." *Arshile* 5 (1996): 111-115.

———. *The New York School: A Cultural Reckoning*. Harmondsworth: Penguin, 1972.

Balken, Debra Bricker. *Philip Guston's Poem-Pictures*. Andover, Massachusetts: Addison Gallery of American Art, 1994.

Banes, Sally. *Greenwich Village 1963: Avant-Garde Performance and the Effervescent Body*. Durham: Duke University Press, 1993.

Belgrad, Daniel. *The Culture of Spontaneity: Improvisation and the Arts in Postwar America*. Chicago: The University of Chicago Press, 1998.

Berkson, Bill. "A New York Beginner." *Modern Painters* (Autumn 1998): 49-53.

———. "Bluhm Paints a Picture." *Art News* 62, no. 3 (May 1963): 38-41, 50, 52.

———. *Elaine de Kooning: Portraits*. New York: Salander O'Reilly, 1999.

———. "Poet and Painter Coda." In *Franz Kline: Art and the Structure of Identity*. Edited by Stephen C. Foster, 141-153. Barcelona: Fundació Tàpies, 1994.

Berkson, Bill, and Joe LeSueur, eds. *Homage to Frank O'Hara*. Berkeley: Creative Arts Book Co., 1980.

Bledsoe, Jane K. *Elaine de Kooning*. Athens: Georgia Museum of Art, 1992.

Bluhm, Norman. "26 things at once." *Lingo* 7 (1997): 10–18.

Boone, Bruce. "Gay Language as Political Praxis: The Poetry of Frank O'Hara." *Social Text* 1 (Winter 1979): 59-92.

Brainard, Joe. *I Remember*. New York: Penguin, 1995.

Breslin, James E.B. *From Modern to Contemporary: American Poetry, 1945–1965*. Chicago: The University of Chicago Press, 1984.

Campbell, Lawrence. "Elaine de Kooning: Portraits in a New York Scene." *Art News* 62, no. 2 (April 1963): 38-39, 63-64.

Castleman, Riva. *Jasper Johns: A Print Retrospective*. New York: The Museum of Modern Art, 1986.

Chassman, Neil A. *Poets of the Cities: New York and San Francisco, 1950–65*. Dallas: Dallas Museum of Fine Arts, 1974.

Dancers on a Plane: Cage, Cunningham, Johns. London: Anthony d'Offay Gallery, 1989.

Dannatt, Adrian. "Norman Bluhm." *The Independent* (20 February 1999).

De Kooning, Elaine. *The Spirit of Abstract Expressionism: Selected Writings*. New York: Braziller, 1994.

De Salvo, Donna, and Paul Schimmel. *Hand-Painted Pop: American Art in Transition, 1955-62*. Los Angeles: The Museum of Contemporary Art, 1992.

Denby, Edwin. *Dancers, Buildings and People in the Streets*. Introduction by Frank O'Hara. New York: Horizon, 1965.

Diggory, Terence. *Grace Hartigan and the Poets: Paintings and Prints*. Saratoga Springs, New York: Skidmore College, 1993.

————. "Questions of Identity in *Oranges* by Frank O'Hara and Grace Hartigan." *Art Journal* 52, no. 4 (Winter 1993): 41–50.

Di Prima, Diane. *Memoirs of a Beatnik*. New York: Olympia, 1969.

Doty, Robert M. *John Button*. Essays by Bill Berkson and Robert Rosenblum. Manchester, N. H.: The Currier Gallery of Art, 1989.

Elledge, Jim, ed. *Frank O'Hara: To Be True to a City*. Ann Arbor: The University of Michigan Press, 1990.

Feldman, Alan. *Frank O'Hara*. Boston: Twayne Publishers, 1979.

Ferdani, Roberto. *O'Hara, Bluhm & Goldberg: Un Poeta e Due Pittori a New York Negli Anni 50*. Chiavari, Italy: Centro per l'Arte Contemporanea di Palazzo Rocca, 1999.

Francis, Richard. *Jasper Johns*. New York: Abbeville, 1984.

Frank O'Hara, A Poet Among Painters. New York: Whitney Museum of American Art, 1974.

Frank O'Hara Read, Performed, Remembered. Cambridge: The Poets' Theatre, 1990.

Friedman, B. H. "Young American." *Artforum* 37, no. 8 (April 1999): 30.

Gooch, Brad. *City Poet: The Life and Times of Frank O'Hara*. New York: Alfred Knopf, 1993.

Gruen, John. *The Party's Over Now: Reminiscences of the Fifties*. New York: Viking, 1972.

Guilbaut, Serge. *How New York Stole the Idea of Modern Art: Abstract Expressionism, Freedom, and the Cold War*. Translated by Arthur Goldhammer. Chicago: The University of Chicago Press, 1983.

Hartung, Philip T. "What is Truth?" *The Commonweal* (23 October 1964): 134-136.

Hills, Patricia. *Alice Neel*. New York: Harry N. Abrams, 1983.

Hunter, Sam. *Alex Katz*. New York: Rizzoli, 1992.

————. *Larry Rivers*. New York: Rizzoli, 1989.

Joe Brainard: Retrospective. New York: Tibor de Nagy Gallery, 1997.

Johns, Jasper. *Jasper Johns: Writings, Sketchbook Notes, Interviews*. Edited by Kirk Varnedoe. New York: The Museum of Modern Art, 1996.

Johnston, Jill. *Jasper Johns: Privileged Information*. New York: Thames and Hudson, 1996.

Katz, Alex. *Invented Symbols*. Edited by Vincent Katz. Ostfildern, Germany: Cantz, 1997.

Katz, Jonathan. "The Art of Code: Jasper Johns and Robert Rauschenberg." In *Significant Others*, edited by Whitney Chadwick and Isabelle de Courtivron. London: Thames and Hudson, 1993.

Kertess, Klaus. *Joan Mitchell*. New York: Harry N. Abrams, 1997.

Kingsley, April. *The Turning Point: The Abstract Expressionists and the Transformation of American Art*. New York: Simon and Schuster, 1992.

Koestenbaum, Wayne. *Double Talk: The Erotics of Male Literary Collaboration*. New York: Routledge, 1989.

Lee, Rensselaer W. *Ut Pictura Poesis: The Humanistic Theory of Painting*. New York: Norton, 1967.

Lehman, David. *The Last Avant-Garde: The Making of the New York School of Poets*. New York: Doubleday, 1998.

Leja, Michael. *Reframing Abstract Expressionism: Subjectivity and Painting in the 1940s*. New Haven: Yale University Press, 1993.

Marshall, Richard. *Alex Katz*. New York: Whitney Museum of American Art, 1986.

Mattison, Robert Saltonstall. *Grace Hartigan; A Painter's World*. New York: Hudson Hills Press, 1990.

McDarrah, Fred W. *The Artist's World, in Pictures*. New York: Dutton, 1961.

McDarrah, Fred W., and Gloria S. McDarrah. *Beat Generation: Glory Days in Greenwich Village*. New York: Schirmer, 1996.

Metzger, Robert P. *Reuben Nakian: Centennial Retrospective, 1897-1986*. Reading, Penn: Reading Public Museum, 1998.

The Museum of Modern Art at Mid-Century, At Home and Abroad. Studies in Modern Art 4. New York: The Museum of Modern Art, 1994.

Myers, John Bernard. *Tracking the Marvelous: A Life in the New York Art World*. New York: Random House, 1983.

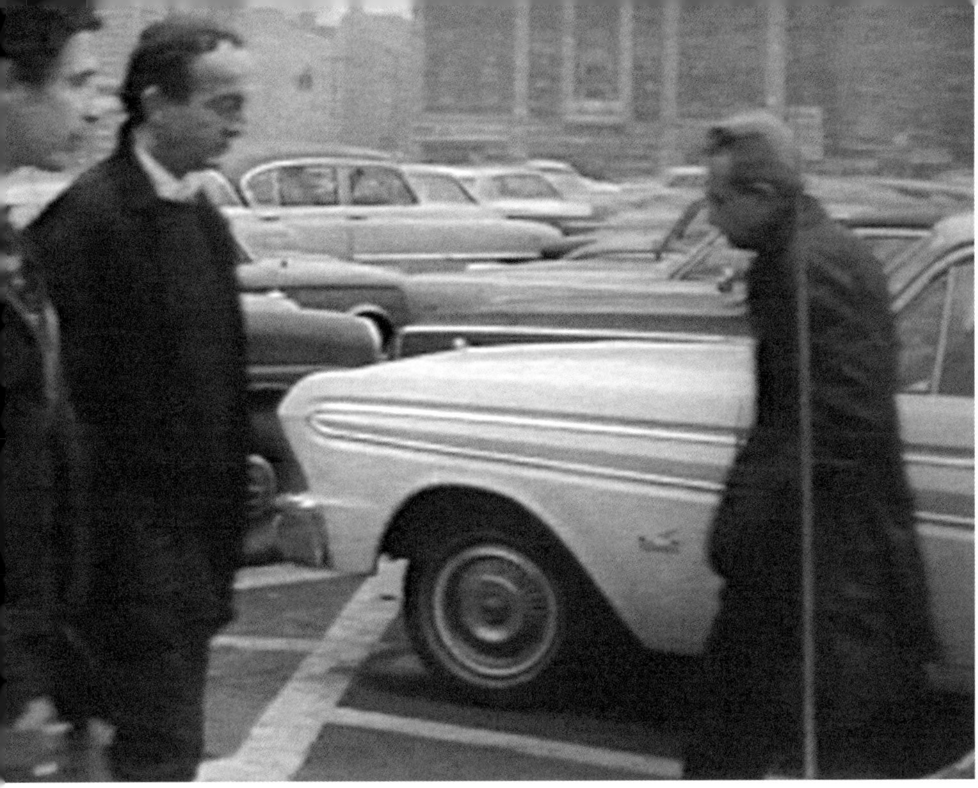

ill from
SA Poetry: Frank O'Hara,
966

Myers, John Bernard, ed. *The Poets of the New York School*. Philadelphia: University of Pennsylvania, 1969.

Naifeh, Steven, and Gregory White Smith. *Jackson Pollock: An American Saga*. New York: Potter, 1989.

Norman Bluhm: A Tribute Exhibition. Essay by James Harithas. Howland, Ohio: The Butler Institute of American Art, 1999.

Notley, Alice. "O'Hara in the Nineties." *Arshile* 6 (1996): 123-137.

O'Hara, Frank. *Amorous Nightmares of Delay: Selected Plays*. Baltimore: Johns Hopkins University Press, 1996.

———. *Art Chronicles, 1954-1966*. 2nd edition. New York: Braziller, 1990.

———. *Biotherm (for Bill Berkson)*. With lithographs by Jim Dine and an essay by Bill Berkson. San Francisco: Arion Press, 1990.

———. *The Collected Poems of Frank O'Hara*. Edited by Donald Allen. Berkeley: University of California Press, 1995.

———. *David Smith*. New York: The Museum of Modern Art, 1966.

———. *Early Writing*. Edited by Donald Allen. Bolinas, California: Grey Fox Press, 1977.

———. *In Memory of My Feelings: A Selection of Poems*. Edited by Bill Berkson. New York: The Museum of Modern Art, 1967.

———. *Jackson Pollock*. New York: Braziller, 1959.

———. *Nakian*. New York: The Museum of Modern Art, 1966.

———. *New Spanish Painting and Sculpture*. New York: The Museum of Modern Art, 1960.

———. *Odes*. New York: Tiber Press, 1960.

———. *Oranges, 12 Pastorals*. New York: Tibor de Nagy Gallery, 1952.

———. *Poems*. With lithographs by Willem de Kooning. New York: The Limited Editions Club, 1989.

———. *Poems Retrieved*. Edited by Donald Allen. San Francisco: Grey Fox Press, 1996.

———. *Robert Motherwell*. New York: The Museum of Modern Art, 1965.

———. *Standing Still and Walking in New York*. Edited by Donald Allen. Bolinas, California: Grey Fox Press, 1975.

———. *Twoja Pojedynczość*. Edited by Piotr Sommer. Warsaw: Pánstwowy Instytut, 1987.

———. *What's With Modern Art?* Edited by Bill Berkson. Austin, Texas: Mike & Dale's Press, 1999.

Orton, Fred. *Figuring Jasper Johns*. Cambridge: Harvard University Press, 1994.

Padgett, Ron, and David Shapiro, eds. *An Anthology of New York Poets*. New York: Random House, 1970.

Parker, Alice C. *The Exploration of the Secret Smile: The Language of Art and Homosexuality in Frank O'Hara's Poetry*. New York: Peter Lang, 1989.

Perl, Jed. "Pop Theater." *Yale Review* (January 1995): 31-75.

Perloff, Marjorie. *Frank O'Hara: Poet Among Painters*. Chicago: The University of Chicago Press, 1998.

———. *Poetry On and Off the Page: Essays for Emergent Occasions*. Evanston: Northwestern University Press, 1998.

Phillips, Lisa. *Beat Culture and the New America: 1950-1965*. New York: Whitney Museum of American Art, 1995.

Prather, Marla. *Willem de Kooning: Paintings*. Essays by David Sylvester and Richard Shiff. Washington, D.C.: National Gallery of Art, 1994.

Rand, Harry. *The Martha Jackson Memorial Collection.* Washington: Smithsonian Institution Press, 1985.

Rivers, Larry, with Arnold Weinstein. *What Did I Do?: The Unauthorized Autobiography.* New York: HarperCollins, 1992.

Rodman, Selden. *Conversations with Artists.* New York: Devin-Adair, 1957.

Rosand, David, ed. *Robert Motherwell on Paper.* New York: Harry N. Abrams, 1997.

Rosenthal, Nan. *The Drawings of Jasper Johns.* Washington: National Gallery of Art, 1990.

Roth, Moira. "The Aesthetic of Indifference." *Artforum* 16, no. 3 (November 1977): 46-53.

Rubenfeld, Florence. *Clement Greenberg: A Life.* New York: Scribner, 1997.

Sandler, Irving. *Alex Katz: A Retrospective.* New York: Harry N. Abrams, 1998.

————. "Avant-Garde Artists of Greenwich Village." In *Greenwich Village: Culture and Counterculture,* edited by Rick Beard and Leslie Cohen Berlowitz, 320-332. New Brunswick: Rutgers University Press, 1993.

————. *The New York School.* New York: Harper & Row, 1978.

————. *The Triumph of American Painting: A History of Abstract Expressionism.* New York: Harper & Row, 1970.

Schimmel, Paul. *Action/Precision: The New Direction in New York, 1955-60.* Newport Beach: Newport Harbor Art Museum, 1984.

Schimmel, Paul, and Judith E. Stein. *The Figurative Fifties: New York Figurative Expressionism.* Newport Beach: Newport Harbor Art Museum, 1988.

Schuyler, James. *The Diary of James Schuyler.* Edited by Nathan Kernan. Santa Rosa, California: Black Sparrow Press, 1997.

————. *Selected Art Writings.* Edited by Simon Pettet. Santa Rosa, California: Black Sparrow Press, 1998.

Shapiro, David, Jeremy Gilbert-Rolfe, and Elisabetta Longari. *Michael Goldberg.* Viterbo: Primaprint, 1997.

Shapiro, David, and Dianne Vanderlip. *Poets and Painters.* Denver: Denver Art Museum, 1979.

Smith, Alexander, Jr. *Frank O'Hara: A Comprehensive Bibliography.* New York: Garland, 1979.

Sontag, Susan. *Against Interpretation: and Other Essays.* New York: Anchor, 1986.

Spike, John. *Fairfield Porter: An American Classic.* New York: Harry N. Abrams, 1992.

Stein, Judith, and David Shapiro. *Alfred Leslie: The Killing Cycle.* St. Louis: The St. Louis Art Museum, 1991.

Stern, Robert A.M., Thomas Mellins, and David Fishman. *New York 1960: Architecture and Urbanism between the Second World War and the Bicentennial.* New York: The Monacelli Press, 1995.

Sylvester, David, ed. *Alex Katz: Twenty Five Years of Painting.* London: Saatchi, 1997.

Varnedoe, Kirk. *Jasper Johns: A Retrospective.* New York: The Museum of Modern Art, 1996.

Varnedoe, Kirk, with Pepe Karmel. *Jackson Pollock.* New York: The Museum of Modern Art, 1998.

Waldman, Diane. *Willem de Kooning.* New York: Harry N. Abrams, 1988.

Wolf, Reva. *Andy Warhol, Poetry, and Gossip in the 1960s.* Chicago: The University of Chicago Press, 1997.

Index

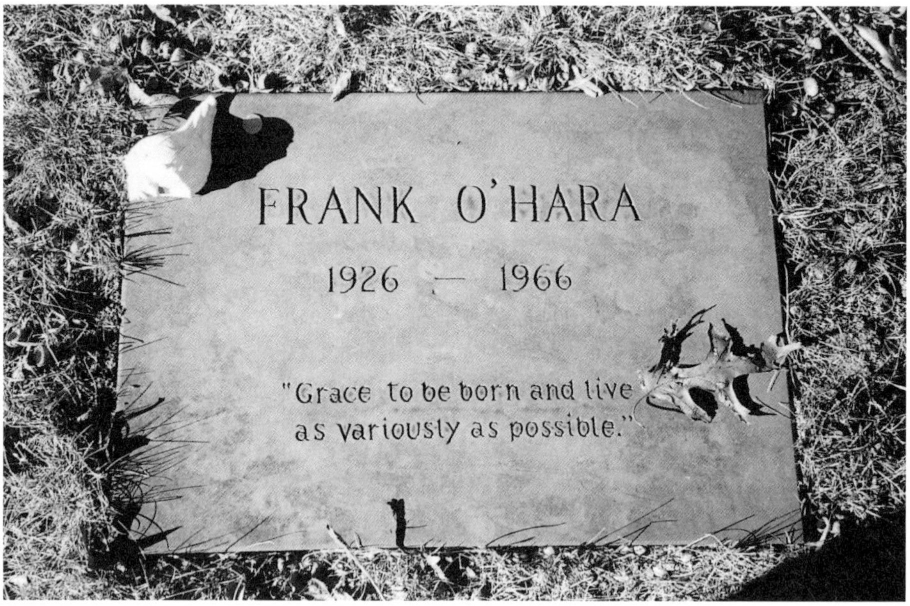

Photo Credits

All photographs appear courtesy of the lenders and/or the following: © Fred W. McDarrah, pages 2, 39, 43, 103, 117, 118; Brian Forrest, pages 14, 19, 29-34, 46-47, 48 top, 69, 70 bottom, 95 (© Alex Katz/ Licensed by VAGA, New York), 104-105, 107-111, 113, 115; © Camilla McGrath, Courtesy Earl McGrath Gallery, page 18; Eric Pollitzer, New York, Courtesy Allan Stone Gallery, page 21; © Douglas M. Parker Studio, Los Angeles, pages 26, 100; Courtesy Tibor de Nagy Gallery, New York, page 37; © Beth Phillips, pages 38, 96-97; Tim Lee, pages 41, 106, 114, 142-143; Anne Diggory, page 45; Don Ross, pages 49, 64 left; © Hans Namuth, pages 50-51; Larry Rivers/Licensed by VAGA, New York, pages 52-58, 81, 91; John D. Schiff, pages 59, 61-63, 65-67; Roy M. Elkind, New York, pages 70 top, 71-74; Photograph © 1999 The Museum of Modern Art, New York, page 75; John Back, pages 77, 139-141; Isberner Photography, Chicago, pages 78, 88; Zindman/Fremont, page 83; Tim Thayer, page 84; © The Estate of Alice Neel, page 86, 87 (Courtesy Robert Miller Gallery); © Alex Katz/Licensed by VAGA, New York, Courtesy Robert Miller Gallery, pages 99, 116, 120-121, and cover; Rudolph Burckhardt, page 98; Photo by Robert McElroy, Courtesy Claes Oldenburg/Coosje van Bruggen, page 101; © 1999 z/s, page 112; Ezra Stoller © Esto. All rights reserved, page 122; © George Cserna, page 123; © 1999 Dedalus Foundation, Inc./Licensed by VAGA, New York, pages 124, 125, 137; © Jasper Johns/Licensed by VAGA, New York, 128, 129 (Photo © Museum of Contemporary Art, Chicago), pages 132-133 (© Dorothy Zeidman), 135, 136 (photo by Rudolph Burckhardt); Robert Rauschenberg/ Licensed by VAGA, New York, 134; and Russell Ferguson, 160.

Editor: **STEPHANIE EMERSON**; *Editorial Assistant:* **JANE HYUN**; *Designers:* **LORRAINE WILD** *with* **BELE DUCKE** *and* **AMANDA WASHBURN**
Printer: **CANTZ**, *Ostfildern*

Frank O'Hara's grave,
Springs Cemetery, Long Island, New York

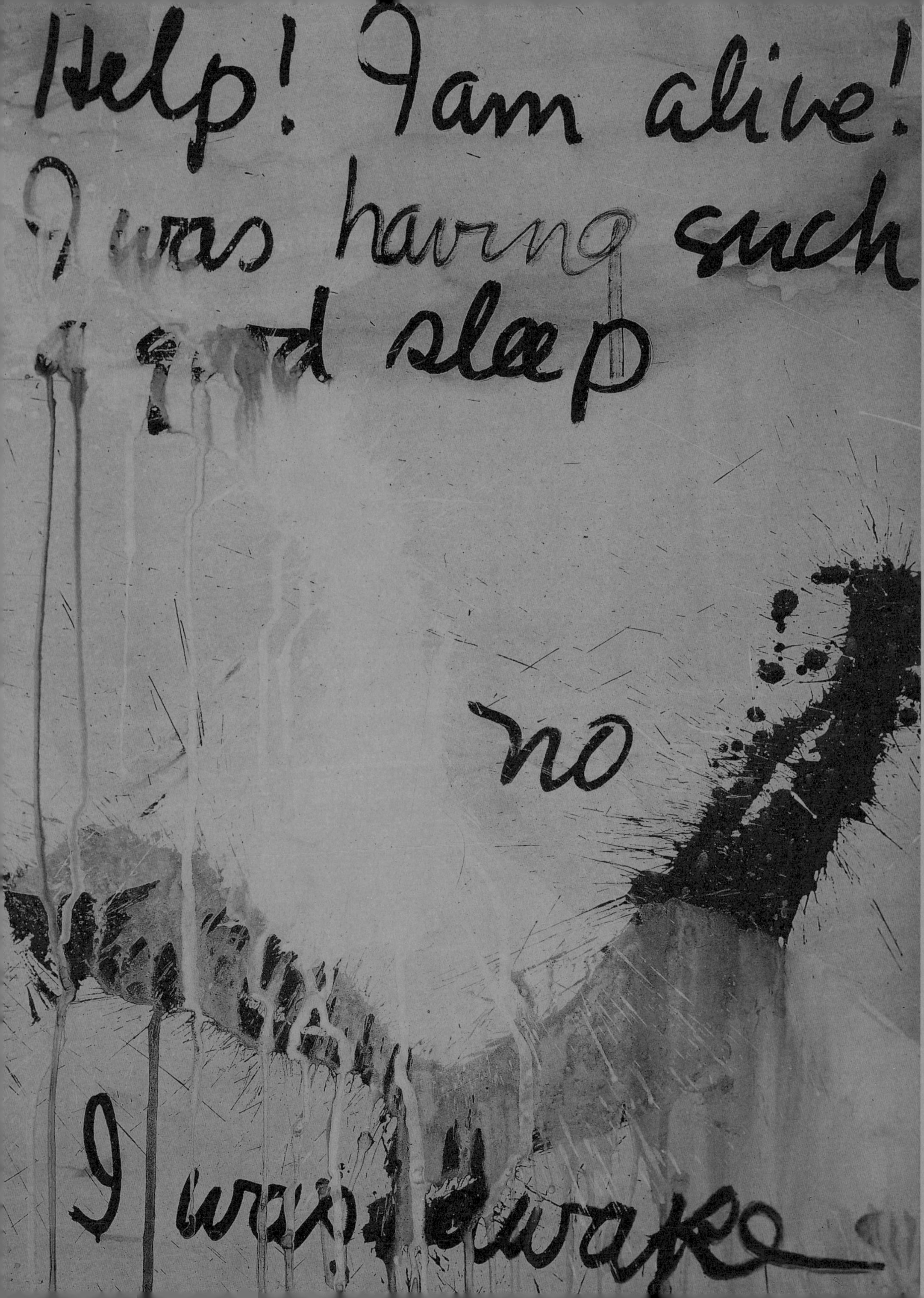
Help! I am alive!
I was having such
a good sleep
no
I was awake